More Than Heaven

More Than Heaven

A Biblical Theological Argument for a Federal View of Glorification

T. JEFF TAYLOR

WIPF & STOCK · Eugene, Oregon

MORE THAN HEAVEN
A Biblical Theological Argument for a Federal View of Glorification

Copyright © 2022 T. Jeff Taylor. All rights reserved. Except for brief quotations in critical publications or reviews, no part of this book may be reproduced in any manner without prior written permission from the publisher. Write: Permissions, Wipf and Stock Publishers, 199 W. 8th Ave., Suite 3, Eugene, OR 97401.

Wipf & Stock
An Imprint of Wipf and Stock Publishers
199 W. 8th Ave., Suite 3
Eugene, OR 97401

www.wipfandstock.com

PAPERBACK ISBN: 978-1-6667-3554-3
HARDCOVER ISBN: 978-1-6667-9272-0
EBOOK ISBN: 978-1-6667-9273-7

06/08/22

Unless otherwise noted, Scripture quotations are taken from the New American Standard Bible® (NASB®), copyright © 1995 by The Lockman Foundation. Used by permission. All rights reserved. www.lockman.org

Scripture quotations marked ESV are from The Holy Bible, English Standard Version® (ESV), copyright © 2001 by Crossway, a publishing ministry of Good News Publishers. Used by permission. All rights reserved.

Scripture quotations marked NIV are taken from the Holy Bible, New International Version® (NIV®), copyright © 1973, 1978, 1984, 2011 by Biblica, Inc.™ Used by permission of Zondervan. All rights reserved worldwide. www.zondervan.com

New Testament Greek citations are from the *SBL Greek New Testament*, copyright © 2010 by the Society of Biblical Literature and Logos Bible Software.

Hebrew text is from the Westminster Leningrad Codex, public domain.

To Meredith G. Kline
(1922–2007)

Exegete and Defender of the Gospel of the Kingdom

Contents

Preface | ix
Abbreviations | xi

Section One: Two Federal Heads

1. Temple of the King | 3
   The King of Glory | 3
   Created in the King's Image | 14
   Created for Glory | 20

2. The Covenant of Works: Adam | 23
   Historical Recognition | 23
   The "Covenant" of Works | 27
   The Covenant of Works at Creation | 44
   Covenant of Works, Not Grace | 55

3. The Covenant of Works: Jesus (Pactum Salutis) | 57
   The Pactum Salutis | 57
   The Ministry of Christ | 78

Section Two: The History of Redemption

4. The King Will Come | 97
   Adam | 97
   Job's Champion | 99
   The King of Israel | 101

   5   The Kingdom Will Come (the Abrahamic Covenant) | 105
          The Kingdom Promise | 105
          The Twelve Tribes | 111
          The Fulfillment | 119

   6   The Toy Kingdom (The Old Covenant) | 125
          Covenant of Works | 131
          The Angel and the Glory Presence | 137
          The Toy Temple and the Real Temple | 144

   7   The King and the Kingdom (the New Covenant) | 150
          The Kingdom of the Lord Jesus | 150
          Kingdom of Priests | 153
          Temple Builder | 158
          Putting on Christ | 160
          The Gospel | 166

Section Three: The Reward

   8   The New Covenant Blessing | 179
          The Reward | 179
          Talents and Minas | 195
          What Jesus Said about Degrees of Reward | 200

   9   The Judgment According to Works | 206
          The Judgment | 206
          The Judge | 218
          The Justified | 223
          Law of the Harvest | 237
          The Savior's Invitation | 241

 10   The Temple Builder: 1 Corinthians 3 | 244
          The Problem | 244
          The Lord's Temple | 245

 11   The Hope of Glory | 267
          The Appearance of the Glory | 268
          The Lord of Glory | 270
          The Especial People | 271

Bibliography | 273
Scripture Index | 279

Preface

THE PROTESTANT CHURCH HAS struggled since the Reformation with how to reconcile the teaching that believers will be rewarded in heaven in degrees commensurate with their works on earth with the teaching that the believer is saved by grace alone apart from the believer's works. The majority of Protestants have sought to resolve this tension by contending that the believer is saved by grace, but rewarded in degrees based on their works. This book takes the minority view and contends that the Scriptures do not teach degrees of reward.

The first three chapters argue that all of history is theologically centered on the two federal representatives, Adam and Jesus. The former transgressed the Covenant of Works with God, and because of his sin, all died. Jesus is the Second Adam, who obeyed the Pactum Salutis covenant of works with the Father. In him, the elect are counted righteous and given the glory of heaven he merited. All his rewards are theirs by faith. Chapters 4–7 turn to what has at times been called the Covenant of Grace, the application of Christ's saving work to believers in history. Throughout, it is clear that God administers his kingdom through covenants. The third section, chapters 8–11, focuses specifically on the reward passages, and how those rewards fit in the broader kingdom history and consummation.

This book is written from a commitment to a Reformed and Evangelical view of the inerrant Scriptures. I am thankful for the theological education I received from Robert Godfrey, Dennis Johnson, John Frame, Robert Strimple, and Meredith M. Kline. However, I am forever indebted to Meredith G. Kline for the radical reformation he brought me in exposing me to the world of biblical theology in the legacy of Geerhardus Vos. Kline's keen theological and exegetical insights have contributed the foundational structure for this book's application to the topic of glorification and final glory.

I have in large measure used the NASB 1995 translation. Other translations have been used where noted, and I have noted where the translation is my own. Though the Greek and Hebrew have been used on occasion, I have provided transliteration and sufficient explanation to give access to those who do not read these languages.

T. Jeff Taylor

Abbreviations

AT	author's translation
BDAG	Walter Bauer, Frederick W. Danker, W. F. Arndt, and F. W. Gingrich, *Greek-English Lexicon of the New Testament and Other Early Christian Literature*, 3rd ed. (Chicago: University of Chicago Press, 2000)
ESV	English Standard Version (2001)
KJV	King James Version (1611)
NASB	New American Standard Bible (1995)
NEB	New English Bible (Cambridge University Press and Oxford University Press, 1961, 1970)
NIV	New International Version (2011)
OED	*Oxford English Dictionary*, 3rd ed., online (June 2021)
REB	Revised English Bible (Cambridge University Press and Oxford University Press, 1989)
WCF	Westminster Confession of Faith

Section One

Two Federal Heads

1

Temple of the King

THE KING OF GLORY

Moses' prologue to Genesis (1:1—2:3) is a summary statement of God's final purpose for all of creation. More than recounting the origin of the world, Moses sets forth the metanarrative of creation. He recounts God creating the cosmos, describes the relationship of heaven and earth, and sets forth creation's final state.

Even without detailed exegesis, it is clear that the relationship of heaven and earth is prominent. In verse 1, God creates "the heavens and the earth." In verse 2, the Spirit hovers over the earth. In verses 26ff., God addresses the angelic council regarding making man in his own image.[1] On each of the creation days, God commands from heaven what is brought into existence on earth. The passage concludes with God entering his heavenly sabbath rest and consecrating the sabbath rest for man on earth. The archetype/replica relationship of the heavens and earth gains clarity as one understands the nature of "the heavens."

"Heavens" in verse 1 refers to the invisible part of creation. In the geocentric account, "earth" includes all the creation normally visible to man including the expanse above the earth. Colossians 1:16 uses the same language and then appositionally supplies its meaning, "For by

---

1. See Gen 3:22–24; 11:7.

Him all things were created, both in the heavens and on earth, visible and invisible, whether thrones or dominions or rulers or authorities—all things have been created through Him and for Him." "Heavens" is "invisible," and "earth" is "visible." Nehemiah 9:6 uses this inclusive language to praise God as Creator of all:

> You alone are the LORD.
> You have made the heavens,
> The heaven of heavens with all their host,
> The earth and all that is on it,
> The seas and all that is in them.
> You give life to all of them
> And the heavenly host bows down before You.

Heaven is not just the blissful dwelling of God. Heaven is the throne of God, the King. Colossians 1:16 intimates this by reference to "thrones" that owe their existence to the Creator. He is the one to whom the mighty angelic army[2] of heaven bows. More explicitly, Psalm 103:19–21 declares that God's throne is surrounded by the angelic hosts who serve him:

> The LORD has established His throne in the heavens,
> And His sovereignty rules over all.
> [20] Bless the LORD, you His angels,
> Mighty in strength, who perform His word,
> Obeying the voice of His word!
> [21] Bless the LORD, all you His hosts,
> You who serve Him, doing His will.[3]

Isaiah 66:1 expands the description of God's sovereign rule to include the visible world: "Heaven is My throne and the earth is My footstool." He is Lord over all creation. He is the sovereign of heaven who rules over the affairs of men on earth. Daniel describes God sitting on his throne in heaven to adjudicate the claims of the nations:[4]

> I kept looking
> Until thrones were set up,
> And the Ancient of Days took *His* seat;
> His vesture *was* like white snow
> And the hair of His head like pure wool.
> His throne *was* ablaze with flames,

---

2. *sabaoth*, "host"; Luke 2:13; Gen 32:1–2; Josh 5:13–15.

3. Cf. Ps 148:1–4.

4. See Dan 7:3–8.

> Its wheels *were* a burning fire.
> ¹⁰ A river of fire was flowing
> And coming out from before Him;
> Thousands upon thousands were attending Him,
> And myriads upon myriads were standing before Him;
> The court sat,
> And the books were opened. (Dan 7:9–10)

Likewise, when Jesus reveals the purposes of God to the apostle John, John records, "I was in the Spirit; and behold, a throne was standing in heaven, and One sitting on the throne" (Rev 4:2). To this King the angels do not stop giving praise, saying, "Holy, holy, holy *is* the Lord God, the Almighty, who was and who is and who is to come" (Rev 4:8). The twenty-four elders cast their crowns at his feet, confessing, "Worthy are You, our Lord and our God, to receive glory and honor and power; for You created all things, and because of Your will they existed, and were created" (Rev 4:11). This King who created all things will sit in final judgment: "Then I saw a great white throne and Him who sat upon it, from whose presence earth and heaven fled away, and no place was found for them" (Rev 20:11). From Genesis to Revelation, the Scriptures proclaim in unison that heaven is the throne of God.

The description of the throne of God in Revelation 4 also makes it clear that heaven is his temple. The hosts of heaven do not cease their worship of the King, "Holy, holy, holy." While one may think that thrones and temples occupy separate jurisdictions, God did not separate them in creation. Heaven is the throne of God, but it is also the temple of the King. Isaiah 6:1–4 says,

> In the year of King Uzziah's death I saw the Lord sitting on a throne, lofty and exalted, with the train of His robe filling the temple. ² Seraphim stood above Him, each having six wings: with two he covered his face, and with two he covered his feet, and with two he flew. ³ And one called out to another and said,
> "Holy, Holy, Holy, is the Lord of hosts,
> The whole earth is full of His glory."
> ⁴ And the foundations of the thresholds trembled at the voice of him who called out, while the temple was filling with smoke.

Isaiah sees the throne of the Lord in the temple filled with God's Glory. Isaiah describes the King seated in Glory in his temple in Isaiah 40:21–23:

> Do you not know? Have you not heard?
> Has it not been declared to you from the beginning?
> Have you not understood from the foundations of the earth?
> ²² It is He who sits above the circle of the earth.
> And its inhabitants are like grasshoppers,
> Who stretches out the heavens like a curtain
> And spreads them out like a tent to dwell in.
> ²³ He it is who reduces rulers to nothing.
> Who makes the judges of the earth meaningless.[5]

The use of the "tent" of God refers to the tabernacle and temple. God stretches out the heavens like a "curtain"—like a "tent to dwell in." God, enthroned in his royal temple, sovereignly rules over the kings of the earth. The psalmist identifies the throne of the King of Heaven with the temple of heaven when he writes, "Yahweh is in His holy temple, His throne is in the heavens" (Ps 11:4 AT). Similarly, Micah identifies God's heavenly temple with his throne when he warns of the judgment to come on Israel:

> Hear, O peoples, all of you;
> Listen, O earth and all it contains,
> And let the Lord God be a witness against you,
> The Lord from His holy temple.
> ³ For behold, the LORD is coming forth from His place.
> He will come down and tread on the high places of the earth.
> (Mic 1:2–3)

The doom is certain. God, the conquering King, will come forth from his temple in heaven and conquer Israel's fortified mountains. They have broken the King's covenant, and there is no defense that can withstand him.

Deuteronomy 26:15 speaks of the day when Israel will enter the land of their inheritance and keep the requirements before the priests to be a "consecrated people" and will pray to the Lord to pour out from his heavenly temple onto their holy land the blessings of the covenant. Moses writes, "Look down from Your holy habitation, from heaven, and bless Your people Israel, and the ground which You have given us, a land flowing with milk and honey, as You swore to our fathers."[6]

Genesis 1:1 starts with the proclamation that God created his heavenly royal temple. But verse 2 immediately informs the reader that heaven itself is the created epiphany of God. Moses' use of "the Spirit" is not just a reference to "God" in verse 1 but actually references the King in

---

5. See Beale, *Temple*, 39; Ps 19:4.
6. Deut 26:15; see Jer 25:30.

his royal temple of Glory. This is easily lost on the modern reader, but the unique vocabulary Moses uses in Genesis 1:2 alerts the Hebrew reader to the Spirit's connection with the theophany[7] of God in the wilderness described in Deuteronomy 32.

Moses didn't write Genesis 1 without context. He wrote Genesis for Israel in the context of their experience. Richard Pratt contends, "Moses wrote the book of Genesis to teach his readers that leaving Egypt and possessing Canaan was God's design for Israel."[8] While Pratt's proposed purpose is considerably narrower than Moses' purpose, it does make the point that Moses' original readers would have connected vocabulary, categories, and concepts in Genesis to their own experience in the exodus, the wilderness, and conquest. The reader is not left to interpret Genesis 1 in isolation from Moses' selected words and concepts used elsewhere in the Pentateuch. His word choice connects Genesis 1:2 to Deuteronomy 32:10–11. Genesis 1:2 reads,

> The earth was formless and void,
> and darkness was over the face of the deep,
> and the Spirit of God was hovering
> over the face of the waters.

These rare terms would have taken the first readers to Deuteronomy 32:

> He found him in a desert land,
> And in the howling waste of a wilderness;
> He encircled him, He cared for him,
> He guarded him as the pupil of His eye.
> 11 Like an eagle that stirs up its nest,
> That hovers over its young,
> He spread His wings and caught them,
> He carried them on His pinions. (Deut 32:10–11)

Though the word is translated "waste" in Deuteronomy 32 and "formless" in Genesis 1, the same word is used in Hebrew, *tōhû* (תֹהוּ). M. G. Kline explains the connection between these two passages:

> The intention to portray the exodus history as a replay of Gen 1:2 is made clear by the use in Deut 32:10,11 of two rare words (the noun *tōhû* and the verb *rḥp*), found in the Pentateuch only in these two passages. In the Song of Moses, the wilderness becomes the new *tōhû*, the waste land, equivalent to the primeval

---

7. God's visible manifestation to man.
8. Pratt, *Stories*, 281.

deep-and-darkness, and it is the Shekinah-cloud that is referred to as hovering (the verb *rḥp*) over Israel in the wilderness-*tōhû*.⁹

The Spirit "hovers" (*rḥp*, רָחַף) over the "formless" (*tōhû*, תֹהוּ) in Genesis 1:2 as the visible Shekinah "hovers" (*rḥp*) over the "waste" (*tōhû*) in Deuteronomy 32:10–11. Moses uses the terms in Deuteronomy to describe the exodus as a new creation. Likewise, the Spirit hovering over the earth at creation is an obvious reference to the theophany of the Glory-cloud in the wilderness and the Shekinah-cloud in the tabernacle and temple. Later writers will also note the identity of the Spirit of God and the theophany with Israel. Nehemiah connects the presence of the "Spirit" with the cloud theophany when he writes,

> Even when they made for themselves
> A calf of molten metal
> And said, 'This is your God
> Who brought you up from Egypt,'
> And committed great blasphemies,
> ¹⁹ You, in Your great compassion,
> Did not forsake them in the wilderness;
> The pillar of cloud did not leave them by day,
> To guide them on their way,
> Nor the pillar of fire by night, to light for them the way in which they were to go.
> ²⁰ "You gave Your good Spirit to instruct them,
> Your manna You did not withhold from their mouth,
> And You gave them water for their thirst. (Neh 9:18–20)

Isaiah also describes the visible presence of the Holy Spirit with Israel in the exodus and journey through the wilderness:

> But they rebelled
> And grieved His Holy Spirit;
> Therefore He turned Himself to become their enemy,
> He fought against them.
> ¹¹ Then His people remembered the days of old, of Moses.
> Where is He who brought them up out of the sea with the shepherds of His flock?
> Where is He who put His Holy Spirit in the midst of them,
> ¹² Who caused His glorious arm to go at the right hand of Moses,
> Who divided the waters before them to make for Himself an everlasting name,

---

9. Kline, *Glory*, 11; see *Images*, 14.

> 13 Who led them through the depths?
> Like the horse in the wilderness, they did not stumble;
> 14 As the cattle which go down into the valley,
> The Spirit of the LORD gave them rest.
> So You led Your people,
> To make for Yourself a glorious name. (Isa 63:10–14)

Isaiah identifies the glorious arm of the Lord as the Holy Spirit.[10] Exodus 14 identifies the Lord's presence as the theophany pillar of fire and cloud:

> . . . the pillar of cloud moved from before them and stood behind them. 20 So it came between the camp of Egypt and the camp of Israel; and there was the cloud along with the darkness, yet it gave light at night. Thus the one did not come near the other all night. 21 Then Moses stretched out his hand over the sea; and the LORD swept the sea back by a strong east wind all night and turned the sea into dry land, so the waters were divided. 22 The sons of Israel went through the midst of the sea on the dry land, and the waters *were like* a wall to them on their right hand and on their left. 23 Then the Egyptians took up the pursuit, and all Pharaoh's horses, his chariots and his horsemen went in after them into the midst of the sea. 24 At the morning watch, the LORD looked down on the army of the Egyptians through the pillar of fire and cloud and brought the army of the Egyptians into confusion. (Exod 14:19–24)

This formative event in Israel's history furnishes Haggai with the background for the promise. Just as God was present in the theophany in the past, God promises a coming glory: "As for the promise which I made you when you came out of Egypt, My Spirit is abiding in your midst; do not fear!" (Hag 2:5) The pillar of cloud is the theophany of God, the Spirit.

The cloud theophany Israel knew as God's presence was bright and identified with the Lord's Glory. The theophany was a "Glory-cloud."[11] Moses uses the "glory" to refer to the theophany synonymously with the "cloud." Exodus 24 records,

> Then Moses went up to the mountain, and the cloud covered the mountain. 16 The glory of the LORD rested on Mount Sinai, and the cloud covered it for six days; and on the seventh day He called to Moses from the midst of the cloud. 17 And to the eyes

---

10. See too "The phrase 'hand of the Lord' refers to the Spirit." Kline, *Covenant Witness*, 17; cf. Ezek 3:22–24; 8:1; 11:5.

11. Kline, *Images*, 14.

of the sons of Israel the appearance of the glory of the LORD was like a consuming fire on the mountain top. ¹⁸ Moses entered the midst of the cloud as he went up to the mountain; and Moses was on the mountain forty days and forty nights. (Exod 24:15–18)

The Glory of God's theophanic presence, the "Spirit," led Israel in the wilderness. Exodus 40 concludes,

> Then the cloud covered the tent of meeting, and the glory of the LORD filled the tabernacle. ³⁵ Moses was not able to enter the tent of meeting because the cloud had settled on it, and the glory of the LORD filled the tabernacle. ³⁶ Throughout all their journeys whenever the cloud was taken up from over the tabernacle, the sons of Israel would set out; ³⁷ but if the cloud was not taken up, then they did not set out until the day when it was taken up. ³⁸ For throughout all their journeys, the cloud of the LORD was on the tabernacle by day, and there was fire in it by night, in the sight of all the house of Israel. (Exod 40:34–38)

Israel was not witness just to an unusual cloud; they were in the presence of God. Kline writes,

> God's theophanic glory is the glory of royal majesty. At the center of the heavens within the veil of the Glory-cloud is found a throne; the Glory is preeminently the place of God's enthronement. It is, therefore, a royal palace, site of the divine council and court of judgment. As royal house of a divine King, the dwelling of deity, it is a holy house, a temple.[12]

The Glory-cloud theophany, the pillar, and subsequently the Shekinah-cloud were the local manifestation of the presence of the King in heaven. God was with his people.

By using the unique vocabulary to reference Deuteronomy 32, Moses is identifying the "Spirit" in Genesis 1:2 with the visible theophany in the wilderness.[13] The localized theophany of the Glory-cloud in the wilderness was a manifestation of the Glory-Spirit of heaven (Gen 1:2 "the Spirit"). The "Spirit" in Genesis 1:2 is the Glory of the divine presence

---

12. Kline, *Images*, 17–18.

13. Kline, *Kingdom Prologue*, 30: "The usage in Genesis 1:2 is similar, thought the Spirit here is probably best understood as the heavenly reality, the invisible cosmos-filling *Glory* of the divine presence, of which the *Glory*-cloud was a localized manifestation."

of heaven. Like the Glory-cloud theophany hovered over Israel, so the Glory-Spirit hovered over the earth. Deuteronomy 32:11 says,

> Like an eagle that stirs up its nest,
> That hovers over its young,
> He spread His wings and caught them,
> He carried them on His pinions.

The theophany of the Spirit in the wilderness cared for Israel like an eagle cares for it's young.[14] So too Genesis 1:2 describes the Spirit hovering. Kline explains the connection:

> To describe the action of the Glory-cloud by the figure of outspread wings was natural, not simply because of the overshadowing function it performed, but because of the composition of this theophanic cloud. For when prophetic vision penetrates the thick darkness, the cloud is seen to be alive with winged creatures, with cherubim and seraphim.[15]

The "Spirit" in Genesis 1:2 is heaven itself filled with the Glory of the divine presence. But just as the Glory-cloud was the localized presence of God, so the "Spirit" references the Glory of God and his royal temple. Heaven is the epiphany of the Glory of the Spirit, just as the Glory-cloud was the visible manifestation of God.

Just as the Second Person of the Trinity became incarnated in history, so the Third Person of the Trinity became endoxated. Heaven is the created manifestation of the Glory of God. Kline writes, "The creation of heaven was an epiphany."[16] The psalmist writes,

> Praise the LORD, my soul.
> LORD my God, you are very great;
> you are clothed with splendor and majesty.
> ² The Lord wraps himself in light as with a garment;
> he stretches out the heavens like a tent. (Ps 104:1–2 NIV)

Kline observes that the splendor with which God is clothed "is identified with the theophanic light of the Lord."[17] Kline concludes,

> As an epiphany, the Glory that constitutes heaven is identifiable with God. At the same time, this Glory epiphany is a created

---

14. See Exod 19:4.
15. Kline, *Images*, 14.
16. Kline, *God*, 13.
17. Kline, *Glory*, 21.

> phenomenon... The heavenly Glory is then an embodiment of Deity... a permanent embodiment.[18]

Heaven is a created manifestation of the Glory of the Spirit, like the incarnation is of the Son. Kline coined the term "endoxation" to describe the "creational projection of the eternal procession of the Spirit..."[19] Kline later again says,

> ...the creating of heaven itself was a replicating of the eternal, uncreated Glory of God...the replicating of eternal divine Glory in the creation of the cosmos points back to a radiating of divine Glory involved in the dynamic forms of subsistence with the Trinity apart from creation.[20]

The Genesis 1:2 reference to the "Spirit" speaks not just of the Holy Spirit, but to the "heavens" as the endoxation of the Holy Spirit—the God of Glory in his royal temple. This does not in any way confuse the creation with the Creator any more than the incarnation does. The "Spirit" references the holy court of the triune God. The Son is present in heaven as the Angel of the Presence. That is not to say that the Son is an angel and not the Son of God. He is God. The Son, in his preincarnate state, is present in creation as the "Angel of the Lord" or the "Angel of the Presence." The Father is King of Glory. God is one and is seen in the created invisible heavens.

Many people assume that heaven has always existed, and that God made the visible world. The first verse of Genesis starts with the declaration that God created the invisible heavens. Genesis 1:1 is the alpha point, the beginning of creation. God is Creator of all existence outside himself. This is the point everything outside of God comes into existence. The creation was not, and then it was. Time, space, matter, creation was not, and then God created it. Moses starts with the starting point—the distinction between the Creator and the creation. God created *ex nihilo*, out of nothing, and *in nihilum*, into nothing. There was not a void. There was not blackness. There was not emptiness. There was not an infinite passing of time before God created the creation. There was God. Proverbs 8 affirms this aseity[21] of God. God's self-existent wisdom forms his architectural wonder. No one taught him. God's Wisdom confesses,

---

18. Kline, *God*, 13.
19. Kline, *God*, 14.
20. Kline, God, 31.
21. Self-existent.

> The LORD possessed me at the beginning of His way,
> Before His works of old.
> ²³ From everlasting I was established,
> From the beginning, from the earliest times of the earth.
> ²⁴ When there were no depths I was brought forth,
> When there were no springs abounding with water.
> ²⁵ Before the mountains were settled,
> Before the hills I was brought forth;
> ²⁶ While He had not yet made the earth and the fields,
> Nor the first dust of the world.
> ²⁷ When He established the heavens, I was there,
> When He inscribed a circle on the face of the deep,
> ²⁸ When He made firm the skies above,
> When the springs of the deep became fixed,
> ²⁹ When He set for the sea its boundary
> So that the water would not transgress His command,
> When He marked out the foundations of the earth;
> ³⁰ Then I was beside Him, *as* a master workman;
> And I was daily *His* delight,
> Rejoicing always before Him. (Prov 8:22–30)

Before God created his "works of old," when there were "no depths," before the springs that bring forth water, before the mountains were even set as the foundational pillars of the earth, prior to making the dust of the earth, God's Wisdom existed in himself. God did not get his Wisdom from anywhere, anyone, or anything. Bruce Walke explains,

> The metaphor "brought forth" signifies that Solomon's inspired wisdom comes from God's essential being; it is a revelation that has an organic connection with God's very nature and being, unlike the rest of creation that came into existence outside of him and independent from his being.[22]

The apostle John also starts his gospel account with the same contrast between the triune God and creation. John writes,

> In the beginning was the Word, and the Word was with God, and the Word was God. ² He was in the beginning with God. ³ All things came into being through Him, and apart from Him nothing came into being that has come into being. (John 1:1–3)

Note how John echoes the words of Genesis 1:1, "In the beginning." The Second Person of the Trinity, the Word, was with God. Indeed, the Word

---

22. Walke, *Proverbs*, 1:409.

himself is God. He is the Wisdom of Proverbs 8. The one who would become incarnate (John 1:14) created all things. Verses 3 excludes the thought of anything having existence in creation that God, the Word, did not bring into being.

What is astonishing is that God created heaven as part of creation and then stepped into time and space. God, who exists in himself before creation and does not need anything, created the invisible heavens and made himself knowable to the creation by dwelling in heaven as his royal temple. When Solomon was making the tiny replica of the temple of heaven, he confessed, "But who is able to build a house for Him, for the heavens and the highest heavens cannot contain Him?" (2 Chr 2:6).[23] Solomon was taken aback by the thought that if the invisible created heavens filled with the Glory of God could come anywhere close to containing the eternal God, then how could his sixty-by-twenty-cubit temple replica![24] It is this created endoxation of the Glory of the Spirit of God, the royal temple of the King, that hovered over the earth at creation to replicate heaven on earth.

CREATED IN THE KING'S IMAGE

The Glory-Spirit is the archetype for the creation of the earth and its vassal king. In Genesis 1:26, the King of Glory in heaven addresses the divine angelic council,[25] "Let Us make man in Our image, according to Our likeness." The vassal king would represent the King of Heaven on earth. But more, the image bearer would bear the resemblance of his heavenly Father. The Spirit of the Lord hovers as a father giving life to his son. Though only a man created from the dust of the earth, Adam would resemble his Father, the God of heaven. Genesis 5:1, 3 says,

> In the day when God created man, He made him in the likeness of God . . . **3** When Adam had lived one hundred and thirty years, he became the father of *a son* in his own likeness, according to his image, and named him Seth.

Adam's son was in his likeness as Adam was created in the likeness of God. Luke's genealogy also uses this same language: "the son of Enosh,

---

23. Cf. 6:18; 1 Kgs 8:27.
24. See 1 Kgs 6:2.
25. See Gen 3:22; 11:7; Isa 6:5; Isa 41:21–22; Rev 4.

the son of Seth, the son of Adam, the son of God" (Luke 3:38). After the fall of Adam, man's image identity continues to be acknowledged in a very broken and perverted form. The end of the first section of Genesis culminates with the judgment on the pagan kings who called themselves "the sons of gods."[26]

The hovering of the Spirit in order to father is seen at other inceptional events. The Glory-cloud hovered over and fathered Israel in the wilderness. The angel announced that the Spirit would overshadow the virgin Mary.[27] The Spirit came as a violent noise of a rushing wind on the church at Pentecost.[28] In these subsequent events, the Spirit was birthing a son. Israel was called "son,"[29] as his covenant people. Gabriel announced that Jesus is the "Son of God." And the New Covenant church birthed at Pentecost would call God "Abba! Father."[30] Adam is the son of God, created in the Glory-Spirit's image. As the Glory-Spirit is the temple of God in heaven, so Adam is the Spirit's replica on earth. Adam himself is the temple of God. The Spirit breathes life into Adam (Gen 2:7). The Spirit fills Adam.

Many find it awkward to think of Adam himself as a temple of God. But as the dwelling of God's Spirit, that is what he was. John 1:14 uses the same architectural language when John writes that Jesus "tabernacled"[31] (or as is usually translated "dwelt") among us. Paul uses the unusual mixed metaphor of being clothed and being temples in 2 Corinthians 5:1–4:

> For we know that if the earthly tent which is our house is torn down, we have a building from God, a house not made with hands, eternal in the heavens. **2** For indeed in this *house* we groan, longing to be clothed with our dwelling from heaven, **3** inasmuch as we, having put it on, will not be found naked. **4** For indeed while we are in this tent, we groan, being burdened, because we do not want to be unclothed but to be clothed, so that what is mortal will be swallowed up by life.

---

26. בְּנֵי הָאֱלֹהִים, *Bene ha'elohim*; Gen 6:2, 4.
27. Luke 1:35.
28. Acts 2:1–4.
29. Hos 11:1; Exod 4:22–23.
30. Rom 8:15; Gal 4:6; see Matt 6:9; Eph 3:14–15.
31. ἐσκήνωσεν, *eskenosen*.

Paul likens putting on the image to being clothed with Christ.[32] To be the image is to be the temple of God.[33] Kline notes, "God created man in the likeness of the Glory to be a spirit-temple of God in the Spirit."[34] The Spirit endoxated is the temple of God. So Adam, made in the likeness of the Spirit, is a replica temple of God.

The Genesis 2:7 infilling of the Adamic temple becomes a foundational event referenced by later writers. Ezekiel 36 promises a re-creation of Israel, when her desolation will be removed and she will again "become like the garden of Eden" (Ezek 36:35) when God puts his Spirit in his people (Ezek 36:27). Ezekiel 37:1–10 describes the "breath"[35] of God coming on the dry bones and bringing them to life. Ezekiel 37:14 summarizes the promise, "And I will put my Spirit within you, and you will come to life." Lamentations 4:20 alludes to Genesis 2:7 in the parallelism of the Lord's anointed, "breath of our nostrils." After the resurrection, Jesus promised the Spirit would come on the disciples. John 20:22 records, "He breathed in[36] them, and said to them, 'Receive the Holy Spirit'" (AT). Beasley-Murray notes the clear connection of these passages: "'He breathed in' is perhaps needlessly literal, but it harks back to the unusual term in Gen 2:7 and Ezek 37:9–10." He continues,

> The symbolism is a clear application of the notion of resurrection, and that in an eschatological context (deliverance for the kingdom). It is not surprising that it came to be viewed as a representation of resurrection in the time of the kingdom. In v. 22 the symbolic action primarily represents the impartation of life that the Holy Spirit gives in the new age, brought about through Christ's exaltation in death and resurrection.[37]

As the Spirit gave indwelling life to Adam, so now in the new age of the kingdom Christ would give the Spirit's indwelling life to believers.

Adam, the image of God, would rule as vassal over the kingdom of God on the earth. God's address to the divine council continues in Genesis 1:26: "let them rule over the fish of the sea and over the birds of the sky and over the cattle and over all the earth, and over every creeping

---

32. Eph 4:24; Col 3:10.
33. 1 Cor 3:16; 6:19.
34. Kline, *Images*, 21.
35. Or "Spirit"; רוּחַ, *ruach*.
36. Ἐνεφύσησεν *enephysesen*.
37. Beasley-Murray, *John*, 380–81.

thing that creeps on the earth." The creation of Adam is the culmination of the six days of replicating the kingdom of heaven on earth. The reader can hear the edicts of the King, "Let there be," and the actualization on earth, "and it was so." The "greater light" is created to "rule" the day, the "lesser light" to "rule" the night. The first three days of creation bring forth dominions that are filled on the following three days by their respective rulers—the creatures of the sea and fowl of the sky on the fifth day and the animals on the sixth day. Over this earthly kingdom, the image of God is placed as vassal king. Each creature is created "after its kind." Adam is in the likeness of God.

Not only would Adam be vassal king over the kingdom of God on earth; he would be a priest in the kingdom. This kingdom is holy, the temple of God on earth. Adam would be a priest/king. He would fill and subdue as king, but he was also tasked to guard the holiness of the kingdom. Genesis 2:15 says, "And the LORD God took the man, and put him into the garden of Eden to cultivate it and to guard it" (AT). Although some scholars translate *"shamar"* (שָׁמַר) with "guard," most translate it "keep." Kline points out that the same word used for "keep" (*shamar*) in Genesis 2:15 is also translated "guard" (*shamar*). When Adam is cast out of the garden, it is the cherubim who "guard"[38] (*shamar*) the entrance to the holy garden.[39] Adam is a priest in the temple of Eden. Kline explains,

> Elsewhere in the Bible, especially in passages dealing with functions of the priests and Levites in Israel, the verb *shamar* occurs frequently in the sense of guarding the holiness of God's sanctuary against profanation by unauthorized "strangers" (cf. E.g. Num 1:53; 3:8, 10, 32; 8:26; 18:3ff; 31:30, 47; 1 Sam 7:1; 2 Kgs 12:9; 1 Chr 23:32; 2 Chr 34:9; Ezek 44:15f, 48:11).[40]

Beale too affirms that Adam is a priest: "he was the archetypal priest who served in and guarded (or 'took care of') God's first temple."[41] So Beale affirms the dual role of the image: "Adam should always best be referred to as a 'priest-king.'"[42]

Ezekiel calls Eden the "holy mount of God" (Ezek 28:14). Eden is the "garden of God" (Ezek 28:13; 31:8–9; Isa 51:3). John describes the new

---

38. NASB.
39. Gen 3:24.
40. Kline, *Kingdom Prologue*, 86.
41. Beale, *Temple*, 68.
42. Beale, *Temple*, 70.

heavens and new earth in Revelation 21–22 as the temple/tabernacle of Eden; it is the city of God, the new Jerusalem (21:2). The loud voice from heaven's throne announces, "Behold, the tabernacle of God is among men, and He will tabernacle among them" (Rev 21:3 AT). The great city temple is reminiscent of Eden, the mountain of God.[43] Revelation's description is like the temple of God described in Ezekiel 40–47.[44] Revelation 22:1ff. describes the ultimate paradise in terms of Eden. There is the river and the tree of life, and there is no more curse. This is the throne of God. Beale contends, "in the end time an Eden-temple will be established as a new Jerusalem that will extend throughout the whole earth."[45]

Some have objected that although the temple has Edenic characteristics, that doesn't mean that the garden of Eden is a temple. Daniel Block acknowledges that he is "swimming against an overwhelming current of scholarly opinion and even against positions" he once held.[46] He even acknowledges the notable similarities of the garden of Eden to the temple. But Block finally objects to considering the garden of Eden a temple. He writes,

> In my response to reading Gen 1–3 as temple-building texts, I have hinted at the fundamental hermeneutical problem involved in this approach. The question is, should we read Gen 1–3 in the light of later texts, or should we read later texts in light of these? If we read the accounts of the order given, then the creation account provides essential background to primeval history, which provides background for the patriarchal, exodus, and tabernacle narratives. By themselves and by this reading the accounts of Gen 1–3 offer no clues that a cosmic or Edenic temple might be involved. However, as noted above, the Edenic features of the tabernacle, the Jerusalem temple, and the temple envisioned by Ezekiel are obvious. Apparently their design and function intended to capture something of the original environment in which human beings were placed. However, the fact that Israel's sanctuaries were Edenic does not make Eden into a sacred shrine. At best this is a nonreciprocating equation.[47]

---

43. Rev 21:10.
44. Beale, *Temple*, 346–53.
45. Beale, *Temple*, 345.
46. Block, "Eden," 4.
47. Block, "Eden," 20–21.

But Block's criticism misses Moses' argument on two levels. First, in terms of hermeneutical method, rarely does one read the first words of a book without contextual aid. The first readers of Genesis were no different. Genesis 1–3 does not exist by itself. The children of Israel had extensive history going back to Abraham and before. Their more recent experiences brought them through the Egyptian bondage, exodus, and wilderness wanderings. As a result of their history and experiences, they did not read Genesis 1–3 without contextual assistance. It was not difficult for the Israelites to understand "In the beginning" as the beginning of creation. As argued already, they would connect "the Spirit" to their daily exposure to the Glory-cloud. Genesis 1–3 gives much more than "clues" that a cosmic or Edenic temple might be involved. Second, the criticism fails to understand the direction of Moses' teaching. Moses' argument is not to show that Eden is a temple because it has the architectural features of the temple in Israel. Rather, the argument runs the opposite direction. God created heaven, the royal temple of the King. The Spirit of this royal heavenly temple replicates himself on earth. This starts in Eden, but finally the whole earth will be the royal temple of God. The miniature temple in Israel bears the details of Eden because it too is representative of the temple in heaven.

Isaiah 66:1 is not hyperbole. God declares, "Heaven is My throne and the earth is My footstool." The whole of the created cosmos is the royal temple of God. As the Glory-Spirit was in heaven, so would be the earth. Kline writes,

> The cosmic structure was built as a habitation for the Creator himself. Heaven and earth were erected as a house of God, a palace of the Great King, the seat of sovereignty of the Lord of the covenant.[48]

What began in Eden would be true of the whole earth.

The realities of sin cloud our minds from contemplating the incredible cultural achievements Adam and this royal humanity would have achieved as image bearers of the King of Heaven in a world without sin. One can only begin to imagine the exploits to outer space, the knowledge of the depths of the sea, and the transformation of the earth itself as mankind would have multiplied without death and filled the earth with image bearers of the King. The shadows of human giftedness in a world filled with sin only darkly points to the achievements man would have

---

48. Kline, *Kingdom Prologue*, 27; cf. Isa 66:1a; Matt 5:34–35; Ps 93; Isa 40:21–23.

realized serving God to the ends of the earth. Though man's ruling over the royal temple on earth would have seen many cultural achievements, the most important would be the filling the earth with the generations upon generations of image-bearing temples of God. God made Adam and Eve in his own image and commissioned them to fill and subdue the earth. The earth would be filled with human temples.

CREATED FOR GLORY

God, who exists in himself, spoke creation into existence, entered time and space, and made heaven his dwelling place. He spoke and made the earth to be a replica of heaven and Adam to bear the likeness to his holy kingship. This is not the end. This is "In the beginning" (Gen 1:1). Adam's commission to rule, guard, and fill was not a commission without end. He would subdue. He would fill the earth. There is a seventh day!

The seventh day is the culmination of the creation story. The ultimate relationship of the two dimensions is promised on the last day. Moses introduces the seventh day with an inclusio[49] that connects the end to the beginning. Genesis 1:1 speaks of the creation of "the heavens and the earth," and verse 2 says the earth was without form and empty. Now after six days of creation of forming and filling, Moses concludes,

> Thus the heavens and the earth were completed, and all their hosts. ² By the seventh day God completed his work which He had done, and He rested on the seventh day from all his work which He had done. ³ Then God blessed the seventh day and sanctified it, because in it He rested from all His work which God had created and made. (Gen 2:1–3)

God, who in 1:1ff. created, now has finished his work and "rested" from all his work. God didn't rest by taking an afternoon nap. God "rested"—he completed his kingdom and sat enthroned. The psalmist uses the same language of God "resting" in the tabernacle and the temple:

> Let us go into His dwelling place;
> Let us worship at His footstool,
> ⁸ Arise, O Lord, to Thy resting place;
> Thou and the ark of Thy strength. (Ps 132:7–8)[50]

---

49. Literary device to bracket. In this case, 1:1 "heavens and earth" and 2:1 "heavens and earth."

50. Cf. 132:13–14; 1 Chr 28:2; Isa 66:1; 2 Chr 6:41.

Beale explains,

> God's rest both at the conclusion of Genesis 1–2 and later in Israel's temple indicates not merely inactivity but that he demonstrated his sovereignty over the forces of chaos (e.g. the enemies of Israel) and now has assumed a position of kingly rest further revealing his sovereign power.[51]

This sabbath rest of God is his enthronement in heaven. Isaiah 66:1 also explicates God's enthronement with his rest: "Heaven is My throne and the earth is My footstool. Where then is a house you could build for Me? And where is a place that I may rest?" Hebrews 4:4 says, "For He has said somewhere concerning the seventh day: 'And GOD RESTED ON THE SEVENTH DAY FROM ALL HIS WORKS.'" The author of Hebrews then connects this sabbath[52] rest with God's enthronement in heaven:

> Therefore, since we have a great high priest who has passed through the heavens, Jesus the Son of God, let us hold fast our confession. 15 For we do not have a high priest who cannot sympathize with our weaknesses, but One who has been tempted in all things as *we are, yet* without sin. 16 Therefore let us draw near with confidence to the throne of grace, so that we may receive mercy and find grace to help in time of need. (Heb 4:14–16)

So the King enthroned in heaven created Adam in his image to rule with the promise of entering the King's sabbath rest. This was signified by the consecration of the seventh day of Adam's week.[53] Adam would work six days and rest on the seventh in worship to God. But intrinsic in the weekly sabbath observance is the hope of the completion of his commission and ultimate entering the consummation sabbath enthronement. The argument of Hebrews 4 is based on this eschatological promise of the sabbath. As God finished and rested, so Adam's completed mission would be met with royal enthronement of the final sabbath. Hebrews says Joshua taking the Israelites into the promised land of rest did not fulfill that promise. There would be one greater than Joshua who would bring the redeemed into God's unending sabbath.

It is important to note here that the promise of entering God's rest in Hebrews 4 does not originate with the redemptive work of Christ. The promise of entering the sabbath rest of God was given from the beginning.

---

51. Beale, *Temple*, 62.
52. Heb 4:9.
53. Gen 2:3: וַיְקַדֵּשׁ, *qadosh*, "sanctified"; Exod 20:8–11.

Starting on the seventh day of creation, God entered his sabbath rest and made the sabbath rest for man.

Heaven and earth were distinguished in the beginning. But there would be a sabbath when heaven and earth, the invisible and visible, would be transformed into the one visible royal temple of the King of Heaven dwelling with his people in Glory. Man was made for the "better country" (Heb 11:16) that exceeds what a man's mind can imagine. God predestined man's glorified existence in the Glory of the King before creation. Paul writes,

> Yet we do speak wisdom among those who are mature; a wisdom, however, not of this age nor of the rulers of this age, who are passing away; 7 but we speak God's wisdom in a mystery, the hidden *wisdom* which God predestined before the ages to our glory . . . (1 Cor. 2:6–7)

Paul quotes Isaiah 64:4 regarding "our glory":

> . . . but just as it is written,
> "THINGS WHICH EYE HAS NOT SEEN AND EAR HAS NOT HEARD,
> AND *which* HAVE NOT ENTERED THE HEART OF MAN,
> ALL THAT GOD HAS PREPARED FOR THOSE WHO LOVE HIM." (1 Cor. 2:9)

This is what the presence of the "Spirit" at creation promised. As Kline observes,

> The Glory-Spirit was present at the beginning of creation as a sign of the telos[54] of creation, as the Alpha-archetype of the Omega-Sabbath that was the goal of creation history."[55]

This consummate purpose is confirmed by the revealing of the new heavens and the new earth in Revelation 21–22. The final realization of God's creation is seen in heaven and earth being transformed into the royal temple of God. God created all things with the eschatological purpose of eternal life together with a glorified humanity.

---

54. Ultimate purpose.
55. Kline, *Images*, 20.

2

The Covenant of Works
Adam

HISTORICAL RECOGNITION

THE OPENING CHAPTERS OF Genesis inform the reader that God created Adam in a covenant relationship dependent on Adam's obedience. Though the word "covenant" is not used in these opening chapters, the covenant relationship between God and Adam is clearly described. To use an obvious example, the reader will immediately understand what is in view when a woman is shopping for her "wedding dress" though the word "marriage" is not used!

The Protestant reformers were not the first to recognize this covenant. Even the Genesis Rabbah (written 300–500 AD), a midrash of ancient rabbinical interpretations on Genesis, comments on Hosea 6:7,

> It is written, 'But they are like a man [Adam], they have transgressed the covenant' (Hosea 6:7) 'They are like a man,' specifically, like the first man . . . 'In the case of the first man, I brought him into the garden of Eden, I commanded him, he violated my commandment, I judged him to be sent away and driven out . . . So too in the case of his descendants, I brought them into the Land of Israel, I commanded them, they violated my commandments, I judged them to be sent out and driven away.'[1]

---

1. *Gen. Rab.* 19:9, cited in Fesko, *Death*, 239.

The fifth-century Babylonian Talmud also understood Hosea as referring to Adam:

> Rab Judah also said in Rab's name: Adam was a Min[2], for it is written, And the Lord God called unto Adam and said unto him, Where art thou? i.e., whither has thine heart turned? . . . For here it is written, But like man, [Adam] they have transgressed the covenant.[3]

Abarbanel (1437–1508 AD) comments on Hosea, "The meaning is that they acted like Adam, or the first man, who I put in the Garden of Eden and he transgressed my covenant."[4] Far from being an innovation of the Protestant Reformation, even within the rabbinical tradition there were those who understood there was a covenant between God and Adam.

Post-apostolic fathers recognize this first covenant. Irenaeus (125–202 AD) writes, "For this reason were four principle covenants given to the human race: one prior to the deluge, under Adam . . ."[5] Clement of Alexandria's (150—215 AD) *Eclogae Propheticae* refers to the four covenants in the Old Testament with Adam, Noah, Abraham, and Moses.[6] Augustine (354—430 AD) recognizes the law character of this first covenant when he writes, "For the first covenant, which was made with the first man, is just this 'In the day ye eat thereof, ye shall surely die . . .'"[7] Augustine argues for original sin from Romans 5:12ff., that even infants are "born in sin, not actual, but original."[8] He argues,

> But even the infants, not personally in their own life, but according to the common origin of the human race, have all broken God's covenant in that one in whom all have sinned.[9]

The existence of the Covenant of Works with Adam becomes central to Augustine's theology.

Cyril of Alexandria (AD 444) diverges from his Eastern tradition, which followed the LXX in translating Hosea 6:7 "like man." He writes,

---

2. Heretic.
3. Sanhedrin Folio 38B; Babylonian Talmud.
4. Ed. Husen (Leiden, 1686), 270, 282, quoted in Warfield, "Hosea," 117–18.
5. Irenaeus, *Against Heresies*, 429.
6. Clement of Alexandria, *Eclogae Propheticae*, cited in Woolsey, *Unity*, 166.
7. Augustine, *City*, 326.
8. Augustine, City, 326.
9. Augustine, *City*, 326.

> We should at all points be very zealous in investigating the truth; in this case we need to say that in place of like someone the Hebrew text says "like Adam" breaking a covenant, so that we may understand that the breaking by the people of Israel was like that committed by Adam. While it was granted to him, remember, to have a relationship with God, to live without [fear of] corruption, and to be regaled with the delights of paradise, he paid no heed to the divine commandment; he then took a turn for the worse, and was unexpectedly deprived of his former condition. So, too, with them, that is, the people of Israel; though the God of all was benevolent and loving to them, saving and protective, and conferred his mercy on them like an early cloud and like morning dew falling, bringing forth his judgment as a light, and crowning them with worship according to the Law, they became indifferent about what was necessary to them and useful for their prosperity and reputation, and they themselves scorned the God who controls all things. This was in spite of Moses in his great wisdom saying clearly, "You shall not make for yourself an idol or likeness of anything in heaven above or on earth below or in the water under the earth," and again, "You shall have no other gods before me." But since like the first man—Adam, that is—they fell headlong into apostasy, they, too, will be completely estranged from the one who was in the habit of making them prosper, having broken a covenant.[10]

Cyril finds the comparison between the Covenant of Works with Adam and the Old Covenant compelling enough that he follows the Hebrew text. Hosea's meaning is clear to him. Dominican Ambrogio Cartharinus (1483–1553 AD) writes, "So then, God established a covenant with Adam from the beginning."[11] Cartharinus goes so far as to affirm that all humanity was represented by Adam as their federal head in whom sin was imputed.[12] Laynez (1512–1565 AD), Jesuit priest and delegate to the Council of Trent, spoke of "first covenant that the Lord made with Adam."[13]

After the Reformation, there was broad recognition among the Protestants that God made a covenant with Adam before his fall into sin. The Reformed confessions reflect this. The London Baptist Confession of 1689

---

10. Cyril, *Commentary on the Twelve Prophets*, 143.
11. Fesko, *Death*, 73.
12. Fesko, *Death*, 73.
13. Fesko, *Death*, 74.

confesses the covenant with Adam was a covenant of works.[14] The 1689 confession explains that this prelapsarian covenant was based on works:

> God gave to Adam a law of universal obedience written in his heart, and a particular precept of not eating the fruit of the tree of knowledge of good and evil; by which he bound him and all his posterity to personal, entire, exact, and perpetual obedience; promised life upon the fulfilling, and threatened death upon the breach of it.[15]

Arminian John Wesley, though certainly departing from the Reformed soteriology, nevertheless recognized the Covenant of Works with Adam. In fact, Wesley's firm understanding of the contrast between the covenants in Christ and with Adam is the basis of his sermon "The Righteousness of Faith," in which he writes,

> They were ignorant that "Christ is the end of the law for righteousness to every one that believeth;"—that, by the oblation of himself once offered, he had put an end to the first law or covenant, (which, indeed, was not given by God to Moses, but to Adam in his state of innocence,) the strict tenor whereof, without any abatement, was, "Do this, and live;" and, at the same time, purchased for us that better covenant "Believe, and live;" believe, and thou shalt be saved; now saved, both from the guilt and power of sin, and, of consequence, from the wages of it.[16]

And again, he writes,

> And, First, "the righteousness which is of the law saith, The man which doeth these things shall live by them." Constantly and perfectly observe all these things to do them, and then thou shalt live for ever. This law, or covenant, (usually called the Covenant of Works,) given by God to man in Paradise, required an obedience perfect in all its parts, entire and wanting nothing, as the condition of his eternal continuance in the holiness and happiness wherein he was created.[17]

While Wesley was not a Calvinist, his gospel proclamation was founded in the contrast between the Covenant of Works in Adam and the Covenant of Grace in Christ.

14. *London Confession*, 20:1.
15. *London Confession*, 19:1.
16. Wesley, "Righteousness of Faith."
17. Wesley, "Righteousness of Faith."

The Covenant of Works: Adam

James P. Boyce, one of the founders and first president of The Southern Baptist Theological Seminary, writes regarding Adam's federal headship,

> In the covenant, under which he sinned, he acted not merely as an individual man, the sole one of his kind, or one isolated from all others of his kind, but as the head of the race, for his posterity as well as himself.[18]

This recognition of the existence of the covenant made with Adam is found in a broad range of theological persuasions and is seen throughout church history and further back to Old Testament rabbis.

THE "COVENANT" OF WORKS

As the whole picture of Scripture comes into view, the Covenant of Works with Adam is an essential foundation for the subsequent story. There are five areas of evidence to consider. The five areas stand individually, but together will provide a cohesive argument that God created Adam in a "covenant" of works.

Hosea 6:7 and Isaiah 24:5

First, there are verses that speak of a prelapsarian covenant with Adam. Though variously disputed, Hosea 6:7 reads, "But like Adam they have transgressed the covenant." The Septuagint (LXX) translated the word for Adam as a generic reference to "like a man." Calvin and others followed the LXX. However, B. B. Warfield pointed out that it would lack apparent significance to say that Israel broke the covenant like a man without supplying reasons that are not readily evident.[19]

In 1892, Wellhausen suggested emending the text from "like Adam" to the name of a place, "at Adam," because of the following "there"[20] and the other references to places in the text. The emendation changed the *koph* (כ) to a *beth* (ב), "like Adam"[21] to "in Adam" or "at Adam."[22] The only known textual evidence for this change is the fourteenth-century

---

18. Boyce, *Abstract*, 156.
19. Warfield, "Hosea," 127.
20. שָׁם, *sham*.
21. כְּאָדָם.
22. בְאָדָם.

de Rosi Codex 554.[23] Some who follow Wellhausen, but note the lacking textual evidence, have argued for a place name without emending the text itself. Though the translation "at Adam" may be possible, the reference to some great transgression in the town Adam remains unknown. The town is only referenced in Joshua 3:16. Because of this lack of notorious wickedness, some have emended the name to Admah, the town destroyed with Sodom and Gomorrah.[24] But this change lacks any textual support. In choosing which translation to adopt, several things should be noted.

Initially, the use of "there" may lead one to think that "Adam" is a place. But other uses illustrate that "there" does not always reference a place. Psalm 14:5 says, "There they are in great dread, For God is with the righteous generation." Note too that the same use of "like Adam" is used in Job 31:33: "Have I covered my transgressions like Adam, by hiding my iniquity in my bosom." Also, while it is true that Hosea refers to many cities, their reference carries significance. Gilgal and Bethel[25] (Beth-aven) were known for idolatry. Jeroboam built golden calves at Shechem.[26] He built two altars, one at Bethel and one at Dan. The leaders of Israel and Judah used their power, represented by the high place at Mizpah and commanding mountain range at Tabor,[27] for evil. Hosea instructs Gibeah, Ramah, Beth-aven, known for their watchtowers, to sound their alarms.[28] Gilead, in the Transjordanian Israel, is condemned for its streets tracked with blood.[29] Gilead was complicit in the murder of King Pekahiah.[30] But "at Adam"? Adam was a little town mentioned once in Joshua 3. It was north of where Israel crossed the Jordan into the promised land.

Some have found it difficult to believe that Hosea would be the only prophet to mention the man Adam by name. But if Hosea is referring to the town of Adam, he is the only prophet to do so. It is not as though Hosea was not well familiar with Adam. Hosea makes extensive reference to Genesis—the Abrahamic Covenant (Hos 1:10; 2:25), the common grace covenant with creation after Noah exited the ark (Hos 2:20), the creation

---

23. Harper, *Critical Commentary on Amos and Hosea*, 287.
24. NEB, REB; Deut 29:23.
25. Hos 4:15; Amos 4:4.
26. 1 Kgs 12:25–33.
27. Hos 5:1–2.
28. Hos 5:8.
29. Hos 6:8.
30. 2 Kgs 15:25.

account (Hos 4:3), the Lion of the tribe of Judah (Hos 5:14), Ishmael being called a wild donkey (Hos 8:9), the curse on the ground (Hos 9:6), Sodom and Gomorrah (Hos 11:8), Jacob's birth, his struggle at Peniel and dream at Bethel (Hos 12:3–6). Byron G. Curtis counts sixteen references to Genesis in Hosea—without counting Hosea 6:7.[31] In addition, Hosea makes numerous references to other portions of the Pentateuch and the Former Prophets. So it should not be surprising that Hosea would refer to Adam. Really the question that should be asked is: What is Hosea saying? Hosea's argument doesn't rest on an obscure reference, but on the action of the federal head of the Covenant of Works.

Hosea was an eighth-century prophet to Israel. His own marriage to Gomer would be a living parable of God's relationship with Israel. Gomer would be unfaithful to Hosea as Israel was to God. Three times in Hosea 1–3, the adulterer is indicted, the verdict pronounced, a promise of restoration given. The relationship of the Old Covenant to the Abrahamic and New Covenants is of key importance. The first time, the indictment is on Gomer (1:1–2). The three children born to her are named for the verdicts. The first son is named Jezreel "because I will visit the bloodshed of Jezreel on the house of Jehu" (Hos 1:4 AT). God would put an end to Israel and break her bow (Hos 1:3–5). The second child, a daughter, is named Lo-ruhamah (no compassion) because God would have no compassion on Israel to forgive them. They broke the Old Covenant, and God would repay them with judgment without mercy. Because of the Abrahamic Covenant, God would have pity on Judah (Hos 1:7). God had promised the patriarchs the everlasting kingdom. Jacob had pronounced the unending blessing on his son Judah, that through him would come the king of the kingdom of God. God's judgment on Israel and Judah would not stop his unconditional covenant promise to the patriarchs. The third child, a son, was named Lo-ammi (not my people) because God's covenant people would no longer be his people (Hos 1:8–9). The first cycle is completed with a promised restoration in the New Covenant. In that day, God would fulfill his promise the Abrahamic Covenant. Rather than the extermination of Jezreel, the number of the sons of Israel will be as the sand of the sea (Hos 1:10; see Gen 22:17). Rather than Lo-ammi (not my people), they will be "sons of the living God" (Hos 1:10). Finally, they will not be Lo-ruhama (no compassion); they will be Ruhama (compassion;

---

31. Curtis, "Hosea," 189–92.

Hos 2:1). In the day of the New Covenant, they will be gathered under the Messiah and will go forth in a new exodus as a mighty army (Hos 1:11).

The second cycle gives a straightforward indictment, verdict, and promise. The legal complaint is presented in Hosea 2:2–5. Israel has been unfaithful and prostituted herself. The verdict follows in Hosea 2:6–13. God will block her way to Baalism (Hos 2:6–8) and remove her prosperity (Hos 2:9–13). They broke the Old Covenant, and God would repay them with punishment. In spite of their covenant unfaithfulness, God would again make covenant in the wilderness, a New Covenant, and give her again vineyards and hope like she had in the first exodus. They would be the faithful people of God in that day; idolatry would be removed from even their speech. This New Covenant would remove the curse in nature over them. No nations will again threaten them. They will know justice and compassion in that day. They will be God's people (Hos 2:14–23). The three names of Gomar's children are reversed: planted to the Lord in the lane, recipients of compassion, and God's people (Hos 2:23).

The third cycle goes straight to the verdict. Hosea would marry Gomar but she would "have no man" (Hos 3:1–3 AT). Israel in the exile is divorced from God because of the Old Covenant sanctions, but married because of the Abrahamic Covenant. After many days, in the New Covenant, God would redeem them and fulfill the Davidic promise.

What is important to see is the interplay of the Abrahamic, Mosaic, and New Covenants. Throughout Hosea judgment is pronounced on Israel for breaking the Mosaic Covenant. They ignored the former prophets' call to repentance and now are no different than the Gentiles. This indictment is repeated twice. Then the verdict is proclaimed three times. Israel will receive no compassion from God. They will not be God's people any longer. They will be divorced and exiled from the Lord. This covenant breaking and sanctioned punishment accords with the terms of the Mosaic Covenant. But beyond this indictment and pronounced judgment is the grace promised Abraham. This promised restoration based on God's covenant with Abraham is restated three times. Because of the Abrahamic Covenant, the remnant of Judah (1:7) will receive grace. Though exterminated by the judgment of the Mosaic Covenant, God will fulfill his promise to Abraham to make his seed as innumerable as the sand of the sea (Hos 1:10; Gen 22:17). Because of God's grace in the New Covenant fulfillment of the Abrahamic Covenant, they will be "sons of the living God." This development of God's covenant promises pervades the entire book. While the dominant message is certainly on the judgment on Israel for breaking the Mosaic Covenant, the promises of the Abrahamic Covenant point to the blessings to come in the New Covenant.

The promises to the patriarchs will come to pass. The Lion of the tribe of Judah will roar (Gen 49:8–12), and God will gather the people of God from the nations (Hos 11:8–11). The Lord will deliver them as he did in the days of the exodus (Hos 12:9). Death will have no power over his people in the day of restoration (Hos 13:14). In that day God will heal and love them. The anger of his judgment will be no more. He will cause his people to blossom like a lily or like a cedar of Lebanon. He will fill his people with splendor. They will flourish in his grace (Hos 14:2–8).

When the reader approaches Hosea 6 with the awareness of the foundational covenant structures, verse 7 is not a throwaway reference to an unknown town. Hosea calls Israel to repentance at the beginning of chapter 6, but Israel's covenant loyalty (*chesed*)[32] is like a transient cloud (Hos 6:4). She professes, but there is nothing to her promised love. She gives burnt offerings, but she has turned to other lovers. So God's judgment has come (see Hos 6:5). God requires *chesed*, covenant faithfulness.[33] Like Adam, they were put in the kingdom but did not love God and keep his covenant. Like Adam, they will be cast out of the kingdom (Hos 6:7).

Another text that appears to speak clearly of the prelapsarian covenant with Adam is Isaiah 24:5, "The earth is also polluted by its inhabitants, for they transgressed laws, violated statutes, broke the ancient covenant" (AT). This verse is found in the section of Isaiah known as the "Little Apocalypse" (Isa 24–27). Though using the Mosaic typological form, this section looks to the ultimate conquest of the kingdom of God over the dragon and his demonic horde. The section is structured as a chiasm.

24—World judgment; but there is a remnant.

25—God is the Savior from the enemy.

26—God is the Savior to the city of life.

27—Judgment on Israel; but there is a remnant.

Chapter 24 points to the Final Judgment and devastation of the earth. It is the great de-creation. Rather than the earth being filled, it is emptied[34] (Isa 24:1, 3). There is no class of people exempt from the Judgment Day

---

32. וְחַסְדְּכֶם.
33. חֶסֶד (Hos 6:6).
34. בּוֹקֵק, *baqaq*.

(24:2). Like a bottle emptied of its contents, so the earth will be emptied and its inhabitants scattered. For rather than the creation becoming the kingdom of God through Adam's covenant faithfulness, the earth has become a graveyard for sinful man.[35] The earth mourns (Isa 24:4-6) under the weight of death. In the midst of this universal pronouncement of judgment, Isaiah gives the reason: they broke the "ancient covenant."[36] Curse now devours the earth. The word translated "ancient" is 'olam, and though the word is often translated "everlasting" because of indefiniteness, 'olam is not limited to this meaning. Allan MacRae notes, "There are at least twenty instances where it clearly refers to the past. Such usages generally point to something that seems long ago, but rarely if ever refer to a limitless past."[37] For example, in 1 Samuel 27:8 'olam is translated "ancient" in the NASB and "of old" in the ESV to refer to the exodus from Egypt. Isaiah is unambiguous; death reigns because Adam broke the covenant.

Exodus 31:16–17 and Romans 2:6–10

Second, there are passages that imply the existence of the prelapsarian covenant with Adam. As evidenced by other covenants, sometimes the covenant exists even though it is only later that it is referred to as a covenant. 2 Samuel 7:11–16 recounts God's promise to establish the throne of King David forever. He will not be like Saul, whose royal lineage was cut off. David's kingdom will endure forever. There is no mention of a "covenant" in the immediate text. But David understood that God's promise was a covenant, and in his last words he confessed that God had made a "covenant" with him (2 Sam 23:5). And again, Psalm 89:3 says God made a "covenant" with David. In the same way, there are passages that are about a covenant and therefore imply a covenant with Adam. One of these is Exodus 31:16–17. The sabbath was the "sign" of the Mosaic Covenant. So the Law included the sign of the covenant in Exodus 20:8–11. This sign of the Law covenant given at Sinai was based on the original sabbath recorded in Genesis 2:1–3. The "sign" of the covenant given to the kingdom people in the covenant at Sinai looks back to the sabbath given the vassal of the kingdom in the garden of Eden. This relationship

---

35. Rom 8:19–22.
36. בְּרִית עוֹלָם, berith 'olam; Isa 24:5.
37. MacRae, "עוֹלָם (olam)," 672.

between the sign and the covenant with Israel suggests that the earlier relationship between Adam and God was also a covenant. As the sabbath pointed to the promise of shalom in the kingdom if they kept the Law covenant, so the sabbath in Genesis 2:1–3 is a promise to Adam. Both are covenant sanctions—the Mosaic of typological shalom rest, the Adamic of eschatological glory.

Romans 2:6–10 is like Isaiah 24:5 in its universal scope of judgment. Contextually, Paul is not discussing ways of salvation. He has listed the basis of judgment for the Gentiles in chapter 1, and now in chapter 2 he turns to the self-righteous Jew. The Gentiles are without excuse (Rom 1:20). If the Gentile without the written revelation of God is condemned, then how much more the Jew, who has been blessed with the Law (Rom 2:1–5, 12–24). Both Jew and Gentile stand condemned before the righteousness of God (Rom 3:9–10). For the righteousness of God is impartial in judging all according to what they have done. It is a matter of legal righteousness. There is no mercy in the equation. Paul develops this point in the passage in a chiasm. The Final Judgment is according to works (Rom 2:6,11). The righteous will be recompensed with glory and eternal life (Rom 2:7,10), and the unrighteous are rendered wrath (Rom 2:8–9).

6—Judgment according to works
  7—Glory, honor, immortality
    8—Wrath and indignation
    9—Tribulation and distress
  10—Glory, honor, peace
11—No partiality with God

There is only this one impartial standard on Judgment Day. Both Gentile and Jew will be judged according to works. The standard for judgment contains no mercy or grace. Judgment Day is a matter of legal justice before God.

There is a question that is often overlooked. Why does this most foundational standard for the just judgment of God promise "glory, honor, and peace"? Strictly speaking, God could have made a creature and required perpetual service and obedience without any recompense of "glory, honor, and peace." But God made a world where Adam's obedience and service would be repaid with "glory, honor, and peace." What is it about the world that God made that makes the most foundational standard for final judgment require that the righteous receive glory? God made Adam in a covenant-of-works relationship. This covenant is the creational standard of judgment for the final Judgment Day. All men, Gentile and Jew, are accountable to this first covenant. The Final Judgment is not based on a standard prior to this covenant of works. The recompense of "glory, honor, and peace" is the covenant blessing promised Adam if he fulfilled the covenant requirement. Likewise, God recompenses the unrighteous with the wrath threatened Adam if he failed. This latter state of condemnation is the status of every man represented by Adam. There is none righteous. Those receiving glory is an empty set. To them is rendered "peace" (vs. 10, *eirane*, εἰρήνη, the Greek word used in the LXX for *shalom*). Though *shalom* is sometimes used to highlight the deliverance from strife and war, the "peace" here promised is the eschatological promise of completeness and fulfillment—the final state. To this empty set belongs honor and glory. The impartial judgment of God delivers the sanctions of the Covenant of Works made with all men in Adam. Paul here confronts the Jew with his need of the Savior. For there is none righteous. The promise to recompense the righteous "glory, honor, and peace" goes beyond what justice would require of God's righteousness to a creature apart from the Covenant of Works. The promised sanction requires a covenant.

Romans 5:12–21

Scripture's teaching that Adam is the prelapsarian federal head of humanity requires the Covenant of Works with Adam. Paul develops the contrast between the two federal heads in Romans 5:12–21. In the previous section (Rom 5:1–11), Paul writes that the believer exults in the certainty of sharing in the Glory of God (Rom 5:2). Then in 5:12–21 Paul gives the reason the believer can have this certain hope. As all died in Adam's sin, so all believers are given righteousness and life in the obedience of the Second Adam, Christ Jesus.

Paul starts with "Because of this" (Rom 5:12)[38] to connect the basis of the certainty (5:12–21) with the certain hope (5:1–11). Though he will quickly interject a parenthetical thought in verses 13–14,[39] in verse 12 he gives the Adamic part of the comparison:

---

38. Διὰ τοῦτο.
39. See Kline, "Gospel."

> Just as through one man sin came into the world, and through the sin [came] death, and in this way death spread to all men, because all sinned. (AT)

Paul is not a Pelagian. Paul does not say that all sinned like Adam and so died. That would raise several problems. Why do infants die in the womb before being able to consciously sin or even have inclinations of the heart? King David confessed that he was a sinner from conception (Ps 51: 5). Why did every person sin if they come into this world without original sin in Adam? Paul does not say that everyone who came into the world themselves sinned and so also died. Rather, the connection is between Adam's sin and the death of everyone. But why does everyone die because of Adam's sin? All die "because all sinned." As the representative of all, when Adam sinned, they sinned. Paul does not say that sin spread to everyone, but rather that death "spread to all men, because all sinned" (Rom 5:12).

Paul is not ignorant of the fact that sin came into the world before Adam. The demons of heaven had already rebelled. Eve had already sinned. But Adam's sin brought condemnation and death to all. Paul writes in verse 15, "for if by the transgression of the one the many died."[40] Verse 16 says, "the judgment out of one [transgression] unto condemnation" (AT).[41] Again in verse 17 Paul writes, "For if by the transgression of the one, death reigned through the one."[42] Paul is unrelenting in the connection between Adam and mankind's condemnation. In verse 18 he continues, "Therefore then as through one transgression unto all men unto condemnation" (AT).[43] He doesn't stop. Verse 19 says, "For just as through the disobedience of the one man the many were constituted [AT][44] sinners."[45] The word translated here "constituted" is elsewhere used for appointing someone to position. Jesus asks in Luke 12:14, "Who made [constituted] me a judge?" Adam's sin placed all men in the category of sinner and being subject to condemnation.

---

40. εἰ γὰρ τῷ τοῦ ἑνὸς παραπτώματι οἱ πολλοὶ ἀπέθανον.
41. τὸ μὲν γὰρ κρίμα ἐξ ἑνὸς εἰς κατάκριμα.
42. εἰ γὰρ τῷ τοῦ ἑνὸς παραπτώματι ὁ θάνατος ἐβασίλευσεν διὰ τοῦ ἑνός.
43. Ἄρα οὖν ὡς δι' ἑνὸς παραπτώματος εἰς πάντας ἀνθρώπους εἰς κατάκριμα.
44. κατεστάθησαν; *kathistémi*; forensic term used for legally making someone something; e.g., "appointed."
45. ὥσπερ γὰρ διὰ τῆς παρακοῆς τοῦ ἑνὸς ἀνθρώπου ἁμαρτωλοὶ κατεστάθησαν οἱ πολλοί.

On the contrasting side of the comparison is the covenant-keeping obedience of Christ. Paul assures in verse 18, "and in this way through the one act of righteousness unto all men unto justification of life."[46] Paul again says in verse 19, "and in this way through the obedience of the one the many will be constituted righteous" (AT).[47] This finished complete work of Christ is the reason for the certainty that causes the believer to hope (Rom 5:1–11). Adam's sin has not had the last word. Christ has the last word. Paul in his lengthy discussion of the believer's resurrection writes, "For as in Adam all die, so also in Christ all will be made alive" (1 Cor 15:22).

This solid foundation of the believer's hope is the finished work of Christ. This union "in Christ" is a covenant union. Jesus says to the disciples, "And I covenant [*diatithemi*] to you, just as my Father covenanted to me the kingdom" (AT).[48] This verbal form of *diatheke* (*diatithemi*) is elsewhere translated "covenant." In the LXX the Hebrew noun for "covenant" (*berith*) is translated with *diatheke*. Jeremiah 38:31 in the LXX (31:33 in the English) says, "the covenant [*diatheke*] which I will covenant (*diatithemi*) to the house of Israel after those days."[49] The LXX of Deuteronomy 7:2 uses the same combination of the verb and the noun: "you will not covenant a covenant to them."[50] Though there is a need to examine the exact meaning of this covenant union of the believer "in Christ," for now the point is that the work of Christ is in the context of a covenant. The contrast Paul makes in Romans 5:12–21 and 1 Corinthians 15 evaporates without there also being a covenant between God and Adam. The contrast is between the federal heads of two covenants. The first Adam transgressed the covenant. The Second Adam obeyed.

Ezekiel 16

Fourth, the relationship between image and covenant implies that when God created Adam in his image in Genesis 1–2, God was in the same act creating Adam in a covenant relationship with himself. Ezekiel 16 displays the relationship between image and covenant. But what is meant by

---

46. οὕτως καὶ δι' ἑνὸς δικαιώματος εἰς πάντας ἀνθρώπους εἰς δικαίωσιν ζωῆς.
47. οὕτως καὶ διὰ τῆς ὑπακοῆς τοῦ ἑνὸς δίκαιοι κατασταθήσονται οἱ πολλοί.
48. Luke 22:29: κἀγὼ διατίθεμαι ὑμῖν, καθὼς διέθετό μοι.
49. ἡ διαθήκη ἣν διαθήσομαι τῷ οἴκῳ ισραηλ μετὰ τὰς ἡμέρας ἐκείνας.
50. οὐ διαθήσῃ πρὸς αὐτοὺς διαθήκην.

The Covenant of Works: Adam

a "covenant"? In contrast to our modern usage, a "covenant" in the Scriptures is not necessarily a bilateral agreement. When God covenanted with creation after the flood not to destroy the world again by another deluge, that was not a bilateral agreement. Nor is it a "bond-in-blood sovereignly administered"[51] or a redemptive "oath-bound confirmation of promise,"[52] as some theologians have suggested. The postdiluvian covenant with creation is not a promise of redemption, but a common-grace delay of the Judgment Day. Also, the covenant with Adam is not a promise in blood. Redemption was not in the picture. It should be noted here that, though it will be explored much more extensively in later chapters, some covenants are unconditional while others are conditional. The Abrahamic Covenant is unconditional. Paul calls it "the promise" in Galatians 3:17. But the Mosaic Covenant sanctions are conditioned upon obedience. Paul calls it "the Law." The definition of "covenant" has to be broad enough to encompass all the covenants found in Scripture. A "covenant" is an oath with divine sanctions.[53]

What is instructive is to see how Ezekiel connects the Mosaic Covenant with God clothing Israel in the image of his Glory-Spirit.[54] For Israel to be clothed as God's image is for Israel to be in a covenant relationship with God. Ezekiel 16 uses an allegory to portray God's relationship with Israel. He took her from her pitiful condition and made her his own wife. Jeremiah uses this same marital imagery in Jeremiah 31:32 to refer to God's covenant with Israel. God says, "My covenant which they broke, although I was a husband to them." Jeremiah 2:2 refers to Israel's days in the wilderness as her betrothal to God. Ezekiel 16:8 describes God's covenant-making love for Israel: "I spread the corner of my robe[55] over you and covered your nakedness. I swore to you and entered into a covenant with you declares the Sovereign Lord, and you became Mine" (AT). Like a groom putting the wedding ring on his bride's hand, culturally, to spread the robe over the bride was a promise of marital love.

The symbolism is seen in Ruth 3. Naomi instructed her daughter-in-law, Ruth, to bathe, dress up, put on perfume, and then secretly go down to Boaz's place. She waited until he finished dinner, and lay down

---

51. Robertson, *Christ*, 15.
52. Murray, "Adamic Administration," 49.
53. Kline, *Kingdom Prologue*, 4.
54. Kline, *Images*, 50–53.
55. כְּנָפִי, *kanaph*, literally "extremity."

to sleep. She went to where Boaz was sleeping, uncovered his feet, and lay down. He woke in the middle of the night and was shocked to see her lying at his feet. Startled, he said, "Who are you?" Ruth proposed to Boaz. She asked him as her kinsman redeemer to marry her. She said, "I am Ruth your maid. So spread your covering over your maid" (Ruth 3:9). As the story continues, he did take Ruth in the marriage covenant.

This use of "corner of the robe" (*kanap*, כָּנָף) is used also twice in Deuteronomy to prohibit a son from having immoral relations with his father's wife. Though it is often translated as "uncover the nakedness of his father," a better translation[56] would be "uncover the edge of his father's robe" (Deut 22:30 AT).[57] The issue is not revealing the father's nakedness by uncovering him, but rather to reverse the covenant his father has with his wife in covering her with the edge of his robe.

Ezekiel 16:8 pictures God taking his bride at Sinai. God spread his robe over Israel and promised protection. He took her as his own. But more than protection is in view. He cleansed her. He clothed her in embroidered fine linen, gold, silver and precious jewels. He put sandals on her feet. He put a crown on her head. He clothed her with his Glory. Literally, God's Glory-cloud was over Israel at Sinai. Psalm 105:39 says, "He spread a cloud for a covering, And fire to illumine by night." The word used for "spread" (*paras*, פָּרַשׂ) is the same used in Ezekiel 16:8. God covered his bride, Israel, with his Glory, and he made her in his image.

The allegory of Ezekiel 16 uses the same clothing, provision, and crown for the bride that were given to Aaron the high priest and the tabernacle where the Glory-cloud dwelt. Aaron represents Israel, the bride. Aaron's clothing and crown and the materials used for the tabernacle replicate the Glory-cloud. The gems, gold, silver, linen embroidered, even the material used for the sandals, the washing, and the fine flour and oil are all what was seen in Aaron and the tabernacle. Israel is "clothed" with the Glory-Spirit. In the allegory, the bride bears the Glory-image of the Glory-cloud. Israel is taken by God in the Mosaic Covenant and "clothed" to be the image of God's Glory.[58]

This connection between the image of God and covenant relationship is present in other covenants in Scripture. When Jesus fulfilled the

---

56. See NASB: "uncovered his father's skirt. יְגַלֶּה כְּנַף אָבִיו

57. Masoretic text 23:1 and 27:20, יְגַלֶּה כְּנַף אָבִיו.

58. Kline, *Images*, 52–53.

The Covenant of Works: Adam

Pactum Salutis[59] between himself, as the Second Adam, and the Father, the Spirit of God raised Jesus from the dead (Rom 8:11) and clothed him with the Glory-Spirit. Paul asserts that Jesus is the image of God.[60] Having fulfilled his covenant mission, Revelation 1:13ff. presents Jesus in his glorified state. He is clothed in the Glory-Spirit. His faithfulness to the Pactum Salutis then is the basis for the New Covenant. Jesus is the archetype for his bride to be transformed in his image and clothed with his Glory. Paul writes,

> And we know that God causes all things to work together for good to those who love God, to those who are called according to His purpose. **29** For those whom He foreknew, He also predestined to become conformed to the image of His Son, so that He would be the firstborn among many brethren; **30** and these whom He predestined, He also called; and these whom He called, He also justified; and these whom He justified, He also glorified. (Rom 8:28–30)

In the three verses, Paul connects being conformed to Christ's "image" and the ultimate glorification that awaits the believer. The condensed references here are to point to this interconnectedness of being in God's image and being in a covenant relationship with God.

This coalescence of "covenant" and "image" demonstrates the existence of a covenant made with Adam before the fall. Kline notes,

> Thus ingeniously the prophetic parable interweaves the concepts of the covenant and the image of God, revealing their mutuality by covering them both under the one symbol of investiture in the divine Glory.[61]

Like Ezekiel 16, Genesis 1 describes God's covenant with Adam, though it uses "image." Kline writes,

> Discovery of the biblical nexus between the concepts of image of God and divine covenant validates Covenant Theology's identification of the Creator's relation to man at the beginning as a covenantal arrangement. In light of the interrelation we have found between covenant and image of God, the fact of man's

---

59. Covenant between God the Father and God the Son.
60. Col 1:15.
61. Kline, *Images*, 53.

creation in God's image, explicitly affirmed in Genesis 1:27, would in and of itself signify the existence of a covenant.[62]

To be the image of God is in fact to be in a covenant relationship with God.

Genesis 1:2

Fifth, the Spirit's hovering presence at creation immediately signals the reader the formation of a covenant. Consider the constituent parts: the Spirit, the creation, the kingdom of God, and the covenant. The reference to the Spirit of God "hovering" in Genesis 1:2 immediately connects the reader to Deuteronomy 32:10–11, where the Glory-cloud hovers over Israel in the wilderness. This Glory-cloud was the visible representation of God's presence with his people. This is the point of Moses' pleading with God in Exodus 33. God says he will send the Angel of the Lord, but not his Presence, the Glory-cloud.[63] God relents, and his Glory-Presence attends Israel to the promised land. As the representation of the King, the theophany of the Glory-cloud takes on the form of the King. At Sinai, "the finger" of God writes the Law on tablets of stone.[64] It is the "glorious arm" of God that delivered Israel in the Exodus.[65] Moses was not allowed to see the "face" of God, but saw his "back" when God covered Moses with his "hand."[66] The most prominent description of the King's theophany is of his feet. They are called "pillars."[67]

Daniel described the Glory theophany in the context of Israel's Babylonian exile. In Daniel 8:15–17, Daniel saw what looked like man over the Ulai River. Daniel was overcome with fear and fell on his face. In Daniel 10:4–9, Daniel saw the same theophany. The man was dressed in linen and girded with a golden belt. His body was a transparent yellow. His face was like lightning. His eyes were like torches. His feet were like a highly polished bronze. When Daniel saw this theophany, he turned deathly pale and fell to the ground. Again, a third time, in Daniel 12:5–7,

---

62. Kline, *Images*, 55.
63. Kline, *Images*, 71–74.
64. Exod 31:18; see Exod 8:19; 2 Cor 3:3; The "finger of God" is the Spirit. Jesus says in Luke 11:20, "But if I drive out demons by the finger of God" (NIV). The parallel in Matthew 12:28 says, "But if it is by the Spirit of God that I drive out demons" (NIV).
65. Isa 63:12.
66. Exod 33:19–23.
67. Kline, *Images*, 19.

Daniel saw the man over the river dressed in linen like a priest. The man raised his hands to heaven and swore by God. God's revelation to John refers to this same Glory-theophany in Revelation 10:1–3. John saw the angel[68] clothed in the Glory-cloud with the rainbow on his face and his face shining like the sun. Do not miss this. His feet are like pillars of fire! He put one foot on the land and one on the sea and roared! He lifted his hand to heaven and swore by himself! This image of the Lord standing in Israel's midst is referenced by Haggai 2:5: "when you came out of Egypt, and My Spirit stood[69] in your midst." The pillar-cloud "stood" at the entrance to the tabernacle to talk with Moses like a friend (Exod 33:10–11).[70] The Glory-cloud dwelt in the tabernacle above the mercy seat, which was called the "footstool" of God.[71]

When the King, in theophany, stands at the entrance to the tabernacle and talks with Moses, the size discrepancy is such that they only see his "feet." This Glory-cloud represents the King. Before Israel crossed the Red Sea, the King went and stood between Israel and the Egyptian army (Exod 14:19ff.). The blast of the King's "nostrils" piled the water for Israel to cross (Exod 15:8) while the "right hand" of the King slew the enemy (Exod 15:6). When the King stopped, Israel stopped. When the King rose up, Israel rose up and followed. Numbers 9:17 says,

> Whenever the cloud was lifted from over the tent, afterward the sons of Israel would then set out; and in the place where the cloud settled down, there the sons of Israel would camp.

The Glory-cloud led Israel to the promised land. When he was not walking before Israel, the King sat enthroned above the mercy seat between the cherubim.[72]

Kline observes that Moses presents Israel's exodus and national formation as a re-creation. As the "Spirit of God was hovering" over the "formless" (*tōhû*) at creation, so the Glory-cloud "hovers" over Israel in the "formless" (*tōhû*, trans. "wilderness") to make a new creation. The re-creation image is seen in the exodus out of the water and through the "formless" wilderness to the promised land flowing with milk and honey. The beginning of the year, the *rosh* (רֹאשׁ, Exod 12:2), started with the

---

68. Jesus in his glorious state; see Rev 1:13–16; see Beale, *Book of Revelation*, 522.
69. עָמְדָה, *amad*.
70. See Num 12:5; Deut 31:15; Ezek 9:3; 10:4, 18.
71. 1 Chr 28:2; Ps 132:7.
72. Lev 16:2; Num 7:8–9.

exodus Passover. The de-creational plagues are superseded by the creation of Israel. The light covered the Israelites while Egypt was in blinding darkness (Exod 10:21–23). The waters were divided for the dry land to appear as Israel crossed (Exod 14:21–22). The construction of the tabernacle itself copied the divine edicts to "make" in Exodus 25–31 with the compliance "they made" in Exodus 35–40. Echoing Genesis 2:2, Moses finished his work (Exod 40:33).[73] Finally, as the sabbath was given as the promise in Genesis 2:1–3, so Israel was brought to the promised land of sabbath rest.[74] But as the author of Hebrews notes, it was not the actual sabbath (Heb 4:8–9). This re-creation of Israel is the reason the Spirit hovered over Israel.

The third part to consider is that God was creating his kingdom. Exodus 19:6 says, "you shall be to Me a kingdom of priests and a holy nation." The fact that God is creating his kingdom is central to the story. God promises to make Abraham a great nation.[75] This kingdom promise shapes the remainder of the Old and New Testaments. Israel was to be that kingdom in the Old Testament. Even the Law God gave Israel was written in the form a suzerainty treaty common to other kingdoms of the period.[76] Even before the kingdom of Israel had an earthly king, Israel recognized they were a nation. The elders of Israel came to Samuel and begged to have a king like the other nations.[77] God told Samuel that it was God that Israel rejected as King. They had rejected him since the exodus.[78]

Finally, consider that God created his kingdom by making a covenant with Israel at Mt. Sinai. Kingdoms were created and administered by covenants. Deuteronomy 32:8 references the dividing of the nations in Genesis 10. God said,

> You yourselves have seen what I did to the Egyptians, and *how* I bore you on eagles' wings, and brought you to Myself. [5] Now then, if you will indeed obey My voice and keep My covenant, then you shall be My own possession among all the peoples, for all the earth is Mine; [6] and you shall be to Me a kingdom of priests and a holy nation. (Exod 19:4–6)

---

73. Kline, *God*, 125–26.
74. Josh 1:13; Gen 49:15; Num 10:33–36; Deut 12:9.
75. Gen 12:3.
76. See Kline, *Treaty*; Kline, *Structure*.
77. 1 Sam 8:4–5.
78. 1 Sam 8:7–8.

As has been referenced, Hosea pictures the time from the exodus to Sinai as the betrothal. But the vows are taken in the covenant at Mt. Sinai. Then Israel became his bride, his kingdom people. It is then that the Glory-cloud of the King stood as witness to the covenant with his kingdom people. Haggai 2:5 says, "As for the word which I covenanted with you, when you came out of Egypt, and My Spirit stood[79] in your midst" (AT). This same oath stance by the Spirit-theophany is seen in Daniel 12 and Revelation 10. This fits the significance of pillars as witnesses in legal transactions. M. M. Kline explains,

> The Spirit-pillar dwelling between the cherubim above the mercy-seat which was set on top of the ark of the covenant parallels the conceptions of the dwelling presence of deities found in surrounding cultures. Images of the gods were set upon portable throne boxes which were carried by four men carrying a platform on which the throne stood. These images of the gods could then be taken in processions throughout the city. It was these objects which were brought to the treaty makings so that the gods could be considered as witnessing the oaths which were sworn. Similarly, the pillar of cloud which dwelt upon the mercy-seat throne in the tabernacle was the presence of God which witnessed the covenant cutting at Sinai and the renewal of that covenant made before the people crossed the Jordan River.[80]

Note the connection between kingdom and covenant. The kingdom was formed by the covenant. The tablets of the covenant are in the ark under the mercy seat of the King. Another passage that bears to the witness function of the pillar is the covenant renewal in the days of Josiah. Second Kings 23:3 is often translated, "The king stood by the pillar and renewed the covenant in the presence of the Lord" (NIV). It could also be translated, "The king stood in front of[81] the pillar and renewed the covenant in the presence of the Lord." The reference is to the pillars at the entry to the temple. As the Glory-pillar stood at the entrance with Moses, Solomon made pillars at the entry of the temple. The pillar theophany forms the frame for the entrance into heaven. The Glory-pillar represents God standing and witnessing the making of the covenant.[82] Also, the people

---

79. עָמְדָה, amad.
80. Kline, *Covenant Witness*, 60.
81. עַל, "in front of"; Holliday, *Concise Hebrew*, 272.
82. Kline, *Glory*, 204; Kline, *Images*, 40.

stood to covenant, as the rest of the verse says, "all the people stood in covenant" (AT).[83]

The first readers would have seen the clear parallel between the Glory-Spirit hovering over Adam at the creation of the kingdom of God by the covenant and the Glory-cloud hovering Israel at the re-creation of the kingdom of God by the covenant at Sinai. The covenant with Adam was described using the language of "image," but the reader would not have missed the connections. For decades Israel had seen the Glory-cloud, who made them his kingdom people through covenant making and renewal. The "hovering" in Deuteronomy 32 called to mind all that they had seen. The "hovering" in Genesis 1:2 immediately brought to mind the original kingdom made through covenant. The role of the covenant in the kingdom makes it inconceivable that Genesis 1:2 could refer to God's kingdom without a covenant. While not all covenants indicate the presence of a kingdom, without a covenant, there is no kingdom.

THE COVENANT OF WORKS AT CREATION

The Covenant—Genesis 1:1—2:3

Genesis 1:1—2:3 provides the broad parameters of God's covenant with Adam. Then in Genesis 2:4ff. Moses focuses on the specifics of the covenant probation. First, when God created Adam (Gen 1:26ff.) and "the earth" (Gen 1:2), that creative act was the creation of the Covenant of Works. Adam never existed as a creature before or outside of the covenant relationship. The covenant with Adam is not an addendum to creation. Along with the other edicts of the creation week, God gave the edict to create Adam in his image. As has been argued before and will be elaborated here, this was the act of creating Adam as party to the covenant. Before God made Eve, he planted the tree of the knowledge of good and evil and the tree of life (Gen 2:9). Both of these trees would play a central role in the covenant probation. Before God made Eve, God gave the covenant prohibition to Adam, "you must not eat from the tree of the knowledge of good and evil, for when you eat from it you will certainly die" (Gen 2:17 NIV). Within the creation week, God set apart the sabbath day to remind Adam of the glory promised in the covenant. Adam never existed in a state of nature outside of the Covenant of Works.

---

83. וַיַּעֲמֹד כָּל־הָעָם בַּבְּרִית.

The Covenant of Works: Adam

Likewise, "the earth" (Gen 1:1) did not exist prior to or outside the Covenant of Works. Creation was a covenantal enterprise. From the beginning, the King administered his kingdom on earth by creating Adam and the visible cosmos in a covenant. Nature was created for the Covenant of Works with Adam. Not only did Adam's breaking the covenant have lasting effects on humanity, but it resulted in creation itself bearing the consequences of Adam's sin. Paul highlights this in Romans 8:19–22:

> For the anxious longing of the creation waits eagerly for the revealing of the sons of God. 20 For the creation was subjected to futility, not willingly, but because of Him who subjected it, in hope 21 that the creation itself also will be set free from its slavery to corruption into the freedom of the glory of the children of God. 22 For we know that the whole creation groans and suffers the pains of childbirth together until now.

Paul personifies[84] the subhuman creation anticipating the day it was made for, the glorification of the King's people. But as a result of Adam's breaking the covenant, the purpose of creation has been frustrated during this age. Creation didn't change with the breaking of the covenant, but the gardener did. Now it produces thorns and thistles[85] instead of being filled and subdued to be the kingdom of God on earth. But the visible creation did not revert to some natural state after Adam sinned. Creation was created as the stage for the Covenant of Works. That was its raison d'être.[86] It was the building supplies for the temple delivered to the site, but left unbuilt.

So the creation now bears witness against all men in their sin. Paul writes in Romans 1:20,

> For since the creation of the world His invisible attributes, His eternal power and divine nature, have been clearly seen, being understood through what has been made, so that they are without excuse.

Creation witnesses with constant clarity to the Glory of the King. It is not some natural law that condemns man. The visible world made for the Covenant of Works with Adam condemns all as covenant breakers in Adam. The contrast is between what man was made for and man as a sinner. Psalm 19:1–6 declares,

84. See Ps 65:12–13, "singing for joy"; Isa 24:4, "earth mourns."
85. Gen 3:18.
86. Reason for being.

> The heavens are telling of the glory of God;
> And their expanse is declaring the work of His hands.
> ² Day to day pours forth speech,
> And night to night reveals knowledge.
> ³ There is no speech, nor are there words;
> Their voice is not heard.
> ⁴ Their line has gone out through all the earth,
> And their utterances to the end of the world.
> In them He has placed a tent for the sun,
> ⁵ Which is as a bridegroom coming out of his chamber;
> It rejoices as a strong man to run his course.
> ⁶ Its rising is from one end of the heavens,
> And its circuit to the other end of them;
> And there is nothing hidden from its heat.

Imagine, if you will, an amazing movie director. He is brilliant in his creativity and production. He has written a fabulous script and chosen the perfect cast. He also is extremely sensitive to the needs of the crew and cast. He provides for their luxury housing and delights their palate. He is scandalously generous in the contracted salaries. His sets bear the marks of genius. But one day the lead male actor decides to quit without provocation. To everyone's amazement, without reason, he storms off the set. He goes immediately to the press and spews every lie imaginable. He says the director is unreasonable, tight-fisted, and doesn't know what he is doing. He says the director has been starving the cast and crew and refuses to provide any housing while they are on the road. He says the set designs are amateurish, and he will no longer associate with such a sham. But the evidence says otherwise. The empty sets show the exquisite attention to detail of a master. The bills from the caterers and hotels show the lavish expense he has paid. The other actors are profuse in their praise of the director. To use our illustration, the creation is the set designed for the glorious production. The creation was made for the creation mandate assigned to Adam. Now the set testifies to what would have been, to the Creator's magnificence, and to Adam's rebellion.

Some have suggested that God made a separate covenant with creation. They argue from Genesis 9:9, "Now behold, I Myself do establish My covenant," and Jeremiah 33:20–22:

> If you can break My covenant for the day and My covenant for the night, so that day and night will not be at their appointed time, ²¹ then My covenant may also be broken with David My servant so that he will not have a son to reign on his throne, and

with the Levitical priests, My ministers. 22 As the host of heaven cannot be counted and the sand of the sea cannot be measured, so I will multiply the descendants of David My servant and the Levites who minister to Me.

The argument from Genesis 9 centers around the word "establish." When God makes a covenant, he "cuts" the covenant. When he causes a covenant to come to pass, he "establishes" the covenant. So it is argued that after the flood God is promising to establish the covenant made with creation before the flood at creation. As has been argued, this is not supported by the Genesis creation account. The covenant being "established" in Genesis 9 refers to the covenant just made in Genesis 8:21–22:

> The LORD smelled the soothing aroma; and the Lord said to Himself, "I will never again curse the ground on account of man, for the intent of man's heart is evil from his youth; and I will never again destroy every living thing, as I have done.
> 22 While the earth remains,
> Seedtime and harvest,
> And cold and heat,
> And summer and winter,
> And day and night
> Shall not cease.

Jeremiah 33:20–22 too refers to this common grace covenant made after the flood. This unconditional covenant cannot be broken. So too, God's unconditional covenant to David cannot be nullified. It is the fulfillment of the unconditional covenant promise to Abraham. There is not a prelapsarian covenant made with creation separate from the Covenant of Works with Adam. The covenant is made with Adam. Creation is the set.

Second, the account of God's image gives the basic components of the covenant. Kline notes the three elements that comprise the "image of God" in Adam: "Made in the likeness of this holy Lord of Glory, man was invested with dominion (like the angels, cf. Ps 8:5), moral excellence (cf. Eph 4:24; Gal 3:10), and the prospect of glorification (cf. 1 Cor 15:49ff.)."[87] While these three elements—dominion, righteousness, and glorification—define "image," they also designate the parts of the covenant. Adam is given dominion as the vassal son of the King of Heaven to build the kingdom of God on earth. He is to fulfill the commission in conformity to the righteous character and commands of the King. This is

---

87. Kline, *Genesis*, 13; see too Kline, *Images*, 26–34.

the stipulation. Upon obedient completion of this mandate, Adam would be glorified and enter into the enthronement of his Father. This is the sanction. After setting forth the covenant relationship in the kingdom of God in the context of the cosmic metanarrative (Gen 1:1—2:3), Moses recounts the covenant probation (Gen 2:4—3:24).

The Probation—Genesis 2:4—3:24

The narrative delineates the parties, sanctions, and stipulations of the probation in a chiasm. The narrative follows the four parts of the probation, and in turn the concomitant results of Adam's failure.

> A—Sanctions—kingdom and vassal son, "tree of life" (Gen 2:4-14)
>> B—Stipulations—covenant stipulation, "Tree of knowledge of good and evil" (Gen 2:15-17)
>>> C—Vassal—righteous dominion, "naked" (Gen 2:18-25)
>>>> D—Sovereign—covenant broken, "Did God really say" (Gen 3:1-6)
>>> C'—Vassal—unrighteous subjugation, "naked" (Gen 3:7)
>> B'—Stipulations—Judgment Day (delayed and interrupted), "to dust you will return" (Gen 3:8-21)
> A'—Sanctions—banished from the kingdom, "tree of life" (Gen 3:22-24)

First, the dual sanctions are presented. Adam was created and placed in the garden of God in anticipation of the day when he would be glorified with God in the God's royal temple. This inchoate manifestation of the kingdom of God shouted God's promises to Adam. The paradise itself was a place of wonder and wealth. The garden of Eden was a place of beauty, shelter, and provision. God planted trees "pleasing to the sight and good for food" (Gen 2:9). The well-watered paradise was a treasure of minerals and precious gems such as gold, bdellium, and onyx (Gen 2:12). The King's garden was filled with all kinds of wildlife—beasts and birds (Gen 2:19). Adam would not be lonely. God made the woman from the man (Gen 2:18-25). But what made the garden of Eden heaven on earth was the presence of God.

The garden of Eden was the dwelling place of God on earth. Later writers would refer to this paradise as the "holy mountain of God" (Ezek

28:13–16), the "garden of God" (Ezek 28:13; 31:8–9), or the "garden of the Lord" (Isa 51:3). The temple would be built with architectural detail to liken it to the garden of Eden.[88] Revelation 21 and 22 liken the final temple of God to the garden of Eden. Genesis 1:2 and 1:26f. immediately signal the reader to the presence of God in Eden. That this presence is the Glory-Spirit theophany becomes clear in chapters 2 and 3. The Lord forms Adam from the ground and breathes life into him (Gen 2:7). After Adam broke the covenant, Adam "heard the sound of the LORD God" (Gen 3:8). When Adam is banished from the garden of Eden, the angels of the court of God are stationed at the entrance of the garden (Gen 3:24).

Not only did Adam see and hear the presence of the Glory-Spirit, but God spoke to Adam in audible language. Adam knew from the creation much regarding God, but God instructed Adam concerning his commission and the particulars of the covenant probation. Before Adam's sin, God verbally prohibited Adam's eating of the tree of the knowledge of good and evil (Gen 2:16–17). After the fall into sin, God spoke on Judgment Day (Gen 3:9–19). Adam lived with God in the garden. God did not set everything in motion and leave. Adam's life was to be one lived in constant communion with the presence of God. The garden of Eden was only the nascent presence of the kingdom of God. Adam would fill the earth and subdue it to be the holy kingdom of God on earth, which would be transformed with heaven itself to be the one royal temple of God. God's presence with Adam would be central to Adam's kingdom work.

God planted the tree of life in the center of the garden to sacramentally represent the promise. If Adam obeyed the covenant probation, he would eat of the tree of life and be confirmed in his future glory. He would eat and "live forever" (Gen 3:22). The tree of life promised the final eschatological glorification promised also in the sabbath day. Revelation 2:7 promises Christians, "To him who overcomes, I will grant to eat of the tree of life which is in the Paradise of God." This promise is realized in the final royal temple of God. Revelation 22:1–2 says,

> Then he showed me a river of the water of life, clear as crystal, coming from the throne of God and of the Lamb, **2** in the middle of its street. On either side of the river was the tree of life.[89]

But Adam sinned. He was banished. He would die. God

---

88. Kline, *Kingdom Prologue*, 48–49.
89. See Ezek 47:7, 12.

> ... drove the man out; and at the east of the garden of Eden He stationed the cherubim and the flaming sword which turned every direction to guard the way to the tree of life. (Gen 3:24)

As is certainly clear even in the midst of judgment, God's grace has begun to intervene so the reader sees not only the terms of the Covenant of Works, but the mitigation by God's grace. Nonetheless, sinful man was cast out of the garden, condemned under the sanction of the covenant. He broke the covenant and would not build the kingdom of God on earth to be transformed into the eschatological temple. He would not live in constant communion and righteousness with the King under the terms of the Covenant of Works. He would not eat of the tree of life and live forever. He ate of the forbidden tree.

Second, the text presents the probation's stipulation. Also in the center of the garden, God planted the tree of the knowledge of good and evil. The tree looked like all the other beautiful beneficial trees. Nothing about its appearance set it apart. But God told Adam,

> From any tree of the garden you may eat freely; [17] but from the tree of the knowledge of good and evil you shall not eat, for in the day that you eat from it you will surely die." (Gen 2:16–17)

That was the only stated prohibition. Adam saw the incredible creation that God made. He smelled what seemed like an unending variety of fragrances and odors. He felt the rocks and grass. He felt the soft blossoms. And it was all good! Adam's nature, created as image bearer in righteousness, was to think God's thoughts after him, to conform to his will, to commune with him in uninterrupted joy. But God said this one thing that was different. The Lord God forbid Adam from eating of this one tree. There was no other reason for the prohibition. This stipulation of the probation confronted Adam with the core question of the covenant: Would Adam be the image of God in righteousness?

The tree of the knowledge of good and evil was not the entry way to moral knowledge. Adam was created in the image of the holy and righteous King. Rather, the tree was a visible reminder of what it meant for Adam to be righteous like the King. As Adam exhibited dominion as the vassal king, he was to do so in complete accord with the righteousness of his Father in heaven. As vassal king, Adam was commanded to know good and evil and rule accordingly. The famous account of Solomon determining the true mother is instructive. Solomon prayed to the Lord, "give Your servant an understanding heart to judge Your people to discern between good and evil. For who is able to judge this great people of Yours?" (1 Kgs 3:9). Solomon judged with wisdom that astounded. First Kings 3:28 tells us, "When all Israel heard of the judgment which the king had handed down, they feared the king, for they saw that the wisdom of God was in him to administer justice." He ruled with wisdom. He discerned good and evil.

Second Samuel 14:17 recounts when Joab sent the woman from Tekoa to persuade David to allow Absalom to return. She appealed,

> Then your maidservant said, 'Please let the word of my lord the king be comforting, for as the angel of God, so is my lord the king to discern good and evil. And may the LORD your God be with you.'

The allusion is to the divine judicial court of the King of Heaven. She is saying that King David is like the angels of the court of heaven, exercising righteous rule. The king makes legal pronouncement distinguishing good and evil. Another example is Micah 3:1–2, where the prophet denounced the rulers of Israel because they "hate good and love evil." To know good and evil summed up what it meant for the king to rule in righteousness. Adam failed as priest-king to rule in righteousness. He broke the stipulation. So, Judgment Day came.

The Spirit who created all things, who was visibly present in theophanic form in the garden of Eden, who made Adam in his image, came to pronounce judgment. Moses writes,

> They heard the voice [קוֹל, *qol*] of the Lord God coming [הָלַךְ, *halak*] in the garden as the Spirit [רוּחַ, *ruach*] of the Day, and the man and his wife hid themselves from the presence of the Lord God among the trees of the garden. (Gen 3:8 AT)

This verse does not describe Adam and Eve late for their evening stroll with God, "in the cool of the day" (Gen 3:8). What they heard shook them to their inner being. They heard the voice or sound (*qol*) of God! One may remember the scene in the movie *Jurassic Park* when the people hear the dinosaur coming and the earth shakes with every step, the cup of water shakes, and they are in terror! Adam and Eve heard God coming, and they had sinned! They heard the *qol* of the Lord God. When God comes, it is loud. At Sinai the whole mountain quaked violently and the Israelites trembled in fear (Exod 19:16–18) as God's *qol* proclaimed the covenant with Israel (Exod 19:19; Deut 4:12, 33; 5:22–26). When David fought the Philistines, they heard the *qol* above as they advanced (2 Sam

5:24). At Pentecost, they heard a loud roar (Acts 2:2).[90] Ezekiel gives a detailed description of the Glory of the Spirit theophany. He fell down on his face as he heard the "*qol* of one speaking" (Ezek 1:24–25, 28). The *qol* of God is like the sound of a loud earthquake or the roar of many waters (Rev 14:2).

They heard God coming as the Spirit (*ruach*), not wind (*ruach*), of the day. "Wind of the day" became to translators "cool of the day." No. It is the Spirit (*ruach*) who comes in the Day of Judgment. In a twisted way Adam has become like the divine council, knowing good and evil (Gen 3:24). Adam exercised judicial judgment, determining good and evil. But he did not judge as the image bearer of the King, but as king like the King! Adam judged evil to be good and good to be evil based on his own determinations, contrary to what the King had said. The creature of dust pretended to be God!

Third, before Adam sinned, the narrative sets forth Adam's initial righteousness as vassal king. All the animals are brought before Adam to see what name he would assign each one. Just as Adam would later name the woman "woman" because she was taken from the "man" (Gen 2:23), so Adam named the animals according to what the Creator had made each to be. As vassal king, he exercised dominion in assigning the names. But each name acknowledged what the King had created. There was correlation between the created reality and the acknowledgment by the vassal. This naming the truth was itself an ethical expression of Adam's righteousness. The truth was that there was not animal suitable for Adam. So God created a helper suitable for Adam. This wife was not merely his companion. She was flesh of his flesh, one flesh (Gen 2:23). This institution of the marriage set the course for what would have been the propagation of humanity to fill the earth (Gen 2:24; see 1:28). They knew each other intimately. They were naked and were not ashamed (Gen 2:24). They were created righteous. They were not morally ignorant. There was no sin. The vassal was righteous. However, it was not the righteousness Adam would have if he had passed the probation. Then he would have the confirmed righteousness as the vassal who kept the covenant. Then he could eat of the tree of life, symbolizing his sure participation in the final glory, and "live forever." Then he, and all he represented, would have been confirmed in covenant-keeping righteousness that guaranteed the eschatological promise of glory in the temple of the King. Adam acted

---

90. Kline, *Images*, 100; Heb 12:19; Exod 19:16.

alone, but his actions were not for himself alone. He was the federal head under the Covenant of Works.

Though the narrative's focus is on the immediate probation Adam faced, the broader context makes it clear that the story is about the federal head of humanity. He is the vassal king to fill the earth with humanity. He, and all humanity in him, is promised the sabbath glory. His marriage is the beginning of children leaving their parents to form their own families. When Adam sinned, all died. Genesis 5 immediately testifies to the consequences of Adam's sin:

> This is the book of the generations of Adam. In the day when God created man, He made him in the likeness of God. ² He created them male and female, and He blessed them and named them Man in the day when they were created. ³ When Adam had lived one hundred and thirty years, he became the father of a son in his own likeness, according to his image, and named him Seth. ⁴ Then the days of Adam after he became the father of Seth were eight hundred years, and he had other sons and daughters. ⁵ So all the days that Adam lived were nine hundred and thirty years, and he died.
> ⁸ . . . and he died.
> ¹¹ . . . and he died.
> ¹⁴ . . . and he died.
> ¹⁷ . . . and he died.
> ²⁰ . . . and he died.
> ²⁷ . . . and he died.
> ³¹ . . . and he died. (Gen 5:1–5, 8, 11, 14, 17, 20, 27, 31)

Adam was to fill the earth, but not with coffins in graves.

Because Adam was the federal head of humanity, it was necessary that the probation take place before the multiplication of the holy royal family across the earth. The righteous kingdom-building work of Adam and his posterity could not begin until they were confirmed as the righteous recipients of the promise.

The picture changes dramatically after Adam sinned. Genesis 3:7–8 says,

> Then the eyes of both of them were opened, and they knew that they were naked; and they sewed fig leaves together and made themselves loin coverings. ⁸ . . . and the man and his wife hid themselves from the presence of the LORD God among the trees of the garden.

Now they hid in sin's shame. They tried to hide from each other when they made the makeshift clothes. And they tried to hide from God. The vassal was unrighteous.

Fourth, the reader is brought to central question of the probation, "Did God say?" Who is suzerain of the covenant? This question is introduced in the narrative with profound description that underlines the question and also reinforces again the connection of the covenant and the vassal being in the King's image. The probationary test starts with the intrusion of the enemy into the holy garden. This is the moment when Adam as faithful priest-king should have stepped on the serpent's head! The crisis is introduced in Genesis 3:1, "Now the serpent was more crafty than any beast of the field which the LORD God had made." The word that is translated "crafty" by most translations or "subtle" by the KJV is the Hebrew word *arum* (עָרוּם). What the modern reader misses, the original reader would have understood. There is a word play with "naked" (*arom*; עֲרוּמִּים). Adam and Eve were righteous in the image of God. They were naked (*arom*) and not ashamed in the righteous image of God. But now the enemy comes who is subtle (*arum*). The question is: Will Adam obey as image of the King, or will he abandon that image for a new image, the image of the enemy?

Satan approaches the woman in the serpent. He seeks to overturn the Creator and his creation. The King will not have dominion over the man as head of his wife over the creatures. The creature will subvert the woman, who will subvert the man into rebellion against God. Satan first misrepresents and questions the word of the King: "Indeed, has God said, 'You shall not eat from any tree of the garden'?" (Gen 3:1). Then Satan just contradicts God's word:

> The serpent said to the woman, 'You surely will not die! [5] For God knows that in the day you eat from it your eyes will be opened, and you will be like God, knowing good and evil.' (Gen 3:4–5)

Again, he twists the truth into a lie. Adam was commanded to know good and evil as a vassal imaging the King and thus "be like God." But Adam was not to adjudicate good and evil as God!

When Satan questioned God's word, he attacked the source of all truth. Satan attacked the distinction between the Creator and the creation. In posing the possibility that Eve needed to judge the word of God, Satan challenged that God was God. In declaring God had ill intent, Satan rejected that God was the source of righteousness and blessing. This tree in the middle of the garden confronted Adam with his commission to rule in likeness to his righteous Father. What God said was "good" was by definition good. What God said was "evil" was evil. God is goodness. Goodness is good because it conforms to the moral righteousness of God. This was the starting point for Adam's rule. His epistemology would be based on God's word. God was life, and his word was life and truth. God was the origin of all truth. For Adam to subdue the earth as image of the King would be for Adam to think God's thoughts after him and obey his every word.

This question "Did God say?" was a direct attack on God as Creator of all. But Adam sinned. Adam abandoned the truth and thought he himself would be God and decide for himself. He knew good and evil, not as a vassal conforming to the King's knowledge of evil, but supposing himself to be the King, ruling what would be good and evil. He bought the lie that he was not a creature. He bought the lie that he could decide truth for himself. He bought the lie that there is knowledge that does not originate with God. The Covenant of Works is ultimately a question of covenant fealty to the King of Heaven. Adam gave the wrong answer in cosmic treason.

COVENANT OF WORKS, NOT GRACE

Before moving on, there are four essential truths to note. First, the Covenant of Works with Adam was a covenant of works. Recent discussion distorted this simple truth. There is no grace in this first covenant. Sin had not yet entered human history. There is no demerit for redemptive grace to be applicable. Others have suggested a different use of "grace" to describe God's beneficence to Adam in the covenant. They argue that the promise is not merited by the obedience of Adam. They maintain that the unmerited nature of the sanction makes it grace. This abstraction obfuscates the actual reality. Just as the disobedience of Adam warrants the unending just wrath of the King, the covenant obedience of Adam warrants the glorification in the royal temple of God. To deny the latter is to deny the former. Finally, the question is not one of merit, but of covenant justice. The legal covenant promises the blessing sanction upon fulfillment of the stipulations of the covenant. It is a matter of strict justice for the King to deliver on what was promised if the stipulation is met. It is precisely a covenant of works because the blessing is contingent upon fulfillment of the stipulation. The sanctioned blessing is merited by obedience to the stipulation.

Second, the Covenant of Works was made with one man, Adam. Adam was the federal representative of humanity. The covenant sanctions depended on the actions of this one man. Covenant obedience would render blessing, and disobedience would yield covenant curse. Adam's relationship with his Father was based on this legal structure. Covenant law was foundational to Adam's relationship with God. Here is the point: the blessing of eternity glorified with God was promised to one man contingent on his obedience. The covenant was not made with a million or billion humans to see which ones would prevail. The covenant was made with one man as representative of all. For anyone to see the glory promised in heaven, he would be dependent on Adam fulfilling the covenant requirements. There was no other way into the glorified royal temple of the King.

Someone may object that Jesus told the rich young ruler that he could have eternal life if he kept the commandments. So is it implied that there was a way outside of Adam? But Jesus was not suggesting that there was a way outside of Adam's obedience. The man asked Jesus how he could have eternal life. Jesus replied, "You know the commandments" (Matt 10:19). The man claimed he had kept them. But to show the man his sin, Jesus pointed to his covetousness and told him to sell his possessions. He was not any different than every other person represented by Adam. He was a fallen sinner born with original sin and in bondage to a sin nature. Rather than telling the man he could obtain eternal life, Jesus showed him why he couldn't do something to obtain eternal life. Adam was one of two men promised the glory of heaven through obedience.

Third, the sanctioned blessing was only promised to the federal head if he kept the totality of the covenant. Participation in the eschatological temple was dependent on fulfilling the covenant mandate. Adam's initial righteousness was not sufficient to obtain a place in heaven. Adam's sinless condition did not give him entrance into the glorified state. Adam's active obedience to the covenant requirement was necessary for him to participate in the blessing.

Fourth, the sanctioned blessing was not promised in degrees. Adam was not offered levels of blessing based on his obedience or kingdom work. Adam was promised glorification in the King's temple. Adam's covenant keeping would benefit all humanity with joyous unending glory in the King's house. But Adam failed.

3

The Covenant of Works
Jesus (Pactum Salutis)

THE PACTUM SALUTIS

ADAM'S SIN WOULD NOT have the last word. Before creation, God planned to redeem man in the eternal covenant theologians call the "Pactum Salutis"[1] or "Covenant of Redemption." In this first covenant, God decreed man's salvation and glorification.

Eternal Covenant

Paul begins his letter to the Ephesians with extended praise to God. God the Father has fulfilled his eternal purpose and has given believers the blessings of heaven in the finished work of Christ. Paul writes,

> Blessed be the God and Father of our Lord Jesus Christ, the one who has blessed us in every Spiritual blessing in the heavenly places in Christ, **4** just as He chose us in Him before the foundation of the world. (Eph 1:3–4 AT)

Before creation, God decreed the blessings he would give to those chosen in Christ. Paul not only calls for worship, but he see the clear implications for the believer's life in the present age. He exhorts Timothy to

---

1. Pact of Salvation.

see the persecution they faced in light of God's gift planned in eternity. Paul writes,

> ... join with *me* in suffering for the gospel according to the power of God, **9** who has saved us and called us with a holy calling, not according to our works, but according to His own purpose and grace which was granted[2] us in Christ Jesus from all eternity, **10** but now has been revealed by the appearing of our Savior Christ Jesus, who abolished death and brought life and immortality to light through the gospel. (2 Tim 1:8–10)

Paul and Timothy are witnesses to the fulfillment of salvation decreed in eternity. Paul's theology understands suffering for the gospel as evidence of the fulfillment of the eternal covenant. Though central to Paul's theology, the accomplishment of God's eternal saving decree in Christ is not a novel perspective. Jesus was fully cognizant of the eternal origin of his ministry. In describing the Final Judgment, Jesus said he will welcome believers: "Come, you who are blessed of My Father, inherit the kingdom prepared for you from the foundation of the world" (Matt 25:34).

Jesus called this eternal intra-Trinitarian decree a "covenant." After the Last Supper, Jesus told the disciples,

> And I covenant to you, just as my Father covenanted to me the kingdom, **30** that you may eat and drink at My table in My kingdom, and you will sit on thrones judging the twelve tribes of Israel." (Luke 22:29–30 AT)[3]

In eternity the Father covenanted the kingdom to the Son in the Pactum Salutis. So, the Son covenanted the kingdom to the disciples in the New Covenant (cf. Luke 22:20). Jesus' words came immediately after he instituted the New Covenant meal with the disciples. The connection between "covenant" (Luke 22:20; *diatheke*, διαθήκη) and "covenant" (Luke 22:29; *diatithemai*, διατίθεμαι)[4] is not incidental. Christ's fulfillment of the Pactum Salutis symbolized in the covenant meal was the basis for the New Covenant.

Paul's opening words to the Ephesians summarize this eternal covenant. Paul praises the Trinity. The Father blessed his people in Christ with every Spiritual blessing. "Every Spiritual blessing" (Eph 1:3) doesn't refer to a person's spiritual life. These are the covenant blessings of heaven

---

2. δοθεῖσαν, *didomi*, "was given."
3. See translation discussion on p. 36.
4. Liddell and Scott, *Greek-English Lexicon*, "διατίθεμαι," 167.

"bound up with the Holy Spirit."[5] While the eternal covenant was made before creation, the covenant was fulfilled in time and space by the Son. The covenant outworking of his ministry is referenced by the three names Paul uses in Ephesians 1:3: "Lord Jesus Christ."

The Father sent the Son into the world as the incarnate vassal servant, Jesus. John writes,

> Jesus said to them, "Jesus said unto them, If God were your Father, ye would love me: for I proceeded forth and came from God; neither came I of myself, but he sent me." (John 8:42 KJV)

The Son was obedient to the Father even to death on the cross. He is the Christ (Messiah). So the Father enthroned the Son as exalted Lord. Paul writes,

> For this reason also, God highly exalted Him, and bestowed on Him the name which is above every name, 10 so that at the name of Jesus EVERY KNEE WILL BOW, of those who are in heaven and on earth and under the earth, 11 and that every tongue will confess that Jesus Christ is Lord, to the glory of God the Father. (Phil 2:9–11)

The Son became the vassal who obeyed the Father and received the blessing of the covenant. He did what Adam failed to do. He is the Second Adam.

Paul says "every Spiritual blessing" belongs to the believer. For what Christ did, he did as the believer's federal head. As Adam represented all humanity, so Christ represents those "chosen" (Eph 1:4). As vassal king, Christ represented the elect when he obeyed the covenant stipulations and was enthroned to the right hand of the Father, "in heavenly places" (Eph 1:3). Paul emphasizes this legal federal union when he writes, "who has blessed us ... in Christ (Eph 1:3). Again, in verse 4, Paul writes, "chose us in Him."

Trinitarian Subordination and Meritorious Works

This summary of the Pactum Salutis describes a subordination of the Son to the Father, and further examination would show a subordination of the Holy Spirit to the Father and the Son. Numerous passages demonstrate these subordinations. Jesus said he didn't know the time of the Parousia. Matthew writes, "But of that day and hour no one knows, not even the

---

5. Lincoln, *Ephesians*, 19; see Eph 1:13–14.

angels of heaven, nor the Son, but the Father alone" (Matt 24:36). He testified to his subordination to the Father when he said,

> I can of Myself do nothing. As I hear, I judge; and My judgment is righteous, because I do not seek My own will but the will of the Father who sent Me. (John 5:30 KJV)

The subordination passages are so prevalent and obvious that the early church was confronted by Arius and others who claimed that the Son did not exist before he was created in time. They maintained the Son is not the eternal God. How could God who is omniscient not "know"? How can God say "I can do nothing"? But the early church fathers were quick to refute this heresy with affirmations of the full deity of Christ. One cannot read the New Testament and fail to be confronted with the unyielding claim that Jesus is the eternal God. John is not claiming that Jesus is some demigod when he writes, "the word was God" (John 1:1). John writes, "Through him all things were made; without him nothing was made that has been made" (John 1:3). Everything that falls in the category of creation and not Creator was made by the Son. He is the Creator. Jesus walked on the water to the disciples and reassured them, "I AM" (ἐγώ εἰμι; Matt 14:27). The religious officials had him crucified for claiming to be the eternal Son of God. They understood his claims. John writes, "For this reason they tried all the more to kill him; not only was he breaking the sabbath, but he was even calling God his own Father, making Himself equal with God" (John 5:18). In the fifth century at the Council of Chalcedon (451 AD), the church articulated the doctrine held since the days of Christ's earthly ministry. Jesus is both God and man. In his one person are two natures. He is God. He is man. This formulation answered the subordination passages while affirming the eternal deity of the Son of God. Lee Irons writes,

> When Jesus said that he does not know the day or the hour of his parousia, he is speaking of himself in terms of his self-imposed limitations as one who took on a true human nature. When the Gospels tell us that Jesus died by crucifixion, they are not saying that the divine nature of Jesus died—which is impossible—but that his human nature died, or, more accurately that Jesus the Son of God died according to his human nature.[6]

---

6. Irons, *Son*, 61.

The Covenant of Works: Jesus (Pactum Salutis)

This understanding of the hypostatic union[7] of the natures of Christ is essential, but the church fathers went further in their attempts to respond to the subordination passages. They responded with formulations of the doctrine of the Trinity that involved subordination in the eternal Godhead. Calvin responded to both the heretics and the early church fathers when he commented on John 5,

> Both parties were in the wrong. For the discourse does not relate to the simple Divinity of Christ, and those statements which we shall immediately see do not simply and of themselves relate to the eternal Word of God, but apply to the Son of God, so far as he is manifested in the flesh.[8]

The subordination texts are in the context of the working out of the Pactum Salutis in creation. There is no ontological subordination in God. The Son is God. Aseity, absolute authority, all the communicable and incommunicable attributes belong to the Son. The Son does not derive his attributes from the Father. The Son is God. When the Pactum Salutis was made before creation, there was no subordination. As one confession says, the persons of the Trinity are "equal in power and glory."[9] There is one God who eternally exists in three distinct persons—no subordination. In eternity, the Trinity covenanted what each person of God would do in creation to fulfill the covenant. The Son, equal with the Father, covenanted to become subordinate in the plan of redemption. The Spirit, equal to the Son and Father, covenanted to become subordinate to the Son and Father in the decree that would bring ultimate cosmic glorification. Execution of the Pactum Salutis started with the creation of heaven, the holy throne of the Father. This in no way implies that God the Holy Spirit or God the Son is not worthy of all glory, honor, and praise as Eternal God. God the Son had no need or lack. God the Holy Spirit was no less Almighty God than the Father and the Son. But in the fulfillment of the Pactum Salutis in time and space creation, the Father sits on the throne in heaven. The Spirit endoxated and filled heaven's temple with God's Glory. While the Son did not cease to be God with all his attributes, the Son became the Angel of the Presence and original image of God. The Trinity moved into creation, into time and space, and began to fulfill the Pactum Salutis.

---

7. Union of the divine and human natures in one person.
8. Calvin, *Commentary on John*, 198.
9. WCF 2.5.

Regarding the Son, Hebrews 1:1–4 says,

> God, after He spoke long ago to the fathers in the prophets in many portions and in many ways, **2** in these last days has spoken to us in His Son, whom He appointed heir of all things, through whom also He made the world. **3** And He is the effulgence of His glory and the very image of His being, and upholds all things by the word of His power. When He had made purification of sins, He sat down at the right hand of the Majesty on high, **4** having become as much better than the angels, as He has inherited a more excellent name than they. (AT)

The writer is not describing the Son in his ontological intra-Trinitarian relationship to the Father, but as he is manifest in creation.[10] Verse 1 contrasts the Son with the revelation given through the Prophets. In verse 2, the author says God has now revealed himself through the Son. God created all things through the Son with the covenant promise that the Son would be heir of all things. This subordination is not descriptive of God the Son ontologically as God. God the Son does not possess less authority, power, or glory than God the Father or God the Holy Spirit. The author describes the subordination that fulfilled the eternal intra-Trinitarian covenant.

To use a rough analogy, it would be like two university professors acting out the student-teacher dynamic in front of their class. One of the professors takes the part of the teacher and one the student. For the purposes of the demonstration, one is subordinate to the other. But outside of the play, there is certainly no subordination. They have parity. So, in creation the Son and the Spirit take roles of subordination in fulfilling the Pactum Salutis. The Father appointed the Son to be heir of all things. The Father is the King of Heaven; the Son is the vassal servant. The sanctioned blessing would be for the Son to be exalted at the right hand of the Father in heaven. The stipulation required that the Son go to the cross and make purification for sins. Being the faithful covenant servant, the Son would inherit a glory greater than the angels. This is all within the confines of his messianic work as Second Adam. It is heretical to say that God the Son gained a glory he did not have. It is heretical to say that the Son did not have a glory greater than the angels before the cross! It is in the context of creation, in heaven,[11] that the author says that the Son is

---

10. Kline, *Images*, 16.
11. Kline *Images*, 16.

the "effulgence of His glory and the very image of His being" (Heb 1:3). Kline notes,

> This description of the likeness of the Son to the Father does not refer to the eternal ontological reality of God apart from creation but to the revelation of the Father by the Son in Creation ... The only way to satisfy the contextual requirements then would seem to be to understand verse 3a in terms of pre-incarnation theophany, and in particular, the Glory revelation of the Creator spoken of in Genesis 1:2b.[12]

As the image of God, the Son is the radiance of God's Glory. He is the providential upholder of creation. The author is not referring to the incarnation. He is referring to the Glory of the preincarnate theophany of the Son in heaven before the earth's creation. As vassal of the covenant, he came to earth and fulfilled his mission, making purification for sins. Now he sits glorified at the right hand of the Father in heaven. He sits enthroned in Glory above the angelic council of the King's court. All the parts of the Pactum Salutis are present. He is the image[13] of God in covenant with God.

The author of Hebrews then exalts in praise the finished work of the Son as Second Adam, federal head of the elect. Exalted to the throne, he receives glory and honor greater than the angelic court. Hebrews 1:4 says, "having become as much better than the angels, as He has inherited a more excellent name than they." This exaltation that the Second Adam received is then supported from Old Testament references in Hebrews 1:5–14.

This Second Adam connection is made explicit in Hebrews 2. Hebrews 2:5–8 quotes Psalm 8 to refer to the vassal authority given to Adam under the Covenant of Works. He would rule as vassal king and be glorified to the Father's throne if he obeyed the covenant. Hebrews 2:7–8 says,

> YOU HAVE CROWNED HIM WITH GLORY AND HONOR,
> AND HAVE APPOINTED HIM OVER THE WORKS OF YOUR HANDS;
> 8 YOU HAVE PUT ALL THINGS IN SUBJECTION UNDER HIS FEET.

But Adam sinned, and Hebrews 2:8 notes the obvious outcome: "But now we do not yet see all things subjected to him." But Jesus did keep the covenant. Hebrews immediately proclaims that what Adam failed to do Jesus has done:

---

12. Kline, *Images*, 16.
13. 2 Cor 4:4; Col 1:15.

> But we do see Him who was made for a little while lower than the angels, *namely*, Jesus, because of the suffering of death crowned with glory and honor, so that by the grace of God He might taste death for everyone. **10** For it was fitting for Him, for whom are all things, and through whom are all things, in bringing many sons to glory. (Heb 2:9–10)

Jesus crushed the head of the serpent through the crucifixion to "render powerless him who had the power of death, that is, the devil" (Heb 2:14). Jesus is king (Heb 1:8, 13), and he is priest (Heb 2:17). He passed the temptation probation (Heb 2:18). Jesus is the covenant Son (Heb 3:6). Now exalted to the right hand of the Father, Jesus sends forth the Spirit as the first-fruits of the eschatological Spirit glorification (Heb 2:4). Jesus has secured the sabbath rest (Heb 4:1, 14). As federal head of the elect, he is seated at the right hand of the Father in Glory. Jesus' obedience to the stipulations of the Pactum Salutis has merited his enthronement in Glory at the right hand of the Father. As the believer's federal head, his merit is the believer's merit.

Covenantal *merit* is at the center of this gospel message. Jesus did for the elect what Adam failed to do for humanity! Jesus is enthroned because of his covenant faithfulness. He became the vassal, obeyed the requirements of the covenant, and now is worthy of the blessing of the covenant. There is a legal bedrock underneath redemption and glorification. The sanctioned blessing is not just Jesus' exaltation to the right hand of the Father, but the redemption and glorification of the elect. Jesus merited the glorification of the elect. His enthronement is theirs. The gospel has often been attacked at this very point. Jesus did not just merit the believer's salvation by paying for his sin, but merited the covenant blessing of sabbath glorification by obedience to the stipulations of the covenant. Merit is at the core of redemption and glorification in the work of Christ. But is this what the Scriptures teach? There is a prophet who leaves no doubt. Isaiah's answer is definitive and scandalous!

The message of Isaiah shouts that God will do what man has not! God will come and bring the new creation. He will merit what man has not. The sheer length of Isaiah makes it easy to get sidetracked with all the rich details and miss the message of the book. Israel's impending fall to Assyria is the immediate occasion for the prophet's message. But the judgment is not limited to the northern tribes. Judah too will fall to the Babylonians. The twelve tribes broke the Old Covenant, and God will bring the sanctioned judgment (Isa 1–12). In their desperate state,

The Covenant of Works: Jesus (Pactum Salutis)

they have turned to the nations for deliverance, but there is no god in the nations of the world that can save them. The world and its gods will also be judged; they stand condemned in Adam (Isa 13–35; see 24:5). Hezekiah sees God's mercy in Judah's deliverance from Assyria, but also God's justice in the Babylonian captivity that will come (Isa 36–39). Chapters 1–39 proclaim the covenant judgments that God will send on his people and the world. But, like a dark room with light streaming in through the cracks and crevices from the bright outside, the realities of God's grace shine through. It's like the excited older brother who delivers news to his younger brother that (1) the younger brother is going to lose his 1,500-square-foot house that needs repair to bank foreclosure, and (2) his rich uncle just gave him a gift of a large new house on beautiful land in the younger brother's favorite county. It's hard to deliver the bad news without the good news being revealed! So in the midst of the message of judgment in the first thirty-nine chapters, Isaiah at the same time reveals a day beyond the judgment. God's covenant judgments innumerated in Leviticus 26 and Deuteronomy 28 would be executed because they broke the Mosaic Covenant. But greater is God's grace which he promised Abraham (Isa 41:8, 51:2). The kingdom of God will bring peace (Isa 2:2–4), and God will dwell with his people (Isa 4:2–4). King David's promised son, the Branch (Isa 4:2), will come. He will be God with us, Immanuel (Isa 7:14), Prince of Peace, Mighty Warrior (Isa 9:6). The Spirit of God will be on him and in his kingdom the redeemed of all the earth will gather (Isa 11:1–16). But redemption will not be limited to Israel. Though the nations of the earth are brought to nothing in the Final Judgment, there is a city filled with life that will come. Even Egyptians and Assyrians will be redeemed, and God will say, "Blessed is Egypt My people, and Assyria the work of My hands, and Israel My inheritance" (Isa 19:25). Death, which swallowed the earth, will be itself swallowed by the great eschatological banquet of God (Isa 25:6–8).

This message of a new world eclipses the judgments proclaimed in prior chapters and fills chapters 40–66. Isaiah commissioned to proclaim judgment (Isa 6:8) is here directed to proclaim the good news! "Comfort, Comfort my people" (Isa 40:1). God is coming to deliver (Isa 40:3, 9). He will give the thirsty open rivers and springs, turn the wilderness into a pool of water and a fountain (Isa 41:17–18). Not only will he comfort Israel, but God will redeem to the ends of the earth (Isa 42:5–12). God will come, and he will be the Deliverer. He will be the servant Israel failed to be (Isa 42:18–25). Israel failed to be the obedient servant (Isa 41:8;

44:1, 21; 45:4) and broke the covenant. Inherent in Isaiah's message is this paradox: God will come and deliver, and God will send his servant to deliver. As the New Testament makes clear, Immanuel is the resolution to that tension. God will be the servant of the Lord who will bring God's kingdom (Isa 42:1–4). God's promised coming in Isaiah 35:1–6 is fulfilled in the coming of Christ (Matt 11:1–5). He will not just bring temporary restoration like Cyrus, but will bring the eschatological deliverance that affects the whole cosmos. He will bring salvation to the ends of the earth (Isa 49:1–18). He would be the faithful obedient servant (Isa 50:4–11).

But how will God bring deliverance to Israel from her enemies and ultimately from her own sin? How will God bring deliverance for the nations? How will God's grace surpass the covenant unfaithfulness of Israel? How will he cleanse the treachery of the world and upend the curse on the earth? The consistent message through sixty-six chapters is: "God will deliver!" He will transform Israel's desolation into the paradise of Eden (Isa 51:3). It is a cosmic deliverance resulting in a "new heavens and new earth" (Isa 65:17). He alone is God. The idol gods of the nations are nothing! The message is ultimately a vindication of God! But what is this deliverance that makes all things right?

Isaiah 40:10 says,

> Behold, the Lord Yahweh shall come with might and His arm ruling for Him. Behold, His reward is with Him and His recompense before Him. (AT)

Again, Isaiah 62:11 says,

> Behold, Yahweh has proclaimed to the end of the earth,
> Say to the daughter of Zion, "Lo, your salvation comes;
> Behold His reward is with Him, and His recompense before Him." (AT)

It is within these bookends (Isa 40:10, 62:11) that the four Servant Songs are found (Isa 42:1–9; 49:1–7; 50:4–9; 52:13—53:12). This servant is a "covenant" for the nations (Isa 42:6) bringing salvation to the ends of the earth (Isa 49:6). He is the faithful servant God will vindicate (Isa 50:4–7). The crescendo of the four songs is found in Isaiah 52:13—53:12. He is the suffering servant who will sprinkle the nations to cleanse them from sin (Isa 52:15; cf. Lev 14:7; 4:6; 8:11). So, he will be exalted in Glory (Isa 52:13, 53:12). Structurally, Isaiah tells us that the servant is the cosmic solution:

The Covenant of Works: Jesus (Pactum Salutis)

Isa 40:10—Yahweh shall come with his reward.

Isa 42:1–9—The servant of the Lord is the covenant.

Isa 49:1–7—The servant of the Lord brings salvation to the ends of the earth.

Isa 50:4–9—The servant of the Lord is the obedient servant.

Isa 52:13—53:12—The servant of the Lord obedient to the end, exalted to Glory.

Isa 62:11—Yahweh shall come with his reward.

The deliverance God brings is the reward he secures as the servant of the Lord. This is the cosmic answer! What does it mean that Yahweh comes with his reward? Does it mean that he comes to give a reward? Or does it mean the God comes with the reward he has merited? How can God merit anything when all is his from the start? Here is the scandalous answer. God merited his reward! Isaiah writes,

> Behold, the Lord Yahweh shall come with might and His arm ruling for Him. Behold, His reward [*sakar*, שָׂכָר] is with Him and His recompense [*peullah*, פְּעֻלָּה] before Him. (Isa 40:10 AT)

Sakar is remuneration earned, the reward. *Peullah* is the paid wages for work. E. J. Young writes, "The two words are here virtually synonymous... A workman has earned his hire as the fruits or reward of his work."[14] Cleon Rogers comments on the meaning of *sakar*, "The basic idea of the word is engaging the services of a person in return for pay."[15] These two words are used together for hire and wages in other texts too (Lev 19:13; 2 Chr 15:7; Jer 31:16; Prov 11:18). This is exactly the kind of relationship described in Romans 4:4: "Now to the one who works, his wage is not credited as a favor, but as what is due." Motyer comments,

> Where reward (*śakār*, 'wage') is used with a pronoun (as here) the pronoun is the person receiving the 'wage' (cf. Ezek 29:18f. where it is used of the victor getting the fruits of his victory). So here, the Lord has received the fruits of his victory, and the *recompense* which *accompanies him*/'is before him', 'in his presence' is the flock of his people which his victory has won.[16]

---

14. Young, *Isaiah*, 39–40.
15. Rogers, "שָׂכָר (*sakar*)," 878.
16. Motyer, *Prophecy of Isaiah*, 302.

God has merited, earned, his reward—the redeemed of the earth. This is repeated in Isaiah 62:11. Yahweh comes as cosmic Deliverer. The incarnate servant of the Lord has done what man could not do. He became the faithful covenant vassal servant. In the Pactum Salutis, the Son became the obedient Second Adam to atone for sin and bring the new creation temple. Christ's atonement for sin is part of the stipulation of the covenant. But the bigger picture required Christ to build the eschatological royal temple.

The servant of the Lord is the eschatological temple. Isaiah writes, "Then He shall become a sanctuary; But to both the houses of Israel, a stone to strike and a rock to stumble over" (Isa 8:14). This is Christ the Lord. Paul writes, " but we preach Christ crucified, to Jews a stumbling block" (1 Cor 1:23). The stumbling block is the temple's cornerstone. Peter writes,

> ... you also, as living stones, are being built up as a spiritual house for a holy priesthood, to offer up spiritual sacrifices acceptable to God through Jesus Christ. **6** For *this* is contained in Scripture:
> "Behold, I lay in Zion a choice stone, a precious corner *stone*,
> And he who believes in Him will not be disappointed."
> **7** This precious value, then, is for you who believe; but for those who disbelieve,
> "The stone which the builders rejected,
> This became the very corner stone,"
> **8** and,
> "A stone of stumbling and a rock of offense." (1 Pet 2:5–8)

Through his obedience to the stipulated death, the servant builds the temple. So, the sanctioned reward is enthronement with the Father united with the Son's redeemed in the Glory of the Spirit.

Another Old Testament prophet confirms the meritorious nature of the Messiah's covenant work, and demonstrates that building the eschatological temple is the stipulation. Zechariah uses the language and context of the Old Covenant to prophetically describe Jesus' messianic work fulfilling the Pactum Salutis. He writes in Zechariah 6:9–15,

> The word of Yahweh came to me, saying, **10** "Take an offering from the exiles, from Heldai, Tobijah and Jedaiah; and you go the same day and enter the house of Josiah the son of Zephaniah,

The Covenant of Works: Jesus (Pactum Salutis)

where they have arrived from Babylon. ¹¹ Take silver and gold, make a crown and set it on the head of Joshua the son of Jehozadak, the high priest. ¹² Then say to him, 'Thus says Yahweh of hosts, "Behold, a man—his name is Branch. From his place He will branch forth and He shall build the temple of Yahweh. ¹³ Yes, it is He who shall build the temple of Yahweh, and He who shall wear the royal robes and sit and rule by His throne. Thus, He shall be a priest by His throne, and the counsel of peace will be between the two of them."' ¹⁴ Now the crown will become a reminder in the temple of Yahweh to Helem, Tobijah, Jedaiah and Hen the son of Zephaniah. ¹⁵ Those who are far off shall come and help build the temple of Yahweh." And you will know that Yahweh of hosts has sent me unto you. And it will take place if you completely obey the Yahweh your God. (AT)[17]

The section is structured chiastically:

Zech 6:9–11—Requisition from the nations.

    Zech 6:12–13b—The Branch will build the temple.

    Zech 6:13c-e—The Branch will be enthroned.

Zech 6:14–15—Requisition of the nations.

The historical occasion is presented in Zechariah 6:9–11. Joshua was the first high priest after the Babylonian captivity during the temple reconstruction. The requisition order[18] is given to go to the treasury steward, Josiah, and take gold and silver that had been offered by the returning exiles and make a crown to crown the high priest. Zechariah 6:12 then makes it clear that the symbolism exceeds the historical occasion.

Zechariah 6:12–13b describes the coronation that fulfills the Davidic Covenant. God did not allow David to build the temple, but promised that his seed would. God promises,

> I will raise up your seed after you, who will come forth from your bowels, and I will establish his kingdom. ¹³ He shall build a house for My name, and I will establish the throne of his kingdom forever. (2 Sam 7:12–13 AT)

Isaiah calls this promised king the "Branch" (Isa 4:2; 11:1). Jeremiah 23:5–6 promises,

---

17. See Kline, *Glory*, 219–25.
18. Kline, *Glory*, 228.

> "Behold, *the* days are coming," declares the LORD,
> "When I will raise up for David a righteous Branch;
> And He will reign as king and act wisely
> And do justice and righteousness in the land.
> **6** In His days Judah will be saved,
> And Israel will dwell securely;
> And this is His name by which He will be called,
> 'The LORD our righteousness.'"

Zechariah 6:12–13b takes the reader beyond the crowning of the high priest. This is the crowning of David's promised seed, the Messiah. This is the crowning of the priest-king. He will build the temple, and his throne will be forever.[19] Joshua the high priest is a picture of Christ, the priest-king. He has crown rights.

Zechariah 6:13c–e then speaks of the enthronement of this priest-king. He will wear the royal robes and crown and sit at the right hand of Yahweh—"by his throne."[20] He is not like the high priest of the Old Testament, who had access to the throne of God one day a year, and that with the fear of death.[21] This priest-king is enthroned in the Glory of God. The "counsel of peace" is between this priest-king and Yahweh. The priest-king is enthroned at the right hand of God because of the covenant between them. "Counsel of peace" is synonymous for the covenant between them. Psalm 83:5 uses this language of "counsel" in parallelism to "covenant" when the psalmist writes, "For they take counsel[22] together with one mind; they make a covenant[23] against you" (AT). Yahweh swore a covenant oath to bless this priest-king with a throne forever.[24] This is the sanction of the Pactum Salutis.

Zechariah 6:14–15 elaborates on the inheritance that will be given this priest-king. He will requisition the nations to help in building the eschatological temple. This temple is not made of stone or even precious stones. The redeemed from the nations are the "living stones" (1 Pet 2:5–8). Paul focuses the first half of Ephesians on the truth Isaiah promised, that the temple of God would include the Gentiles. In Ephesians 2:12–13, Paul writes to Gentile believers,

19. See Jer 33:14–17.
20. עַל־כִּסְאוֹ.
21. Heb 9:7.
22. נוֹעֲצוּ, *yaats*.
23. בְּרִית, *berith*.
24. Ps 110:4.

... you were at that time separate from Christ, excluded from the commonwealth of Israel, and strangers to the covenants of promise, having no hope and without God in the world. [13] But now in Christ Jesus you who formerly were far off have been brought near by the blood of Christ.

Paul continues in Ephesians 2:19–22,

So then you are no longer strangers and aliens, but you are fellow citizens with the saints, and are of God's household, [20] having been built on the foundation of the apostles and prophets, Christ Jesus Himself being the corner *stone*, [21] in whom the whole building, being fitted together, is growing into a holy temple in the Lord, [22] in whom you also are being built together into a dwelling of God in the Spirit.

The nations are his inheritance. The psalmist writes,

I will surely tell of the decree of the Lord:
He said to Me, "You are My Son,
Today I have begotten You.
[8] Ask of Me, and I will surely give the nations as Your inheritance,
And the *very* ends of the earth as Your possession . . ." (Ps 2:7–8)

His recompense is enthronement as heir of the eschatological temple, the redeemed of the earth. Zechariah 6:15 promises the inheritance on condition of complete obedience to the covenant. The Son's complete obedience throughout his earthly life, all the way to damnation on the cross, met the demand of the covenant stipulation. Through his obedience he builds the eschatological temple.

Preeminent Role in the Story of Redemption and Glorification

The Pactum Salutis is the basis for redemption and eschatological glory. Adam, vassal of the King of Heaven, was to obey the covenant stipulations, and so build the eschatological temple in Glory. If Adam had kept the Covenant of Works, he, as federal head, and all humanity in him, would have merited, in the terms of the covenant, the sanctioned eschatological life in the glorified creation. Adam sinned. But the Second Adam, Christ, kept the stipulations of the Pactum Salutis and built the eschatological temple and thereby merited the sanctioned blessing of eschatological Glory. Here is the stark point: the only way to receive the sanctioned blessing of eschatological life in Glory is either through the obedience of the federal head Adam or the federal head Christ. A place in the eschatological temple is earned. In the history of creation there are only two men who have been offered access through covenant obedience. Where the first Adam failed, the Second Adam in victory brings "many sons to glory" (Heb 2:10). In the covenant disobedience of the first, all are condemned. The covenant obedience of the Second Adam merits the glory of the elect.

Though both the Covenant of Works with Adam and the Pactum Salutis with the Second Adam are covenants of works, the work of the Second Adam, Christ, is not just the fulfillment of the Covenant of Works by the Lord Jesus. The Pactum Salutis certainly entails the Second Adam doing what the first Adam did not do in filling the kingdom of God with the living temple of God, resulting in eschatological glory, but it required different stipulations and did more than what the Covenant of Works with Adam could have done. Adam's obedience would have confirmed his progeny in righteousness and secured the eschatological glory. The Second Adam, in the Pactum Salutis, brings the elect from a legal status under the sentence of eternal damnation to an enthronement with the God of heaven.

The Pactum Salutis covenant stipulations required both the active obedience and passive obedience of Christ. In his passive obedience, he suffered the punishment for the sin of the elect and so propitiated (*hilasmos*, ἱλασμός),[25] satisfied, the just wrath of God. This atoning sacrifice removes the penalty for sin under the Covenant of Works with Adam. But it is the active obedience of the Second Adam to the covenant stipulations of the Pactum Salutis that gives the believer right to sabbath glory. Just as the righteousness that Adam had when he was created could never obtain eschatological glory, so the righteousness Jesus was born with as the Second Adam was not the righteousness that obtains heaven for the believer. Sinless perfection in the abstract does not obtain the final sabbath. The covenant-keeping righteousness obtains eternal glory. Paul writes,

> So then as through one transgression there resulted condemnation to all men, even so through one act of righteousness there resulted justification of life to all men. **19** For as through the one man's disobedience the many were made sinners, even so through the obedience of the One the many will be made righteous. (Romans 5:18–19)

---

25. 1 John 2:2; 4:10; see Morris, *Apostolic*.

The Covenant of Works: Jesus (Pactum Salutis)

In the context of the Covenant of Works and the Pactum Salutis, the righteousness Christ obtains for the believer is not an abstract return to a sinless condition, but rather the status of one who has kept the stipulations of the covenant and is thus proclaimed a covenant keeper, "righteous." So as Adam's covenant unrighteousness brought condemnation, the sanction for transgression of the covenant, so the Second Adam's covenant obedience gained the covenant sanction of justification, a declaration covenant righteousness resulting in the blessing of eschatological life. Here Paul contrasts the unending damnation with the eschatological Glory in the covenant sanctions.

This two-Adam structure is the story of Scripture. All other personages are ancillary to this primary story. Paul bookends history with these two men when he discusses the final resurrection:

> But now Christ has been raised from the dead, the first fruits of those who are asleep. 21 For since by a man *came* death, by a man also came the resurrection of the dead. 22 For as in Adam all die, so also in Christ all will be made alive. 23 But each in his own order: Christ the first fruits, after that those who are Christ's at His coming, 24 then *comes* the end, when He hands over the kingdom to the God and Father, when He has abolished all rule and all authority and power. 25 For He must reign until He has put all His enemies under His feet. 26 The last enemy that will be abolished is death. 27 FOR HE HAS PUT ALL THINGS IN SUBJECTION UNDER HIS FEET. But when He says, "All things are put in subjection," it is evident that He is excepted who put all things in subjection to Him. 28 When all things are subjected to Him, then the Son Himself also will be subjected to the One who subjected all things to Him, so that God may be all in all. (1 Cor 15:20–28)

Adam brought death. Jesus brought resurrection life. As vassal king, Jesus rules at the right hand of the Father, until all things are in subjection. Then the Son himself is subject to the Father in Glory. Paul continues,

> So also it is written, "The first MAN, Adam, BECAME A LIVING SOUL." The last Adam *became* a life-giving spirit. 46 However, the spiritual is not first, but the natural; then the spiritual. 47 The first man is from the earth, earthy; the second man is from heaven. 48 As is the earthy, so also are those who are earthy; and as is the heavenly, so also are those who are heavenly. 49 Just as we have borne the image of the earthy, we will also bear the image of the heavenly. (1 Cor. 15:45–49)

The Glory-Spirit breathed life into the image of God, Adam, and he became a "living soul." The first Adam was from the dust of the earth, natural. But the Second Adam, the "last Adam," enthroned to the right hand of the Father, sent the "life-giving Spirit." This Second Adam is from heaven, and those who believe bear the image of this one from heaven. Paul is writing of two Adams, two men. The creation and the end of creation are discussed in relationship to these two men. The first Adam was made from the dust of the ground. The Second Adam came from heaven, the incarnation of the Second Person of the Trinity, fully God and fully man. He became a man to do what the first Adam did not do. The Second Adam builds the eschatological temple and brings many sons to dwell forever with the triune God.

Paul's language in 1 Corinthians 15:45–49 demonstrates that the two-Adam contrast is foundational in Paul's writings. For Paul, "flesh" and "Spirit" are but references to the two covenant realities in Adam and in Christ. Herman Ridderbos writes,

> Flesh (body) and Spirit do not stand over against one another here as two "parts" in the human existence or in the existence in Christ . . . Rather, "flesh" and "Spirit" represent two modes of existence, on the one hand that of the old aeon which is characterized and determined by the flesh, on the other that of the new creation which is of the Spirit of God. It is in this sense that the difference is also to be taken between the first Adam as "living soul," i.e., flesh, and the second as life-giving Spirit. The contrast is therefore of a redemptive-historical nature: it qualifies the world and the mode of existence before Christ as flesh, that is, as the creaturely in its weakness; on the other hand, the dispensation that has taken affect with Christ as that of the Spirit, i.e., of power, imperishableness and glory . . . .[26]

Paul's contrast of "flesh" (also "old man")[27] and "Spirit" in Romans 6–8 is based on the two-Adam contrast of Romans 5. Paul writes, "while we were in the flesh . . . at work in the members of our body to bear fruit for death. But now . . . that we serve in newness of the Spirit" (Rom 7:5–6). Jesus also contrasts the two ages with the same language. John writes,

> Nicodemus said to Him, "How can a man be born when he is old? He cannot enter a second time into his mother's womb and be born, can he?" ⁵ Jesus answered, "Truly, truly, I say to you,

---

26. Ridderbos, *Paul*, 66. See Russell, *Flesh*.
27. Rom 6:6: ὁ παλαιὸς ἡμῶν ἄνθρωπος.

> unless one is born of water and the Spirit he cannot enter into the kingdom of God. **6** That which is born of the flesh is flesh, and that which is born of the Spirit is spirit. **7** Do not be amazed that I said to you, 'You must be born again.' **8** The wind blows where it wishes and you hear the sound of it, but do not know where it comes from and where it is going; so is everyone who is born of the Spirit." (John 3:4–8)

Jesus is saying more than that it requires the Holy Spirit to regenerate a man in order for any man to enter the kingdom of God. That is true, but the conversation between the Messiah of Israel and this Pharisee is about the contrast of the ages. A man born of a woman, though a keeper of the Law, is still "flesh" and condemned. Nicodemus responds, "How can these things be?" Jesus points out that Nicodemus is a teacher of the Law that speaks of Christ and yet he does not understand. Yes, Jesus has come from heaven. The kingdom of God has come. This is the contrast between the "flesh" in Adam and the "Spirit" that brings the kingdom. The very miraculous signs that Nicodemus acknowledged attest to Jesus (John 3:2) are the signs of the presence of the "Spirit" of the kingdom of God. There are two Adams, and the keeper of the Law will not enter the kingdom. Though Jesus addresses the contrast between the Mosaic shadows and the arrival of the kingdom of God, the more ultimate contrast is between those of this world, born "flesh," and those of the coming kingdom, "born of the Spirit." The contrast is between two Adams, two worlds.

Erroneous Conflation with the Covenant of Grace

To protect the clarity of the gospel and not obscure the primacy of the work of Christ as the Second Adam in the Pactum Salutis, it is important to distinguish the Pactum Salutis from the Covenant of Grace. "Covenant of Grace" is the common name attached by many in the Protestant Reformation tradition to the gospel promise made throughout the Old Testament scriptures, culminating in the New Covenant. Starting in Genesis 3:15, all through the story of believers before Christ, whether Noah, Job, Abraham, Moses, David, Daniel, is this promise of salvation by faith in the coming Messiah. All believers before Christ, though under different times and covenants, are saved the same way—by faith in the coming Redeemer. The common promise is often called the "Covenant of Grace." This promised salvation is based on the work of Christ under the Pactum

Salutis. Old Testament believers were saved based on what Jesus would do; New Testament believers are saved based on what Jesus did. The story of redemption is centered on the work of Christ. As will be addressed in subsequent chapters, the application of that saving work to believers is seen throughout the unfolding history of redemption.

The Pactum Salutis is closely related to the Covenant of Grace. If Adam had obeyed the stipulation in the probation, he and all he represented would have been confirmed in covenant-keeping righteousness. Though still engaged in filling and subduing the earth until the completion of the kingdom work, they would have been unable to sin and would have had the sure promise of eschatological sabbath glory. In parallel fashion, the Second Adam met the requirements of the Pactum Salutis and has been exalted to the right hand of the King of Heaven in Glory. The Covenant of Grace is the application of the benefits of Christ work to the believer. The believer is forgiven all his sin and is legally already enthroned in Christ at the right of the Father. The Covenant of Grace is intrinsically related to the Pactum Salutis. But they are different covenants. If the difference is lost, the gospel is greatly threatened. Some theologians have tried to combine the two covenants into one covenant while protecting the distinct elements, but this tends to distort the Pactum Salutis.

Christ is more than the mediator of the Covenant of Grace. He is the federal head of the elect. When he was damned, his damnation paid the full penalty for the sin of the elect. His damnation was their damnation for their sin. Moses was the mediator of the Old Covenant, but his obedience could not take the place of Israel's disobedience. Moses could not take upon himself in their place, the covenant punishment poured out on Israel. He was the mediator, but he was not a federal head. His obedience and disobedience did not act in place of Israel's. Some theologians acknowledge that Christ was the federal head in the taking the penalty under the Covenant of Works. His death, as federal head, was in the place of the elect. But this does not go far enough. Christ was not just the federal head to pay for sin, but the federal head in the Pactum Salutis to merit by his obedience the covenant blessing of eschatological Glory. Not only was the sin of the elect imputed to the federal head, but the covenant-keeping righteousness of the federal head was imputed to the elect. In Christ the elect have legal right to the eschatological blessing. To combine the two covenants usually reduces the Pactum Salutis to Christ paying for the sin of the elect. Lost is the federal head's covenant keeping, which merits the covenant blessing. Christ did infinitely more than pay for sin. Christ's exaltation is as federal head of the elect. His covenant obedience is their covenant obedience; his exaltation is their glorification.

The Pactum Salutis and the Covenant of Grace have different parties and different requirements. Jesus is the servant of the Lord in the Pactum Salutis; he is Lord in the Covenant of Grace. The Pactum Salutis is a covenant of works in which the vassal's obedience to the stipulation merits the covenant blessing as a matter of covenant justice. In the Covenant of Grace, the blessing of the covenant is received by faith in the obedience of the federal head, contrary to the demerit of the believer. The righteousness of the covenant servant under the Pactum Salutis is the covenant obedience of the servant. The justifying covenant righteousness of the believer in the Covenant of Grace is completely alien to obedience of the believer. It is the imputed covenant-keeping righteousness of Christ. The Pactum Salutis is law; the Covenant of Grace is grace. To combine the two covenants is to lose grace.

Sometimes theological arguments are too familiar and obscure the actual differences involved. An illustration may help. There was a train that was headed to the Celestial City. In order to obtain entrance, the conductor had to bring the proper construction materials and follow the directions. But the conductor decided to choose for himself the best route, and picked the wrong switches in the tracks. He hit the bottle and neglected to bring the required building supplies. Now on the wrong route, he and all his passengers are headed to an abrupt end in the canyon.

The king of the Celestial City commissioned another conductor. He followed every direction, brought the required construction supplies, and is sure to gain entrance into the city. But the second conductor is also on a rescue mission. He sent rescuers to airlift to safety any passengers on the first train who would abandon their luggage and come to the provisions of the second train. Some came, while others did not. But one thing is clear: only the second conductor earned a place in the Celestial City. His passengers are granted entrance because of his obedience.

This is the difference between the Pactum Salutis and the Covenant of Grace. In the Pactum Salutis, Christ merited the Celestial City. In the Covenant of Grace, he applies the blessing to those he delivers. Christ has legal claim to the city as the obedient servant. The passengers are heirs by grace. What is his, he has made theirs.

Some have muddied the theological waters by raising the question of *conditionality*. Do both the Covenant of Works and Covenant of Grace have conditions? This becomes the basis for confusion between grace and meritorious works. The Covenant of Works requires the fulfillment of the covenant stipulation to receive the covenant blessing. The obedience to the condition is the meritorious basis of receipt of the covenant blessing. The blessing is earned. But in the Covenant of Grace, one receives the covenant blessing contrary to one's demerit. Yes, one must believe and receive the unmerited gift. But to call that a "condition" in an effort to put it on the same ground as the condition of the Covenant of Works is inane. It would be like saying that a Mr. Smith has worked his whole life and gained great wealth and prominence. His later years are filled with prosperity because he has met the required conditions. In contrast, Annie is an orphan who scraps with the boys in the alley for food each day. She is ill-tempered and regularly breaks the laws. But one day Mr. Smith offers to adopt Annie and promises that all that is his will be hers! She accepts the unbelievable offer. Does she meet a "condition"? Yes, in the very narrow sense that she could accept or reject. But does her acceptance in any way merit the blessing? No. So too, it is not helpful to speak of "condition" when speaking of the Covenant of Grace. The Covenant of Grace is not a covenant to be kept, but a promise received by faith. The only condition for the believer is faith in his Redeemer!

Understanding Christ's work as Second Adam in the Pactum Salutis is then foundational to understanding Christ's earthly ministry. Christ did not pay for sins and send the Holy Spirit to empower the believer to obey so the believer could obtain the covenant blessing through the believer's obedience. This is a gross distortion that destroys the gospel. The good news is not that Jesus took away the believer's sin and now empowers the believer to keep the covenant so that the believer will be blessed. The gospel is that the Second Adam came and did what Adam failed to do. The Lord Jesus kept the covenant and merited the eschatological blessing for all who put their faith in him. The blessing is received based on the obedience of Christ alone.

THE MINISTRY OF CHRIST

Jesus fulfilled the eternal covenant, the Pactum Salutis, in history. Mark starts his gospel account by connecting the historical with the eternal. Mark doesn't skip the Christmas story. He shouts at the top of his lungs the significance of the incarnation. God has come to bring cosmic deliverance! He announces the coming of Jesus by identifying him as the

Son of God! He writes, "The beginning of the gospel of Jesus Christ, the Son of God" (Mark 1:1). This identification of Jesus as the Son of God is not just a statement about the natures of Jesus. Mark is referencing the promise of God in Isaiah. He writes,

> THE VOICE OF ONE CRYING IN THE WILDERNESS,
> 'MAKE READY THE WAY OF THE LORD,
> MAKE HIS PATHS STRAIGHT.' (Mark 1:3)

The quote is from Isaiah 40:3:

> A voice is calling,
> "Clear the way for the Yahweh in the wilderness;
> Make smooth in the desert a highway for our God." (AT)

And verse 10:

> Behold, the Lord Yahweh will come with might . . . (AT)

Though Mark only quotes one verse, he is not merely referencing the one verse. He is referencing the entirety of Isaiah's promise that God will do what Adam and Israel failed to do. This technique of scriptural reference is common in Scripture. The specific verse quoted references a much broader content. It is like two lovers who spent a wonderful evening at a cafe in Paris. The food was exquisite; the live music a delight. The time together that evening would never be forgotten. The address of the cafe displayed was 1012 Cafe St., a number that struck the romantic couple since his birthday was on the 10th and hers on the 12th. Years later, when one would say "1012" to the other, it would bring back the whole evening as though they were there! That is how quotes in Scripture often function. Mark is quoting this one verse found at the beginning of Isaiah's new section, "Comfort, O comfort my people" (Isa 40:1), to reference the whole promise of Isaiah. God will bring deliverance and a new creation. Isaiah's promise is the template for Christ's ministry. Isaiah's promises are summed up in "God is coming." The message of Mark's Gospel is, "God has come!" What the Trinity covenanted in eternity, the Trinity has done in Jesus' ministry.

Mark juxtaposes the deity of Jesus with Jesus hanging on the cross in such a stark manner that the tension of the incarnation of God and the damnation under God's wrath can only be understood as the fulfillment of the Pactum Salutis. Mark's confession that Jesus is God in the first verse of the gospel sets the stage for awe evidenced in the following chapters.

John the Baptist is not worthy to untie his sandals (Mark 1:7). He will baptize with the Holy Spirit (Mark 1:8). Heaven opened at his baptism with the Holy Spirit coming down on him like a dove and the Father announcing, "You are My beloved Son, in You I am well pleased" (Mark 1:11). He battled with Satan for forty days in the wilderness in the midst of wild beasts with angels ministering to him (Mark 1:13). He enjoined the disciples to follow him and they left their fathers and fishing nets followed him (Mark 1:16–20). He is the one the unclean spirits called "the Holy One of God" (Mark 1:24). People saw the exorcisms he did and marveled, "What is this? A new teaching with authority! He commands even the unclean spirits, and they obey Him" (Mark 1:27) But at the end, he is hanging on a Roman cross, crying out, "MY GOD, MY GOD, WHY HAVE YOU FORSAKEN ME?" (Mark 15:34). Mark set the stage to understand the finale in the reference to Isaiah in the first verses of the gospel. God the Son has come to fulfill the intra-Trinitarian Pactum Salutis. This is confirmed by the way Mark concludes the gospel. When the women went to the tomb, they found the extremely large stone rolled back from the entrance. When they entered the tomb, an angel told them that Jesus had risen as he had said he would and had gone to meet the disciples, just as he had said he would. The women, though confused, were struck with the reality of who Jesus is. Mark's final verse says it all:

> They went out and fled from the tomb, for trembling and astonishment had gripped them; and they said nothing to anyone, for they were afraid. (Mark 16:8)

They were immobilized by the deep fear. They were confused, but filled with fear. This is the response to the true identity of Jesus throughout the gospel. When Jesus hushed the wind and waves, the disciples responded with fear: "They became very much afraid and said to one another, "Who then is this, that even the wind and the sea obey Him?" (Mark 4:41). When the people saw the legion-filled demoniac delivered sitting clothed and in his right mind, they were filled with fear (Mark 5:15). When the woman who had a hemorrhage for twelve years was healed by touching Jesus' cloak, she was filled with fear (Mark 5:33). When Jesus was transfigured in Glory, the disciples were terrified (Mark 9:6). The final verse takes the reader back to the first verse of Mark.[28] God is the Deliverer, and he has come!

---

28. Lane, *Mark*, 591–92.

The Covenant of Works: Jesus (Pactum Salutis)

The incarnation is not just an affirmation that Jesus is God, but the good news that God has come to deliver! God the Son has come as the covenant vassal servant to bring the kingdom of God through his obedience to the Father. He will be the priest-king and build the royal temple of the King in heaven. He will obey the Father even to damnation on the cross. Victorious over the enemy, he will be exalted to the right hand of the Father. He will bring the eschatological day of glory in the new heavens and new earth. Even the Gentiles will be saved. At the crucifixion, the Roman centurion confesses, "Truly this man was the Son of God" (Mark 15:39).

This fulfillment of the Pactum Salutis is the common confession of the gospel writers. Luke presents Jesus as the "light for revelation to the Gentiles" (AT; Luke 2:32; Isa 42:6; 49:6). John the Baptist will prepare the way of the Lord (Luke 1:17; Isa 40:3; Mal 3:1). In Mary's Magnificat, she draws from Isaiah when she speaks of the "servant" (Luke 1:54-55; Isa 41:8-9).[29] Luke draws a tight web of logic in chapter 3, which connects God's promised coming in Isaiah 40 (Luke 3:4-6) to John's proclamation that he is not worthy to untie the sandal of the coming one who will baptize with the Holy Spirit (Luke 3:16). On this one the Spirit descended and this one the Father calls "Son" (Luke 3:22). Luke then immediately gives Jesus' genealogy: "the son of Enosh, the son of Seth, the son of Adam, the son of God" (Luke 3:38). God the Son has come as the Second Adam, the Son of God. The God who created all things (John 1:1–3) has come. He became a man (John 1:14).

Throughout the gospels, Jesus constantly refers to himself as the "Son of Man." As would become evident, there was a messianic claim attached to that name. But at the most basic level, "Son of Man" is an identity of a man. Jesus calls himself a man. The son of a man is a man, as much as the offspring of an elephant is an elephant. The saying is well known, "Like father, like son." The disciples James and John were like their dad and so received their nickname. Mark recounts the calling of the disciples: "and James, the son of Zebedee, and John the brother of James (to them He gave the name Boanerges, which means, 'Sons of Thunder')" (Mark 3:17). These are the two brothers who blurted out, "Lord, do You want us to command fire to come down from heaven and consume them?" (Luke 9:54). Their father was well known for his aggressive temper; so too the sons. The Son of Man is a man.[30] Isaiah writes with parallelism,

---

29. Isa 42:1; 44:1–2, 21; 45:4; 48:20; 49:3.
30. Ps 80:17; 8:4; Ezek 2:1.

> I, even I, am He who comforts you.
> Who are you that you are afraid of man who dies
> And of the son of man who is made like grass... (Isa 51:12)

Job too writes with parallelism, equating "man" and "son of man,"

> How much less man, *that* maggot,
> And the son of man, *that* worm!" (Job 25:6)

Jesus was a man, but he was a man on a mission from God. When he was only a boy, he reminded his parents that he was about his Father's things (Luke 2:49). Throughout his life, Jesus lived in perfect obedience to the King of Heaven, his Father. Before the sun was up (Mark 1:35), in the midst of his pressing ministry (Luke 5:16), literally all the time, Jesus walked in unbroken dependence on his Father. Jesus understood that he came from heaven. He says,

> For I have come down from heaven, not to do My own will, but the will of Him who sent Me. (John 6:38)

Again, John writes,

> *Jesus*, knowing... that He had come forth from God. (John 13:3)

Jesus testifies to his mission:

> No one has ascended into heaven except the One who descended from heaven: the Son of Man ... For God did not send His Son into the world to condemn the world, but to save the world through Him. (John 3:13, 17 AT)

Jesus' life was found in every word that proceeded from the mouth of the Father:

> Jesus explained, "My food is to do the will of Him who sent Me and to finish His work. (John 4:34; cf. Matt 4:4)

His mission defined him:

> Jesus replied, "The work of God is this: to believe in the One He has sent." (John 6:29 AT)

The clarity of his claim was not lost on the hearers:

> They were asking, "Is this not Jesus, the son of Joseph, whose father and mother we know? How then can He say, 'I have come down out of heaven'?" (John 6:42)

The Covenant of Works: Jesus (Pactum Salutis)

Specifically, Jesus identified himself as the vassal servant of the Pactum Salutis. He referred to Isaiah 53:10–11 when he told the disciples, "For even the Son of Man did not come to be served, but to serve, and to give His life a ransom for many" (Mark 10:45). Jesus told the disciples he was the fulfillment of Isaiah's servant of the Lord when, at the Last Supper, Jesus referenced Isaiah 53:12, saying, "For I tell you that this which is written must be fulfilled in Me, 'And He was numbered with transgressors'" (Luke 22:37).

In the Pactum Salutis, Jesus is the image of the King of Heaven (Col 1:15; cf. Heb 1:3). As Second Adam, he is the vassal priest-king. As the Spirit created Adam as the temple image of the King of Heaven, so likewise the Spirit overshadowed Mary at the conception of Jesus (Luke 1:35). Jesus says, "As the living Father sent Me, and I live because of the Father" (John 6:57). The King has life in himself; the vassal has life from the King. So the one who "eats Me, he also will live because of Me" (John 6:57). Jesus is the federal head of the elect. His covenant remuneration is their recompense. The covenant blessings are bound up in Jesus. Those who are represented by him are blessed by his covenant obedience; they will not be cursed (Luke 6:22–26). He has no authority in himself. He is the vassal image of the King of Heaven. He says, "Truly, truly, I tell you, the Son can do nothing by Himself, unless He sees the Father doing it. For whatever the Father does, the Son also does" (John 5:19 AT). He is the vassal replica of the King of Heaven.

As vassal king, Jesus has the authority of heaven. The Father declares this when he calls Jesus his "Son" at his baptism and transfiguration. The Father says, "This is My beloved Son, with whom I am well pleased; listen to Him!" (Matt 17:5). As Second Adam, he will bring the kingdom of God. The Father has put all things into his hands (John 13:3). Jesus says, "My Father is working until now, and I Myself am working" (John 5:17). He has all authority on earth. The wind and waves obey him (Mark 4:39). He is the vassal king. He is also the vassal priest. At the start of his ministry, Jesus found the money changers in the temple. He drove them out and said, "Take these things away; stop making My Father's house a place of business" (John 2:16). He is the faithful priest guarding the holy place. He, the vassal servant, has authority on earth to forgive sins (Mark 2:10). He casts out evil spirits. His miracles are not proof of divinity, but signs of the kingdom he brings. He heals the sick. He feeds the hungry. This is the vassal that is endowed with the mission and authority to forgive sins. He says, "But so that you may know that the Son of Man has authority on earth to forgive sins . . ." (Mark 2:10). But more specifically, building the kingdom of God means building the King's royal temple. The kingdom of God is the royal temple of the King of Heaven.

The Second Adam priest-king is commissioned to build the royal temple of the King of Heaven. The temple is central to his ministry. He is constantly at the temple. When he was twelve, his parents found him in the temple courts (Luke 2:46). At the beginning of his ministry, he drives the money changers out of the temple. The devil took him to pinnacle of the temple to tempt him (Matt 4:5). He announces, "But I say to you that something greater than the temple is here" (Matt 12:6). Daily he taught at the temple (Mark 14:49). Even after Jesus' ascension, the disciples are gathered at the temple (Acts 2:46; 3:10). The temple is not peripheral to the ministry of Christ. He has come to build the royal house (temple) of the King of Heaven. He is the temple to which the Old Testament temple pointed.

John says that God "tabernacled" among us (John 1:14). Jesus identifies himself as the temple (John 2:19–21). He is the eschatological temple (Rev 21:22). So the elect, as his body, are the temple (1 Pet 2:4–8; Eph 2:19–22). Jesus promises the believer,

> He who overcomes, I will make him a pillar in the temple of My God, and he will not go out from it anymore; and I will write on him the name of My God, and the name of the city of My God, the new Jerusalem, which comes down out of heaven from My God, and My new name. (Rev 3:12)

The eschatological kingdom of God is the royal temple of the King of Heaven.

At each step Jesus uses his authority in obedience to the Father. As the God-man, vassal king, he is bound by the covenant will of the Father. The author of Hebrews writes,

> Therefore, when He comes into the world, He says,
> "SACRIFICE AND OFFERING YOU HAVE NOT DESIRED,
> BUT A BODY YOU HAVE PREPARED FOR ME;
> 6 IN WHOLE BURNT OFFERINGS AND *sacrifices* FOR SIN YOU HAVE TAKEN NO PLEASURE.
> 7 "THEN I SAID, 'BEHOLD, I HAVE COME
> (IN THE SCROLL OF THE BOOK IT IS WRITTEN OF ME)
> TO DO YOUR WILL, O GOD.'" (Heb 10:5–7)

His entire life was to image the King in covenant obedience. Even Jesus' baptism was "to fulfill all righteousness" (Matt 3:15). Unlike Adam or Israel, he obeyed the covenant stipulations. The word of the King provided the directive for everything he did. Immediately after his baptism, he was put to the test when the Spirit drove him into the wilderness for forty days. Like Adam, he was surrounded by animals.[31] But it was no garden paradise. Satan confronted him with three temptations. The responses from Deuteronomy sharpen the focus on the covenant context. First, Satan offered an alternate covenant stipulation for Jesus to use his authority for himself and

> ... command that these stones become bread. (Matt 4:3)

Jesus replied that God's word is the basis of life:

> It is written, "MAN SHALL NOT LIVE ON BREAD ALONE, BUT ON EVERY WORD THAT PROCEEDS OUT OF THE MOUTH of GOD." (Matt 4:4; see Deut 8:3)

Second, Satan took Jesus to the top of the temple and told him he didn't have to be a vassal servant:

> If you are the Son of God, throw Yourself down; for it is written, "HE WILL COMMAND HIS ANGELS CONCERNING YOU" and "ON *their* HANDS THEY WILL BEAR YOU UP, SO THAT YOU WILL NOT STRIKE YOUR FOOT AGAINST A STONE." (Matt 4:6)

But Jesus rejected any other role than the Father had given:

> YOU SHALL NOT PUT THE LORD YOUR GOD TO THE TEST. (Matt 4:7; see Deut 6:16)

Finally, Satan offered Jesus a counterfeit covenant sanction and made the alternate stipulation more obvious:

> ... showed Him all the kingdoms of the world and their glory;
> **9** and he said to Him, "All these things I will give You, if You fall down and worship me." (Matt 4:8–9)

Jesus abhorred the tempter and restated his absolute commitment to the King of Heaven:

---

31. Mark 1:13.

> Then Jesus said to him, "Go, Satan! For it is written, 'You shall worship the Lord your God, and serve Him only.'" (Matt 4:10; see Deut 6:13)

This conflict at the beginning of Jesus' ministry evidenced the greater conflict between the vassal of the kingdom of God and the enemy of the King. Before Jesus' birth, Satan sought his murder at the hands of Herod. As Jesus approached the cross, Satan tempted Jesus through one of his closest disciples, Peter (Matt 16:22–23).

In obedience, Jesus went to the cross. Luke says he "set His face to go to Jerusalem" (Luke 9:51 AT). Luke is referencing Isaiah 50:7:

> For the Lord God helps Me,
> Therefore, I am not disgraced;
> Therefore, I have set My face like flint,
> And I know that I will not be ashamed.

He is the obedient servant of the Lord. He knows the King will recompense him. In his obedience he goes to the cross. For this purpose he was given authority. He says,

> No one has taken it away from Me, but I lay it down on My own initiative. I have authority to lay it down, and I have authority to take it up again. This commandment I received from My Father. (John 10:18)

Jesus is not a powerless victim. He is the obedient vassal king. His authority is from the King, and he uses that authority to go to the cross in obedience to the Father. As the stipulation of the Pactum Salutis, it is a "commandment." He uses that authority as priest-king as he approaches the cross. He requisitions the donkey. Matthew writes that Jesus told them, "Go into the village opposite you, and immediately you will find a donkey tied *there* and a colt with her; untie them and bring them to Me" (Matt 21:2). Jesus was in total control, even to the detailed preparation of the Last Supper. He told Peter and John,

> "Go and prepare the Passover for us, so that we may eat it." [9] They said to Him, "Where do You want us to prepare it?" [10] And He said to them, "When you have entered the city, a man will meet you carrying a pitcher of water; follow him into the house that he enters. [11] And you shall say to the owner of the house, 'The Teacher says to you, "Where is the guest room in which I may eat the Passover with My disciples?"' [12] And he will show you a large, furnished upper room; prepare it there." (Luke 22:8–12)

The Covenant of Works: Jesus (Pactum Salutis)

When the soldiers came to arrest Jesus, he was still in complete control. John writes,

> So Jesus, knowing all the things that were coming upon Him, went forth and said to them, "Whom do you seek?" ⁵ They answered Him, "Jesus the Nazarene." He said to them, "I AM." And Judas also, who was betraying Him, was standing with them. ⁶ So when He said to them, "I AM," they drew back and fell to the ground. (John 18:4–6 AT)

He was not caught by surprise. He knew all that was going to happen. He went to the Roman cohort. He inquired who they sought. When they answered, he said, "I AM" ('Ἐγώ εἰμι *ego eimi*). John emphasizes Jesus' response, "I AM," with the resulting fear of the soldiers. The soldiers fell to the ground! This is God that stood before them. He went to the cross.

As this hour approached, John provides an account of Jesus' intentionality and expectation of the King's covenant blessing. As the crowds gathered in Jerusalem for the Passover Feast, Greeks approached the disciple and asked to see Jesus. Jesus responds they would see him, for "The hour has come for the Son of Man to be glorified" (John 12:23). He would be "lifted up" on the cross and "draw all men to Myself" (John 12:32). He prays to the Father,

> Now My soul has become troubled; and what shall I say, 'Father, save Me from this hour'? But for this purpose I came to this hour. ²⁸ Father, glorify Your name.' (John 12:27–28)

The Father then responds audibly from heaven so the crowds hear, "I have both glorified it, and will glorify it again" (John 12:28). They heard, but couldn't hear. Some attributed the sound to thunder; the devout said it was an angel. Jesus clearly identifies himself as the fulfillment of the Pactum Salutis by referring to Isaiah:

> For a little while longer the Light is among you. Walk while you have the Light, so that darkness will not overtake you; he who walks in the darkness does not know where he goes. ³⁶ While you have the Light, believe in the Light, so that you may become sons of Light. (John 12:35–36)

Jesus is the Light of Isaiah. Isaiah promised,

> He shall make *it* glorious, by the way of the sea, on the other side of Jordan, Galilee of the Gentiles.
> ² The people who walk in darkness

Will see a great light;
Those who live in a dark land,
The light will shine on them. (Isa 9:1–2)³²

And again, referring to the servant of the Lord, Isaiah writes,

> And I will appoint You as a covenant to the people, As a light to the nations. (Isa 42:6)

And,

> I will also make You a light of the nations
> So that My salvation may reach to the end of the earth. (Isa 49:6)

So the one who lives in this light is promised,

> Then your light will break out like the dawn, And your recovery will speedily spring forth; And your righteousness will go before you; The glory of the Lord will be your rear guard. (Isa 58:8)

And,

> Arise, shine; for your light has come, And the glory of the Lord has risen upon you. (Isa 60:1)

But Israel did not see. John then explains and quotes Isaiah 53:1 and 6:10:

> *This* was to fulfill the word of Isaiah the prophet which he spoke: "Lord, who has believed our report? And to whom has the arm of the Lord been revealed?" ³⁹ For this reason they could not believe, for Isaiah said again, ⁴⁰ "He has blinded their eyes and He hardened their heart, so that they would not see with their eyes and perceive with their heart, and be converted and I heal them." ⁴¹ These things Isaiah said because he saw his glory, and he spoke of Him. (John 12:38–41)

Yes, the Greeks would see him, while Israel was blind.

Jesus knew the tree at Golgotha was the ultimate stipulation he faced. He who was sinless willingly became sin. He knew he would not just die on a cross, but be cursed as a covenant breaker and hang on the tree to display God's just condemnation (cf. Deut 21:23). When faced with obedience to damnation, he said, "Father, if You are willing, remove this cup from Me; yet not My will, but Yours be done" (Luke 22:42). He chose the

---

32. See Matt 4:15–16.

The Covenant of Works: Jesus (Pactum Salutis)

cup of wrath[33] over disobeying the King. This was necessary to make a way for sinners in the eschatological temple. Jesus tells the disciples,

> Do not let your heart be troubled; believe in God, believe also in Me. ² In My Father's house are many dwelling places; if it were not so, I would have told you; for I go to prepare a place for you. ³ If I go and prepare a place for you, I will come again and receive you to Myself, that where I am, *there* you may be also. (John 14:1–3)

The one who sweat drops of blood as he went obediently to take the punishment of hell tells the disciples not to be troubled. The contrast in who does the work could not be starker. He went to the cross. For in so doing he prepared a place for the believer.

Paul pulls together the elements of the Pactum Salutis in Philippians 2. Paul writes,

> ... who although He existed in the form of God, did not regard equality with God a thing to be grasped, ⁷ but emptied Himself, taking the form of a bond-servant, *and* being made in the likeness of men. ⁸ Being found in appearance as a man, He humbled Himself by becoming obedient to the point of death, even death on a cross. ⁹ For this reason also, God highly exalted Him, and bestowed on Him the name which is above every name, ¹⁰ so that at the name of JESUS EVERY KNEE WILL BOW, of those who are in heaven and on earth and under the earth, ¹¹ and that every tongue will confess that Jesus Christ is Lord, to the glory of God the Father. (Phil 2:6–11)

God became the covenant servant and obeyed the covenant stipulations, even to bear the unfiltered wrath of God. So the vassal servant is exalted to the highest place! As previously noted, it would be heresy to say that God the Son was not already exalted above every name! But in the eternal covenant, God the Son became a man. Now that vassal servant has been exalted to the highest place, above any every creature in heaven and earth. The vassal Jesus fulfilled the messianic commission and now is seated at the right hand of the King of Heaven, to the Glory of the King!

In the hours before the crucifixion, Jesus prayed to the Father,

> I glorified You on the earth, having accomplished the work which You have given Me to do. ⁵ Now, Father, glorify Me

---

33. Isa 51:17; Jer 25:15; Rev 14:10.

> together with Yourself, with the glory which I had with You before the world was." (John 17:4–5)

He had been the faithful servant, and now, in light of the ultimate act of obedience, Jesus laid claim to the promised sanction of the Pactum Salutis, glory. For this purpose all creation was made. Paul writes,

> For by Him all things were created, *both* in the heavens and on earth, visible and invisible, whether thrones or dominions or rulers or authorities–all things have been created through Him and for Him. (Col 1:16)

Faithful to the requirements of the covenant, Jesus was raised from the dead and ascended to the right hand of the Father in Glory. He has received his sabbath enthronement (Heb 4:14ff.). Having fulfilled the covenant, he could say to the disciples, "All authority has been given to Me in heaven and on earth" (Matt 28:18). Or as Paul writes, "far above all rule and authority and power and dominion, and every name that is named, not only in this age but also in the one to come" (Eph 1:21).

The God-man, the Second Adam, has kept the covenant and sits at the right hand of the King of Heaven in Glory. Daniel writes about this hope of Israel. The kings of the nations, described as wild beasts, claim that the kingdom belongs to them. There are endless wars between the claimants and united persecution against the people of God. But when the day of adjudication comes, Daniel writes,

> I kept looking in the night visions,
> And behold, with the clouds of heaven
> One like a Son of Man was coming,
> And He came up to the Ancient of Days
> And was presented before Him.
> **14** And to Him was given dominion,
> Glory and a kingdom,
> That all the peoples, nations and *men of every* language
> Might serve Him.
> His dominion is an everlasting dominion
> Which will not pass away;
> And His kingdom is one
> Which will not be destroyed. (Dan 7:13–14)

To a man is given everlasting dominion. But this man comes "with the clouds of heaven." He is not just a man; he is the God-man. He is the exalted Son of Man.

By the resurrection, he is declared to be the Son of the King. Paul writes, "who was declared the Son of God with power by the resurrection from the dead" (Rom 1:4). When he ascended, he rose up into cloud. This is not a mere meteorological observation. As the Glory-cloud appeared over Israel, and as the Glory-cloud was present at the theophany, Jesus is received to be seated at the right hand of the King of Heaven. There the angelic army of the King proclaim Jesus' praise. John writes that he saw

> ... myriads of myriads, and thousands of thousands, [12] saying with a loud voice, "Worthy is the Lamb that was slain to receive power and riches and wisdom and might and honor and glory and blessing." (Rev 5:11-12)

At Pentecost, Peter pointed to the presence of the Spirit as evidence of Jesus' ascension to the right hand of the Father. Luke records the conclusion of Peter's sermon:

> Therefore having been exalted to the right hand of God, and having received from the Father the promise of the Holy Spirit, He has poured forth this which you both see and hear. [34] For it was not David who ascended into heaven, but he himself says:
> "THE LORD SAID TO MY LORD,
> 'SIT AT MY RIGHT HAND,
> [35] UNTIL I MAKE YOUR ENEMIES A FOOTSTOOL FOR YOUR FEET.'"
> [36] Therefore let all the house of Israel know for certain that God has made Him both LORD and Christ–this Jesus whom you crucified. (Acts 2:33-36; cf. Psalm 110)

Jesus, enthroned in Glory, sent forth the Holy Spirit. His presence evidenced that Jesus, faithful priest-king, is seated at the right hand of the Father. He entered the Father's sabbath enthronement (Heb 4:14). John writes in Revelation that he saw

> ... one like a Son of Man, clothed in a robe reaching to the feet, and girded across His chest with a golden sash. [14] His head and His hair were white like white wool, like snow; and His eyes were like a flame of fire. [15] His feet *were* like burnished bronze, when it has been made to glow in a furnace, and His voice *was* like the sound of many waters. (Rev 1:13-15)

This glorified Son of Man is the Lord of Glory. John had seen him transfigured. Now he sees him as the image of the Glory-Spirit. Kline writes,

> In the Spirit, John saw Christ in the form of a theophanic blend of the Glory-Spirit and the Angel of the Presence with the anthropomorphic lineaments of the latter dominant and the Glory-cloud features adjectival. The theophanic figure was further, a blend of the "ancient of days" as well as the "son of man" of Daniel 7:9ff., and thus fully trinitarian.[34]

Dressed in high-priestly robes, the Lord is present in the midst of the church, her Bridegroom, preparing her for the wedding day.

The Lord will come on that glorious day. Scandalizing the high priest, Jesus warned him of that day. Matthew writes,

> And the high priest said to Him, "I adjure You by the living God, that You tell us whether You are the Christ, the Son of God." 64 Jesus said to him, "You have said it *yourself*; nevertheless I tell you, hereafter you will see the SON OF MAN SITTING AT THE RIGHT HAND OF POWER, AND COMING ON THE CLOUDS OF HEAVEN." 65 Then the high priest tore his robes and said, "He has blasphemed." (Matt 26:63–65)

Without understanding the exaltation context of the Pactum Salutis, the high priest had no other possible conclusion than that Jesus was making claims to deity. He was, but his claims went far beyond that! He told the disciples of the day in which he would come. Matthew writes,

> And then the sign of the Son of Man will appear in the sky, and then all the tribes of the earth will mourn, and they will see the SON OF MAN COMING ON THE CLOUDS OF THE SKY with power and great glory. 31 And He will send forth His angels with A GREAT TRUMPET AND THEY WILL GATHER TOGETHER His elect from the four winds, from one end of the sky to the other. (Matt 24:30–31)

The vassal king exalted in Glory will come. Note that the angelic army is now described as "His angels." On that day he will judge. John writes,

> Truly, truly, I say to you, an hour is coming and now is, when the dead will hear the voice of the Son of God, and those who hear will live. 26 For just as the Father has life in Himself, even so He gave to the Son also to have life in Himself; 27 and He gave Him authority to execute judgment, because He is *the* Son of Man. 28 Do not marvel at this; for an hour is coming, in which all who are in the tombs will hear His voice, 29 and will come forth;

---

34. Kline, *Images*, 24–25.

those who did the good *deeds* to a resurrection of life, those who committed the evil *deeds* to a resurrection of judgment. **30** I can do nothing on My own initiative. As I hear, I judge; and My judgment is just, because I do not seek My own will, but the will of Him who sent Me. (John 5:25–30)

The Lord will call forth all, to life or to judgment. But even then, the Lord acts as image of the King of Heaven. His judgment is just and righteous because he represents the King. He is the glorified man from heaven.

Section Two

The History of Redemption

4

The King Will Come

THE HISTORY OF THE cosmos, its creation and consummation, revolve around these two Adams. Immediately after Adam's fall, God promised the Second Adam would be victorious. From that promise until the incarnation, believers looked forward by faith for the champion's coming. By faith, believers would receive the covenant blessings this last Adam would secure as their federal head under the Pactum Salutis.

ADAM

In Genesis 3, Adam went from being the federal head to being a sinner saved by grace through faith in the Second Adam. Adam became the first to believe the gospel. God came to the scene of the crime in the Spirit of the day to judge the covenant breach. God pronounced a temporary judgment. God declared to the serpent, "dust you will eat, All the days of your life" (Gen 3:14). To the woman, God declared the consequences of sin on her family:

> I will greatly multiply
> Your pain in childbirth,
> In pain you will bring forth children;
> Yet your desire will be for your husband,
> And he will rule over you. (Gen 3:16)

Then, finally to the failed kingdom builder, Adam, God said,

> Because you have listened to the voice of your wife, and have eaten from the tree about which I commanded you, saying, "You shall not eat from it;"
> Cursed is the ground because of you;
> In toil you will eat of it
> All the days of your life.
> 18 Both thorns and thistles it shall grow for you;
> And you will eat the plants of the field;
> 19 By the sweat of your face
> You will eat bread,
> Till you return to the ground,
> Because from it you were taken;
> For you are dust,
> And to dust you shall return. (Gen 3:17–19)

All man's labors would come to nothing. He would die. This common curse would afflict all who fell in Adam. But Adam heard something more. The serpent would live. The woman would bear children and have a husband. Adam would live and eat the plants of the field! Judgment Day was being continued. Adam's ears were hanging on God's promise. For during this delay between Adam's covenant breaking and God's judgment on all in Adam, God would send a Redeemer, a Second Adam. Adam heard,

> And I will put enmity
> Between you and the woman,
> And between your seed and her seed;
> He shall bruise you on the head,
> And you shall bruise him on the heel. (Gen 3:15)

In the fall into sin, there was no enmity between the woman and her new lord, Satan. But God promised to put enmity between her and the devilish intruder and between the seed of Satan and the seed of the woman. This promised seed of the woman would do what Adam had not—crush the King's enemy. This champion would be wounded, but through the wounding he would crush the head of the serpent.

Before continuing with the account of Adam's response, it is important to recognize the momentous role this promised "seed" would have. The "seed" is not just the Savior who redeems sinners and defeats Satan. He is the man who does what Adam did not do as vassal priest-king. Adam failed to rule in righteousness as image of the King. Adam failed to guard the holy kingdom garden and cast out the enemy of the

King. Adam failed to fill the kingdom with the seed of the woman. Adam brought the judgment of death, though at this point the adjudication was delayed. This promised seed is the man who will fill the kingdom with a seed that will be at enmity with the enemy of the King. This champion will rule with righteousness and will guard the holy temple of the King. He would go to the cross to crush the head of the serpent. This is not just a promised mediator; the champion is the faithful vassal Second Adam.

Adam heard and believed in the coming one, and voiced his faith. Genesis 3:20 reads, "Now the man called his wife's name Eve, because she was the mother of all living" (AT). She would give birth to the champion who would save. So Adam named her "Eve" (playing on the Hebrew word for "life").[1] God would send the faithful Adam, and Adam believed. Sealing this expression of faith, God clothed Adam and Eve with the skin of a sacrificed animal. No longer would they be naked and ashamed. They would not bear the image of the serpent. They were restored as image bearers in covenant. This promise to save is immediately evidenced by the faith and martyrdom of Abel in chapter 4. Hebrews 11:4 says, "By faith Abel offered to God a better sacrifice." So the champion was already filling the new creation with the genealogy of faith. As Adam had been the priest-king, so this champion would be the faithful priest-king.

JOB'S CHAMPION

This promise of the coming champion was passed down through the believing line. Though the suffering of Job is prominent to the book, the underlying question of the book is: Is God really fulfilling his redemptive promise? The account of Job begins as he is presented as an upright God-fearing believer. His seven sons take turns hosting feasts and inviting his three daughters. Job is an exceedingly wealthy man, but he walks humbly before God. After each of these feasts, he makes offerings for his children due to his concern that they might have sinned. He is characteristically pious. But his faith us not a generic trust in God. As the account makes clear, Job believes the gospel promise.

God was redeeming sinners, just as he promised. But Satan doesn't think so, and when God draws Satan's attention to "my servant Job," Satan calls God a fraud, saying, "Does Job fear God for nothing?" Satan says anyone would "serve" God because he is paying them to do so. God has

---

1. חַוָּה, *chavvah*, "Eve"; חַי, *chay*, "living."

protected Job and blessed him with wealth. Who wouldn't "serve" God for the payoff? But is Job evidence of God's redemption? No. Satan challenges God's claims to redeem. Satan protests that if God stops the payoff, Job will show who he really is, and it isn't a "servant" of God. The question is, will Job serve God for nothing? Is he a redeemed believer, or is God tampering with the evidence rather than redeeming man? Obviously Job can't know what is going on behind the scenes in heaven.

Satan takes away Job's health, wealth, and children. He is left sitting among the ashes, covered with boils. His wife tells him to curse God, and he is "comforted" by three friends who are short on the gospel and long on works righteousness. Their message is clear: "You must have really sinned! Look at you! What did you do?" Chapter after chapter the discourses run the same. God is just and Job must be a terrible sinner to be going through this. But that doesn't explain what has happened here. Job protests that his distress is not God's punishment or even discipline for some sin he committed. Job does not claim that he is without sin, but his tribulation is not from his sinning! He challenges God. But he perseveres in faith.

The high point of Job's expressed gospel faith is in chapter 19. The integrity of his faith had been unrelentingly challenged by "his friends." Job looks to heaven and says,

> But I know that my Redeemer lives and at the last He shall stand upon the dust. And after the loss of my skin which is thus destroyed, even from my flesh shall I see God. (Job 19:25 AT)

The "redeemer" (*goel*, גֹּאֲלִי) is the kinsman redeemer. Job's hope is that his kinsman redeemer will come from heaven. After death, there is a day of bodily resurrection, and "from" his flesh he will see God. Yes, Job will serve God for nothing in his current suffering in hope of that day. But it is not just a hope of deliverance. Job says that in that day, "I shall see God!" This is not hyperbole. This is the eschatological promise given to Adam in Genesis 1—2:4. Moses had not been allowed to see but a glimpse of God. Elijah had only been hidden in the cleft of the rock as God passed by. Job is looking to day when he will see God! Jesus would promise, "Blessed are the pure in heart, for they shall see God" (Matt 5:8). Job's hope is not just for redemption; he hopes for his unimaginable glorification in the presence of the King! Job's ultimate hope is God's vindication that God is bringing the redeemed to glory!

THE KING OF ISRAEL

The hope of the coming king was foundational to Israel's history. At the end of Jacob's life, he gathered his sons to bless them. When he came to Judah, he said,

> The scepter shall not depart from Judah,
> Nor the ruler's staff from between his feet,
> Until Shiloh comes,
> And to him *shall be* the obedience of the peoples. (Gen 49:10)

The promised king would come through the line of Judah. The blessings would be his (Gen 49:11f.). Of his line would come David and David's promised son, Jesus. Even the enemies of Israel could not stop this king from coming. Numbers 24 describes the Canaanites hiring Balaam to curse Israel. But he cannot curse what God has blessed. Balaam speaks of the victorious "star" that will arise from Jacob and exercise universal dominion (Num 24:17–24). Even when the tribes of Israel had no king, their hope was bound up in this coming king.

The twelve tribes took possession of the land of Canaan. Though God was her King, she was governed by judges. In her sin, Israel repeatedly fell into the cycle of disobedience and subsequent judgment. Israel would break God's law, and God would give them over to their oppressors. They would cry out, and he would raise up a judge to deliver them. There were great victories, such as Deborah and Commander Barak over the Canaanite king Jabin and his military commander Sisera, and Gideon over the Midianites. These would be followed by a time of peace. But then Israel would forsake God, and the cycle would begin again. Was there anyone in Israel who could bring lasting peace? Judges ends with the words, "In those days there was no king in Israel; everyone did what was right in his own eyes" (Judg 21:25). This sets the stage for the coronation of Israel's kings.

When Samuel was old and his sons, who were judges, did not walk in obedience to God, the elders asked for a king "like all the nations" (1 Sam 8:5). God told Samuel that their wanting a king like the nations was a rejection of God the King, not a rejection of Samuel. So God gave them a king like the nations. No one was as tall and handsome as Saul (1 Sam 9:2). But he did not obey God, and God took the kingdom from him to give it to one after his own heart, David (1 Sam 13:14). David was the youngest of the eight sons of Jesse. He didn't fight like the kings of the nations. He would choose a sling instead of the king's armor (1 Sam 17:39–40). He was clothed with the Spirit of God. Samuel had anointed him, and "the Spirit of the Lord came mightily upon David from that day forward" (1 Sam 16:13).

David became Saul's armor bearer. Israel was in a standoff with the Philistines. Every morning and evening, for forty days, the Philistine champion, Goliath, would come out and challenge Israel to send out their champion. Goliath was 9 feet and 9 inches tall. He wore a bronze helmet and a coat of armor weighing 126 pounds, and he had bronze knee and shin protectors. He carried a bronze javelin, and a curved sword. The head of his spear weighed 15 pounds. His shield bearer carried a large rectangular shield to protect him. Who in Israel would represent Israel against the giant? King Saul didn't go out to meet him in combat. King Saul tried to find someone to fight, and offered wealth, freedom, and his daughter to the man who would kill Goliath. There was no one to fight for Israel. Goliath continued day and night to taunt Israel. But God had anointed the new deliverer of Israel, David. David, a youth, made clear he represented Israel in the name of God, who would give the victory. David downed Goliath with a stone and then cut off his head with the giant's own sword. David, anointed to be king, was the victorious champion! Was he the one who would deliver Israel and establish God's kingdom? Was he the king for whom they had been waiting? His adultery with Bathsheba and the murder of one his mighty men, Uriah, made it clear he was not. But God promised that David's son would sit on the throne that would have no end. God told Nathan to tell David,

> When your days are complete and you lie down with your fathers, I will raise up your descendant after you, who will come forth from you, and I will establish his kingdom. **13** He shall build a house for My name, and I will establish the throne of his kingdom forever. (2 Sam 7:12–13)

This coming king would build the temple for the Glory of the King of Heaven. David believed God's promise. Peter proclaimed at Pentecost that David

> ... knew that GOD HAD SWORN TO HIM WITH AN OATH TO SEAT *one* OF HIS DESCENDANTS ON HIS THRONE, **31** he looked ahead and spoke of the resurrection of the Christ, that HE WAS NEITHER ABANDONED TO HADES, NOR DID HIS FLESH SUFFER DECAY. (Acts 2:30–31)

Who would this son of David be? Solomon had it all. He was endowed with incomparable wisdom. He had wealth to match. If ever the resources were there to build the kingdom of God, Solomon had them. The author of 1 Kings notes, "So Judah and Israel lived in safety, every man under his vine and his fig tree, from Dan even to Beersheba, all the days of Solomon" (1 Kgs 4:25). He built the temple. He conscripted thirty thousand men to obtain the lumber from Lebanon. He used seventy thousand carriers and eighty thousand stonecutters.[2] After the seven years it took to build the temple (1 Kgs 6:38), he spent another thirteen years building his palace (1 Kgs 7:1). The palace was larger than the temple.[3] He enlarged Jerusalem and fortified strategic cities to control the trade routes. He chronicles his achievements and writes,

> Then I became great and increased more than all who preceded
> me in Jerusalem. My wisdom also stood by me. (Eccl 2:9)

But what did he achieve with this unparalleled wisdom and power? Solomon writes,

> Thus I considered all my activities which my hands had done
> and the labor which I had exerted, and behold all was vanity
> and striving after wind and there was no profit under the sun.
> (Eccl 2:11)

Solomon had not escaped the curse on Adam's labors. His palace would decay and his temple would be plundered. He was not the king who would reign forever. He died. Even a cursory reading about the lives of the kings of Israel and Judah disabuses anyone of thinking that one of them was the promised king. When would the promised king come?

The psalmist writes of this coming king,

> Your throne, O God, is forever and ever;
> A scepter of uprightness is the scepter of Your kingdom.
> ⁷ You have loved righteousness and hated wickedness;
> Therefore God, Your God, has anointed You
> With the oil of joy above Your fellows. (Ps 45:6–7)

When would such a king come? A thousand years would still pass, waiting for the king.

---

2. Merrill, *Kingdom*, 294.
3. Merrill, *Kingdom*, 296.

In the fullness of time, God sent the angel Gabriel to the temple to announce to Zacharias that he and his barren wife would give birth to John, who would prepare the way of the king. Then God sent Gabriel to the virgin Mary to inform her that the Holy Spirit would overshadow and she would give birth to "the Son of the Most High." Gabriel said,

> ... and the Lord God will give to him the throne of his father David, 33 and he will reign over the house of Jacob forever, and of his kingdom there will be no end. (Luke 1:32–33)

The promised king was coming in fulfillment of the Davidic promise. Once Zacharias could speak, he too praised God that the promised heir to David's throne was coming (Luke 1:69). After Jesus' birth, God sent the angel to announce to the shepherds, "For unto you is born this day in the city of David a Savior, who is Christ the Lord" (Luke 2:11 KJV). Even the wise men from the East came to see the "King of the Jews" (Matt 2:2). When Jesus was eight days old and presented at the temple, believers were waiting for his coming! Eighty-four-year-old Anna fasted and prayed day and night at the temple, waiting for the "redemption of Jerusalem" (Luke 2:36–38). Righteous Simeon also was waiting for the "consolation of Israel" (Luke 2:25). The Holy Spirit brought Simeon into the temple to see Jesus. He took Jesus in his arms and blessed God. He then referred to Isaiah's promise and said,

> ... my eyes have seen Your salvation
> 31 that you have prepared in the presence of all peoples,
> 32 A LIGHT FOR REVELATION TO THE GENTILES,
> And for glory of your people Israel. (Luke 2:30–32)

The king had come.

5

The Kingdom Will Come
(The Abrahamic Covenant)

THE KINGDOM PROMISE

THE BOOK OF GENESIS is the prologue to the Old Covenant documents (the Old Testament) and provides the kingdom history leading up to the Old Covenant made at Sinai. In short, Genesis promises the king and his kingdom. This makes the literary structure of Genesis of particular interest. As M. G. Kline notes, the "ten toledoth" ("these are the generations"[1]) provide the narrative structure.[2] Central to this structure is the Abrahamic Covenant. The first section (Gen 2:4ff.) describes the pagan kings, and is followed by the covenant line of Seth (Gen 5:1ff.). The flood is the climactic third section (Gen 6:9ff.). The fourth renews the history of the pagan kings (Gen 10:1ff.), and countering, the fifth presents the community of believers (Gen 11:10ff.). Like the first triad, this second triad culminates in a climactic section. God makes a covenant promising the kingdom to Abraham (Gen 11:27ff.). The last four sections alternate between God's exclusion of Ishmael (Gen 25:12ff.) and Esau (Gen 36:1ff.) and inclusion of Isaac (Gen 25:19ff.) and Jacob (Gen 37:2ff.). The flood prefigures God's coming judgment on the kingdoms of the world. The Abrahamic Covenant promises the everlasting kingdom of God.

---

1. אֵלֶּה תוֹלְדוֹת.
2. Kline, *Genesis*, 3-5.

Though the Abrahamic Covenant is formalized in Genesis 15, the surrounding chapters describe the covenant God made with Abraham. Embedded between three genealogical sections (Gen 11:27-32; 16:1-16; 22:20—25:11) are the covenant promises: the first section promises the kingdom (Gen 12:1—15:20); the second Abraham's heir (Gen 17:1—22:19).[3] Each of these promise sections are arranged in parallels that develop the promise, the obstacles, deliverance, and finally the covenant oath:

The Promise
    Inheritance (Gen 12:1-5)
    Heir (Gen 17:1-27)
Obstacles to the Promise
    Inheritance (Gen 12:6—13:17)
    Heir (Gen 18:1—19:38)
Deliverance and Dedication
    Inheritance (Gen 13:18—14:24)
    Heir (Gen 20:1—21:34)
God's Covenant Oath
    Inheritance (Gen 15:1-20)
    Heir (Gen 22:1-19)

God's call to Abram starts with the kingdom promise to make Abram into a great nation in a land God would provide. God's blessing would be on Abram, and through Abram God would bless even the Gentiles. Those who blessed Abram would be blessed, and Abram's enemies would be cursed (Gen 12:1-3). Again, in Genesis 17:1-27, God promised that Abram would be the father of a multitude of nations, and changed his name to "Abraham." God promised the covenant would be everlasting. Kings would come from Abraham, and the kingdom land would be his. God changed Sarai's name to Sarah and promised the heir would come through her. She would be the mother of many nations. Abraham and Sarah would not be defined by the world's obstacles, but by the promises of God.

The circumstances belied the promises of God (Gen 12:6—13:17). The Canaanites lived in the land and were not going to willingly leave. The land itself was incapable of supporting the inhabitants. Famine forced Abram to go to Egypt. How could a land that couldn't feed him be the promised kingdom land for a "great nation"? But Egypt would not be

---

3. Kline, *Genesis*, 4.

a refuge. Pharaoh threatened the kingdom promise when he took Sarah into his harem.

Abram was very rich in livestock, gold, and silver (Gen 13:2). His nephew Lot was also with him, with his herds. They had so much that the land could not sustain the two of them. Their herdsmen were at odds with each other over the land. How could Abraham be a great nation when he couldn't even include his nephew? Lot left for the Jordan Valley, and Abram settled in Canaan among the Canaanites and Perizzites. It wasn't long before Lot was taken captive by Kedorlaomer and his vassals.

Where would Abraham find an heir? Sarah was barren, and the thought she could have a child made her laugh in unbelief (Gen 18:12). Even Abraham's nephew was in danger. God was going to bring judgment on Lot's neighbors. Abraham pled with the Lord, "Will You indeed sweep away the righteous with the wicked?" (Gen 18:23). When God's angels delivered Lot and his daughters, the sons-in-law and wife were judged. What kind of kingdom people would God make from Abraham's family? The kingdom promises of God sounded good, but Abraham's day-to-day experience exclaimed a different story.

Yet though the obstacles were real, God's care for Abraham was greater than the problems. God was with Abraham and made that clear by appearing to him as the Angel of the Lord (the Second Person of the Trinity in preincarnate form)[4] to assure Abraham of the veracity of the promise (Gen 12:7; 17:1; 18:1). When Pharaoh took Sarah from Abram, God intervened and loaded Abram up with the court's wealth (Gen 12:16, 20) as he was ushered out of Egypt. When Lot was taken captive by Kedorlaomer, the Lord enabled Abraham to be victorious. Melchizedek, the priest-king of God at Salem, went out to meet Abram after the victory. He blessed Abram and praised God in celebration of what God had done.

When King Abimelech took Sarah into his household, God threatened his life and delivered Abraham and Sarah. Through this experience, God demonstrated to Abraham and Sarah that he is the God who opens and closes wombs. As promised, Isaac was born a year later. They laughed and named their son Isaac, from the Hebrew word meaning "laugh."[5] Each of these two major sections (the kingdom, Gen 12:1—15:20; Abraham's heir, Gen 17:1—22:19) proclaim the faithfulness of God to Abraham, and they each conclude with the covenant oath.

---

4. Also called the Angel of the Presence. Cf. his appearance to Hagar in Gen 16:7ff., especially v. 13: "You are a God who sees."

5. צָחַק, tsachaq, "laugh"; יִצְחָק, Yitschaq, "Isaac."

In Genesis 15, Abraham has just rescued Lot. As success often does, it exacerbated the questions Abraham had. How could Abraham become a great nation? He was childless? Was he to adopt? God assured Abraham he would have an heir that was biologically Abraham's. Then God showed Abraham the stars and said, "So shall your seed be" (Gen 15:5 AT). God continued, and assured Abraham of the land promise and said, "to give you this land to inherit[6] it" (Gen 15:7 AT). Abraham would be a great nation. He would have an heir and an inheritance. The kingdom would come. But Abraham asked, "How may I know that I will inherit it" (Gen 15:8 AT)?

God instructed Abraham to cut and lay in half the heifer, goat, ram, turtledove, and pigeon. The birds of prey came down on the carcasses, and Abraham drove them off. That night God caused Abram to fall into a deep sleep. God covenanted to Abraham the kingdom. Moses writes,

> And He said to Abram, "Surely, know that your seed will be a stranger in a land that is not theirs, where they will be enslaved and oppressed four hundred years. [14] But I will also judge the nation whom they will serve, and afterward they will come out with great possessions. [15] And you, you shall go to your fathers in peace; you will be buried at a good old age. [16] And in the fourth generation they will return here, for the iniquity of the Amorite is not yet complete."
>
> [17] And it came about when the sun had set, that it was very dark, and behold, there appeared a smoking oven and a burning torch which passed between these pieces.
>
> [18] On that day Yahweh made a covenant with Abram, saying,
> "To your seed I have given this land,
> From the river of Egypt as far as the great river,
> the river Euphrates:
> [19] the Kenite and the Kenizzite and the Kadmonite [20] and the Hittite and the Perizzite and the Rephaim [21] and the Amorite and the Canaanite and the Girgashite and the Jebusite." (Gen 15:13–21 AT)

The animal carcasses symbolized death. God, in a theophany of two pillars of smoke, walked the path of death. God took upon himself the oath to give Abraham the kingdom or God would bear the curse of the covenant. In fact, God would do both. God would give Abraham the kingdom by taking upon himself the curse.

---

6. יָרַשׁ, yarash.

The covenant to give Abraham the kingdom ultimately depends on his heir. Ironically, this was true in two senses. In the typology of the covenant fulfillment, it is obvious that there will be no kingdom without Abraham having a son to populate the kingdom people of Israel. But in the ultimate fulfillment of the Abrahamic kingdom promise, Abraham has an inheritance because of the finished work of his messianic heir.

Just when it looked like God was coming through on his promises, He told Abraham to take Isaac up on the mountain and sacrifice him to the Lord. Abraham got up early—probably because he had not slept all night—and took Isaac and some wood up the mountain. As he raised the knife to take his son's life, the Angel of the Lord stopped him and said, "for now I know that you fear God, since you have not withheld your son, your only son, from Me" (Gen 22:12). Abraham looked and saw a ram and offered him in the place of his son. Abraham called the place "The LORD Will Provide" (Gen 22:14). Then the Angel of the Lord called out a second time from heaven and said,

> By Myself I have sworn, declares the LORD, because you have done this thing and have not withheld your son, your only son, 17 indeed I will greatly bless you, and I will greatly multiply your seed as the stars of the heavens and as the sand which is on the seashore; and your seed shall possess the gate of his enemies. 18 In your seed all the nations of the earth shall be blessed, because you have obeyed My voice. (Gen 22:16–18)

So much more is here than what is spoken! Abraham's kingdom inheritance would not come through him giving his only son. But God the Son, the Angel of the Lord, would be the sacrifice in the path of curse. In order that Abraham would have the kingdom, God the Father did not withhold the judgment knife from his Son. In Abraham's seed all the nations would receive this kingdom.

At every step in Abraham's journey, God was at work to give Abraham the kingdom. God called Abraham with the promise of the kingdom. God delivered Abraham through all the threats and obstacles to the promise. After demonstrating his covenant faithfulness to Abraham, God formally covenanted that God would give Abraham the kingdom. This covenant did not contain stipulations for Abraham to obey in order to be blessed. Abraham's works would not merit the eschatological kingdom. In fact, he demonstrates his own sin in the journey. Twice he places Sarah in danger of being absorbed into harems! Abraham sinfully tries to help

God bring about the promised heir by having relations with Sarah's maidservant, Hagar. This brought forth Ishmael, not the heir.

This contrast between God's justice and righteousness and his grace to Abraham is evident in what is not said in the story of Abimelech (Gen 20). Abraham was afraid of the king as he came into Gerar, so he told the king that Sarah was his sister. The king took Sarah. In some ways, it sounds like the same thing as what happened with Pharaoh. The details are different but the sinner is the same—Abraham had not learned! God came to the king and told him he was a dead man! He had taken Abraham's wife! Abimelech protested that he didn't know and would God judge his people when they didn't know Abraham lied. Sarah too enforced the deception. God acknowledged the sin had been committed in ignorance and gave him an ultimatum. Either the king would restore Sarah to Abraham or God would kill the king and all that were his! He told Abimelech that Abraham would pray for him and he would live if he obeyed! Abimelech restored Sarah and gave livestock, servants, and a thousand pieces of silver to Abraham and told him he was welcomed to settle wherever he wanted! God made Abimelech's wife and maids able to have children again; for God had made them barren because of Abimelech's sin.

The silence of the narrative is deafening! This is the second time Abraham has put the promise in jeopardy! The first time was when they came to Egypt, and he was afraid of the Pharaoh and represented Sarah as his sister. God struck Pharaoh with plagues when he took her into the harem, and Abraham left with sheep, oxen, donkeys, camels, and servants—and not a word of rebuke from God! Now Abraham did it again! He lied to Abimelech and again put the promise in danger! Again, God was ready to come down hard in judgment on the king. But Abraham left as the prophet enriched by the king and he prayed for the sinner Abimelech! But what about sinful Abraham? And again, there is not a word of rebuke from God to Abraham! The reader may object, "Many would accuse God of having a double standard!" Yes, that's the point. While God dealt with Pharaoh and King Abimelech under the righteous requirements of law, God didn't deal with Abraham this way. God dealt with Abraham with grace, grace, and more grace. Abraham's own sin didn't stop God from moving forward in fulfilling his promise!

Yes, Abraham had faith, and obedience, but that did not merit Abraham receiving the eschatological kingdom. Abraham responded to God's kingdom promise with faith. When God called him to the kingdom land, Abraham went. When he came to Canaan, and the Angel of the Lord appeared to him and promised the land, Abraham believed and built an altar "to the Lord who had appeared to him" (Gen 12:7). He went from Bethel to Ai and built altars marking out the land God promised, and he worshiped God. Then he went to the southern border toward the Negev. He believed God's promise. When they came out of Egypt and the land couldn't support Lot and himself, Abraham settled in the land and generously allowed Lot to take the choice land in the valley. God promised Abraham the land he saw and descendants as the numerous as the dust of the earth. God invited Abraham to walk the length and breadth of the land, and Abraham believed God and built an altar to worship the Lord at Hebron. When he heard Lot was taken captive, he did not respond in resentment that Lot had taken the better land. Abraham took his resources and went out to rescue Lot. When he gained the victory, he acknowledged that God had given him the victory and gave tribute to Melchizedek and refused any spoils that would imply that someone else other that God was his king. In faith Abraham circumcised his household in dedication to God. When the Angel of the Lord revealed the judgment to come on Sodom and Gomorrah, Abraham interceded for them in faith. When Isaac was weaned, Abraham celebrated his son with a great feast for what God had done. When God told him to take that son and offer him on an altar, Abraham believed God could raise the dead,[7] and took his knife in his hand to strike his son. When God told Abraham that God would provide, Abraham in faith named the place "The Lord Will Provide." His faith received the promise by grace. Did Abraham obey God? His faith was evidenced by his obedience (Jas 2:21). His faith is seen all the way through by his actions, by his obedience to God. But his obedience was not the basis of receiving the eschatological promise. Could Abraham have had faith and not obeyed God? No. Even Lot's faith, weak as at moments it appeared, was evidenced in his obedience and vexed heart over the wicked. Abraham believed and acted accordingly. But the covenant was a promise based on what God would do, not what Abraham would do!

THE TWELVE TRIBES

When faced with the considerations of the last section, the reader may ask, "What about Genesis 22:16–18?" There Moses records,

---

7. Heb 11:19.

> By Myself I have sworn, declares the Lord, because you have done this thing and have not withheld your son, your only son, ¹⁷ indeed I will greatly bless you, and I will greatly multiply your seed as the stars of the heavens and as the sand which is on the seashore; and your seed shall possess the gate of their enemies. ¹⁸ In your seed all the nations of the earth shall be blessed, because you have obeyed My voice.

God promised Abraham the kingdom blessings because he obeyed. This causal relationship between Abraham's obedience and the promise is reiterated when God gave the kingdom promise to Isaac. The Lord said, "I will establish the oath which I swore to your father Abraham" (Gen 26:3). He promised Isaac that his seed would be as the stars and would receive the land. Through Isaac's seed the nations would be blessed "because Abraham obeyed My voice and kept My charge, My commandments, My statutes and My laws" (Gen 26:5). Moses here draws the continuity between Abraham's obedience to God before the giving of the Law at Sinai and the covenant obedience required from Israel by that covenant. On this typological level, Abraham's obedience and Israel receiving the land, Abraham's obedience is the basis for Israel's entry into the land. Abraham's obedience functions on two levels. As a recipient of the eschatological kingdom promise, his faith evidenced by obedience receives the promise. His obedience is not the basis of receiving the promise. But on the typological level, Abraham's obedience is the basis for Israel's entering the land. The same dual function is seen in Noah. On the ultimate level, Noah's obedience is the fruit of his faith in the promises of God, but as a type of Christ, bringing his family through the judgment in the ark, Noah's obedience is the basis of their deliverance (Gen 6:9; 7:1; Heb 11:7; cf. 1 Pet 3:18–22). The kingdom promise to Abraham is fulfilled on two levels, typologically in Israel under the Mosaic Covenant, and eschatologically in the seed, Christ. It is on the typological level that Abraham's obedience is the basis of the twelve tribes receiving the typological kingdom land. Both the typological and eschatological levels are referenced in Genesis 12–22.

Abraham is called from the land of his fathers to live in a land that God would give him. God brought him to the land of Canaan, and promised, "To your seed, I will give this land" (Gen 12:7 AT). Abraham understood that God was promising the land of Canaan. He walked from length and breadth in Canaan building altars, marking out the promised land. When Lot left for Sodom, Abraham stayed in Canaan. God again promised him the land he saw—north, and south, east and west (Gen

13:14). Again, in Genesis 15:7, God told Abraham, "I am the Lord who brought you out of Ur of the Chaldeans, to give you this land to inherit it" (AT). Then the Lord told Abraham they would be enslaved for four hundred years and then return to Canaan. Then God would bring judgment on the Amorites. He said, "To your seed I have given this land, From the river of Egypt as far as the great river, the Euphrates" (Gen 15:18 AT). God promised Abraham and his seed "the land of your sojournings, all the land of Canaan" (Gen 17:8).

When God reiterated the covenant to Isaac, he told him to sojourn in Canaan and not go to Egypt. God said, "I will give all these lands" (Gen 26:3). When he moved to Rehobath, he named it so because "we shall be fruitful in the land" (Gen 26:22). When Isaac sent Jacob out of Canaan to find a wife, he stopped along the way in what he would name Bethel. That night the Lord told Jacob, "the land on which you lie, I will give to you and to your seed" (Gen 28:13 AT). He assured him that he would bring Jacob back to this land (Gen 28:15).

Because Moses struck the rock, God did not allow him to enter the land. But before Moses died God took him up to Mount Nebo and showed him the land "Gilead as far as Dan." Moses writes,

> And Yahweh said to him "'This is the land which I swore to Abraham, Isaac, and Jacob, saying 'I will give it to your seed'; I have let you see it with your own eyes, but you shall not go over there." (Deut 34:4 AT)

While Moses didn't go into the land, God showed Moses that he was faithful to the covenant promises.

As Joshua led the tribes of Israel into the land of Canaan, God said, "Be strong and courageous, for you shall give this people possession of the land which I swore to their fathers to give them" (Josh 1:6). For forty years Israel had wandered in the wilderness so that the rebellious generation would not see the promised land, "the land which the Lord had sworn to their fathers . . . , a land flowing with milk and honey" (Josh 5:6). Israel took the land in conquest and settled according to tribe. Joshua writes,

> So the Lord gave Israel all the land which He had sworn to give to their fathers, and they possessed it and lived in it. 44 And the Lord gave them rest on every side, according to all that He had sworn to their fathers, and no one of all their enemies stood before them; the Lord gave all their enemies into their hand.

> **45** Not one of the good promises which the Lord had made to the house of Israel failed; all came to pass. (Josh 21:43–45)

Joshua affirms that all the covenant promises God made to Abraham, Isaac, and Jacob were fulfilled! "All came to pass!" When Nehemiah rebuilt the wall, the Levites praised God,

> You are the Lord God,
> Who chose Abram
> And brought him out from Ur of the Chaldees,
> And gave him the name Abraham.
> **8** You found his heart faithful before You,
> And made a covenant with him
> To give the land of the Canaanite,
> Of the Hittite and the Amorite,
> Of the Perizzite, the Jebusite and the Girgashite–
> To give it to his seed.
> And You have fulfilled Your promise,
> For You are righteous. (Neh 9:7–8 AT)

God gave them the land. The author of 1 Kings emphasizes the extent of the land obtained:

> Now Solomon ruled over all the kingdoms from the River *to* the land of the Philistines and to the border of Egypt. (1 Kgs 4:21)

Clearly, the Old Testament presents Israel in Canaan as the fulfillment of the kingdom land promise to Abraham. But more than just land, 1 Kings is presenting a king and his kingdom! Abraham was promised a great nation. At the height of Solomon's reign was a great nation!

The fulfilled promises include more than the land. God promised that the sons of Abraham would be as the sand of the seashore or the innumerable stars in the night sky. When there was famine in the land, God encouraged Jacob to go to Joseph in Egypt. Even in leaving the land temporarily, God would be at work multiplying Jacob's family. God said,

> I am God, the God of your father; do not be afraid to go down to Egypt, for I will make you a great nation there. (Gen 46:3)

God was so faithful to that promise that they posed a threat to the Egyptians. Exodus records,

> All the souls who came from the loins of Jacob were seventy souls, and Joseph was already in Egypt. **6** Joseph died, and all

his brothers and all that generation. ⁷ And the sons of Israel were fruitful and increased greatly, and multiplied, and became exceedingly numerous, so that the land was filled with them. ⁸ And a new king arose over Egypt, who did not know Joseph. ⁹ He said to his people, "Behold, the people of the sons of Israel are more and mightier than we." (Exod 1:5–8 AT)

So they put them in hard labor, a strategy that has a good track record of thinning a population. But it didn't. Exodus 1:12 says,

> But the more they afflicted them, the more they multiplied and the more they spread out, so that they were in dread of the sons of Israel.

So Pharaoh ordered the Israelite midwives to put the male children to death at birth. The midwives, in faith, disobeyed Pharaoh. The result was more of God's blessing. Exodus says,

> So God was good to the midwives, and the people multiplied, and became very numerous. ²¹ Because the midwives feared God, He made families for them. (Exod 1:20–21 AT)

Not only did God multiply Israel all the more, but note the irony: God gave these midwives husbands and children too! Pharaoh would not stop God's promise to Abraham. This note about the midwives gaining families of their own is for emphasis. The very ones Pharaoh tried to order to be instruments of destruction God blessed to fulfill his promise. Deuteronomy starts with Moses' appeal to the people to appoint judges to help with the burden Moses carried. God's blessing was beyond what Moses could bear. Moses says, "The LORD your God has multiplied you, and behold, you are this day as the stars of heaven for multitude" (Deut 1:10). The tribes of Israel didn't receive the promise because of their righteousness.[8] But in spite of their constant rebellion against God, God was faithful to the promises to Abraham, Isaac, and Jacob.[9] Moses reminds them, "Your fathers went down to Egypt seventy persons *in all*, and now the LORD has made you as numerous as the stars of heaven" (Deut 10:22). The psalmist later writes,

> For He remembered His holy word *with* Abraham His servant;
> ⁴³ And He brought forth His people with joy, His chosen ones with a joyful shout. ⁴⁴ He gave them also the lands of the nations,

---

8. Deut 9:4.
9. Deut 9:5.

that they might take possession of *the fruit* of the peoples' labor (Ps 105:42–44)

When God forced Balaam to bless Israel rather than curse, Balaam said, "Who can count the dust of Jacob . . ." (Num 23:10). At the beginning of a description of Solomon's wealth and prosperity, 1 Kings 4:20 notes,

> Judah and Israel *were* as numerous as the sand that is on the seashore in abundance; *they* were eating and drinking and rejoicing.

But this merriment was not lasting, much less everlasting.

Though Israel received the land based on Abraham's obedience, they would only keep it through their own obedience to the Mosaic Covenant. Moses addresses the tribes with Ten Commandments and then the Shema. Then he sets forth the summary sanctions of the covenant,

> Then it shall come about when the LORD your God brings you into the land which He swore to your fathers, Abraham, Isaac and Jacob . . . [14] You shall not follow other gods, any of the gods of the peoples who surround you, [15] for the LORD your God in the midst of you is a jealous God; otherwise the anger of the LORD your God will be kindled against you, and He will wipe you off the face of the earth . . . [17] You should diligently keep the commandments of the LORD your God, and His testimonies and His statutes which He has commanded you. [18] You shall do what is right and good in the sight of the LORD, that it may be well with you and that you may go in and possess the good land which the Lord swore to give your fathers. (Deut 6:10, 14–15, 17–18)

After giving the Law, Moses recounts the curses and blessings of the covenant. Their possession of the kingdom land depends on their obedience to the covenant.[10] Moses concludes,

> But if your heart turns away and you will not obey, but are drawn away and worship other gods and serve them, [18] I declare to you today that you shall surely perish. You will not prolong *your* days in the land where you are crossing the Jordan to enter and possess it. (Deut 30:17–18)

Israel broke the Mosaic Covenant. God sent prophets to call them to repentance. They rejected the prophets.[11] Israel was exiled by the Assyr-

---

10. Josh 23:12–16.
11. Jer 7:24–26.

ians, and Judah was taken into exile by the Babylonians. In the midst of the tragic history, the prophets continually describe Israel's rejection of the Mosaic Covenant and God's faithfulness to still keep his covenant with Abraham, Isaac, and Jacob. The fulfillment of the promise to Abraham would not be nullified by Israel breaking the Mosaic Covenant. The prophets speak of the fulfillment of the Abrahamic Covenant after the judgment for breaking the Mosaic Covenant. Isaiah writes,

> Lebanon will be turned into a fertile field,
> And the fertile field will be considered as a forest?
> 18 On that day the deaf will hear words of a book,
> And out of their gloom and darkness the eyes of the blind will see.
> 19 The afflicted also will increase their gladness in the LORD,
> And the needy of mankind will rejoice in the Holy One of Israel . . .
> 22 Therefore thus says the LORD, who redeemed Abraham, concerning the house of Jacob:
> "Jacob shall not now be ashamed, nor shall his face now turn pale . . . (Isa 29:17–19, 22)

The renewal of all things is described. Israel broke the Mosaic Covenant, but God cannot break the Abrahamic Covenant. God will cause David's son to sit on the throne forever and bring righteousness to the earth. The people of God will live in safety. God says to Jeremiah,

> If you can break My covenant for the day and My covenant for the night, so that day and night will not be at their appointed time, 21 then My covenant may also be broken with David My servant so that he will not have a son to reign on his throne, and with the Levitical priests, My ministers. 22 As the host of heaven cannot be counted and the sand of the sea cannot be measured, so I will multiply the descendants of David My servant and the Levites who minister to Me. (Jer 33:20–22)

God continues. He will answer those who say God failed to keep his promise to Abraham and rejected his people (Jer 33:24). God will fulfill his covenant to Abraham, Isaac, and Jacob. God says, "But I will restore their fortunes and will have mercy on them" (Jer 33:26). Jeremiah can't stop the sun from shining or the stars from the night sky. So too, no one can stop God from keeping his covenant with Abraham. Jeremiah here combines the promise to David with the promise to Abraham with the reference to the stars and the sand (Jer 33:22).

God promised the kingdom. Abraham obeyed God. Israel received the kingdom. They disobeyed, but that didn't stop God's promise. So the Pharisees reasoned that they were still God's people and the kingdom was still theirs! When Jesus came, they said, "We are Abraham's seed" (John 8:33 AT).[12] The rabbis taught, "The circumcised do not go down to Gehenna."[13] But Jesus says the scandalous. When the Roman centurion came to Jesus asking him to heal his servant, the centurion said he was unworthy for Jesus to come to his house. He only needed Jesus to say the word and it would be done. Jesus says,

> Truly I say to you, I have not found such great faith with anyone in Israel. **11** I say to you that many will come from east and west, and recline *at the table* with Abraham, Isaac and Jacob in the kingdom of heaven; **12** but the sons of the kingdom will be cast out into the outer darkness; in that place there will be weeping and gnashing of teeth. (Matt 8:10–12)

But the centurion Gentile from the ends of the earth would feast with Abraham! Jesus tells the story of the rich man and Lazarus. The rich man enjoyed the good things of life, but now he was suffering in hades. The poor Lazarus died and now was in Abraham's bosom. The rich man cried out, "Father Abraham" (Luke 16:24). But the rich man found no relief from the judgment. These were scandalous words to the Pharisees.

Jesus was teaching at the temple and the chief priests and elders asked what was his authority to teach. They were silent in response to his question. So he did not respond to their question. But then Jesus told a couple of stories to drive the point home. The first was about a man who had two sons. When the father told the first son to work, the son refused but then did work. The other son said he would, but he didn't. Jesus asked which son did the will of his father. They answered, and Jesus said,

> Truly I say to you that the tax collectors and prostitutes will get into the kingdom of God before you. **32** For John came to you in the way of righteousness and you did not believe him; but the tax collectors and prostitutes did believe him. (Matt 21:31–32)

Then Jesus told another parable. This one was about a landowner who left his tenants to work the land. When the landowner asked for the fruit of the land, the tenants killed his servants. So he sent his son. They killed

---

12. Cf. Matt 3:9; Luke 3:8.

13. Beasley-Murray, *John*, 134, ref. *Exod. Rab.* 19.81c (Strack and Billerbeck, *Kommentar zum Neuem Testament*, 1:116–21).]

him. Jesus asked what they thought the owner would do when he came. Yes, he would judge the wicked tenants. Then Jesus says the unthinkable:

> Therefore I say to you, the kingdom of God will be taken away from you and given to a people, producing the fruit of it. (Matt 21:43)

They understood his point, and they would have killed him, but they were afraid of the crowd of people who were listening. But the thought that the kingdom could be taken from the leaders of the Jews, from the crème de la crème of the nation, and be given to another was unthinkable! And to say that the kingdom would be given to tax collectors and women of the red-light district was anathema!

Had the Pharisees not read Isaiah or listened to the words of Hosea? "My People" become "Not My People" and "Not My People" become "My People." Paul understood Hosea. He writes,

> ... from among Gentiles. 25 As He says also in Hosea,
> "I WILL CALL THOSE WHO WERE NOT MY PEOPLE, 'MY PEOPLE,'
> AND HER WHO WAS NOT BELOVED, 'BELOVED.'"
> 26 "AND IT SHALL BE THAT IN THE PLACE WHERE IT WAS SAID TO THEM, 'YOU ARE NOT MY PEOPLE,'
> THERE THEY SHALL BE CALLED SONS OF THE LIVING GOD. (Rom 9:24–26)

How was it possible that the Abrahamic Promise would be fulfilled through the kingdom being given to Gentiles? As Paul develops along with the other writers of the New Testament, God's kingdom promise to Abraham was fulfilled typologically in the Old Testament in Israel, but is eschatologically fulfilled in Christ in the New Testament. Unbelieving Israel could not see this, and Jesus' claims and kingdom proclamation were an affront to everything they taught. But the Abrahamic Promise exceeded anything fulfilled in the Old Testament.

THE FULFILLMENT

God promised Abraham, "in you all the families of the earth shall be blessed" (Gen 12:3).[14] And again, "For I will make nations come forth from you" (Gen 17:6). God promised

---

14. See Gen 18:18.

> ... an everlasting covenant,[15] to be God to you and your seed after you. And I will give to you and to your seed after you, the land of your sojournings, all the land of Canaan, for an everlasting possession; and I will be their God." (Gen 17:7–8 AT)

The promise of the kingdom entailed a king. Jeremiah 33:20–26 makes clear that the Davidic Promise is an extension of the Abrahamic Promise. In both God promised a king and a kingdom. To David he promised, "I will establish the throne of his kingdom forever" (2 Sam 7:13). Matthew draws the same connection when he begins his gospel, "genealogy of Jesus the Messiah, the son of David, the son of Abraham" (Matt 1:1). Here is the king promised David. Here is the king promised Abraham. In this brief statement are the three covenants: the Abrahamic Covenant, David king of Israel under the Old Covenant, and Jesus Christ, the Lord of the New Covenant. The temporary typological fulfillment of the Abrahamic Covenant under the Mosaic Covenant gives way to the ultimate fulfillment under the New Covenant.

God promised Abraham the kingdom land. Abraham saw more than the land of Canaan. Hebrews 11:9–10 says,

> By faith he lived as an alien in the land of promise, as in a foreign *land*, dwelling in tents with Isaac and Jacob, fellow heirs of the same promise; [10] for he was looking for the city which has foundations, whose architect and builder is God.

Lest there be any confusion regarding what was promised, the author continues,

> All these died in faith, without receiving the promises, but having seen them and having welcomed them from a distance, and having confessed that they were strangers and exiles on the earth. [14] For those who say such things make it clear that they are seeking a country of their own. [15] And indeed if they had been thinking of that *country* from which they went out, they would have had opportunity to return. [16] But as it is, they desire a better *country*, that is, a heavenly one. Therefore God is not ashamed to be called their God; for He has prepared a city for them. (Heb 11:13–16)

Abraham understood what was really promised, and it wasn't a little piece of real estate in the Middle East. He knew that even this earth did

---

15. Gen 17:13, 19: 22:18.

not hold the fulfillment to the promise God gave him. He was alien on the earth. He looked for the kingdom of heaven.

When God commanded Abraham to offer his son Isaac, Abraham saw more than a son he didn't have to kill. Hebrews says,

> By faith Abraham, when he was tested, offered up Isaac, and he who had received the promises was offering up his only begotten son; **18** it was he to whom it was said, "In Isaac your seed shall be called." **19** He considered that God is able to raise people even from the dead, from which he also received him back in a parable. (Heb 11:17–19 AT)[16]

As the Angel of the Lord withheld Abraham from taking the knife with the promise that God would provide another son to sacrifice, Abraham believed and named that place "The Lord Will Provide" (Gen 22:14). Unlike the Pharisees, Abraham saw and believed. Jesus tells the Pharisees, "Your father Abraham rejoiced to see My day, and he saw *it* and was glad" (John 8:56).

Abraham's hope was beyond the kings and kingdom of twelve tribes. He looked for the "better country" with the better king from heaven. He understood the parable and looked for the reality. He believed God's promise of the seed that would come from his loins and make him heir of the kingdom of God, and by faith he was counted righteous (Gen 15:6). On this eschatological level, his obedience only evidenced his faith. He was justified by faith alone.

Judaism held that Abraham's obedience to God made them heirs of the kingdom. Jubilee 23:10 says, "Abraham was perfect in all his deeds with the Lord, and well-pleasing in righteousness all the days of his life." Paul responds to this. Abraham is the test case of justification precisely because the kingdom was promised to him. Did he inherit it because of his righteousness or because of faith apart from works? Paul makes the antithetical contrast between faith and works in Romans 4. He writes,

> What then shall we say that Abraham, our forefather according to the flesh, has found? **2** For if Abraham was justified out of works, he has something to boast about, but not to God. **3** For what does the Scripture say? "ABRAHAM BELIEVED GOD, AND IT WAS CREDITED TO HIM UNTO RIGHTEOUSNESS." **4** Now to the one who works, his wage is not credited according to favor, but according to what is due. **5** But to the one who does not work, but

---

16. ἐν παραβολῇ ἐκομίσατο.

believes in Him who justifies the ungodly, his faith is credited unto righteousness. (Rom 4:1–5 AT)

Paul has already established that there is "none righteous" (Rom 3:10). Abraham was regarded by God as righteous not because of his obedience and works, but through faith. If he was regarded as righteous because he was righteous, he would receive what was due. But because unrighteous Abraham believed God's kingdom promise, he was counted righteous based on the covenant righteousness of his heir, Christ. By grace, through faith, on the basis of the covenant righteousness of another, Abraham was regarded as righteous. His faith was not counted as righteousness. His heir, in whom he put his faith, was righteous. Abraham was righteous because his federal head was righteous. Abraham believed this. So he understood, as Paul writes,

> For the promise to Abraham or to his seed that he would be heir of the world was not through the Law, but through the righteousness of faith. (Rom 4:13 AT)

Some have tried to make Paul's contrast between a righteous obedience that comes from faith and the righteousness of keeping the Mosaic Law. But Paul's words disallow any thought of Abraham's righteous standing before God based on his own obedience or righteousness. For then, like the worker whose wage is due, Abraham's blessing would be based on Abraham's works. But, as Paul makes clear, Abraham does not receive what is due, but what, contrary to his unrighteousness, is received by grace. The contrast between the promise to Abraham and the Mosaic Law is not merely a contrast to righteousness before the Law and righteousness under the Law. It is a contrast between grace and covenant-keeping righteousness.

Paul develops this contrast at length in Galatians. For Paul, the promise of God to Abraham is fulfilled by grace in Christ. He writes,

> Even so Abraham BELIEVED GOD, AND IT WAS RECKONED TO HIM AS RIGHTEOUSNESS. [7] Therefore, be sure that it is those who are of faith who are sons of Abraham. [8] The Scripture, foreseeing that God would justify the Gentiles by faith, preached the gospel beforehand to Abraham, saying, "ALL THE NATIONS WILL BE BLESSED IN YOU." [9] So then those who are of faith are blessed with Abraham, the believer. (Gal 3:6–9)

In contrast to righteousness through faith, Paul describes the Mosaic Covenant:

> For as many as are of the works of the Law are under a curse; for it is written, "Cursed is everyone who does not abide by all things written in the book of the law, to perform them." 11 Now that no one is justified by the Law before God is evident; for, "The righteous man shall live by faith." 12 However, the Law is not of faith; on the contrary, "He who practices them shall live by them." (Gal 3:10–12)

The unconditional Abrahamic Covenant brought with it the unconditional blessing of the kingdom. But to be under the Mosaic Covenant was to be under a curse. The Law was a conditional covenant that required obedience and threatened curse. The Mosaic Covenant is not like the Abrahamic. Abraham was justified through faith apart from works. The Mosaic Covenant required that the Law be obeyed. It was not life through faith, but life through covenant obedience to the Law. As Paul writes, "the Law is not of faith."

The Abrahamic Covenant could not find fulfillment in the Mosaic Covenant. The Mosaic Law made that clear. The kingdom promise to Abraham finds its fulfillment in his seed, Christ. Paul writes,

> Now the promises were spoken to Abraham and to his seed. He does not say, "And to seeds," as *referring* to many, but *rather* to one, "And to your seed," that is, Christ. 17 What I am saying is this: the Law, which came four hundred and thirty years later, does not invalidate a covenant previously ratified by God, so as to nullify the promise. 18 For if the inheritance is based on law, it is no longer based on a promise; but God has granted it to Abraham by means of a promise. (Gal 3:16–18)

The typological kingdom promise was fulfilled in Israel and her kings. But now the kingdom has come in Christ. Like the promise, the kingdom fulfillment is received by faith. So Paul concludes his words to his Gentile readers, "And if you belong to Christ, then you are Abraham's seed, heirs according to promise" (Gal 3:29 AT). John uses this same type-and-fulfillment language when he sees the assembly of martyred believers. First he describes them in terms of the kingdom people under the Old Testament. He heard "144,000 sealed from every tribe of the sons of Israel" (Rev 7:4). But then he looked,

... and behold, a great multitude which no one could count, from every nation and *all* tribes and peoples and tongues, standing before the throne and before the Lamb, clothed in white robes, and palm branches *were* in their hands. (Rev 7:9)

Both describe the same assembly. He heard and saw. But both refer to the same people. He heard the elders say the Lion of the tribe of Judah had overcome, but when he looked, he saw a Lamb standing as if slain. Here is Israel, the kingdom people from all nations, redeemed by the Lion of the tribe of Judah, the Lamb that was slain.

6

The Toy Kingdom
(The Old Covenant)

CHILDREN PLAY WITH TOYS; they always have. Johnny may run around the yard with a stick pretending to fight off the intruding pirates, but in his play that stick is an AK-47! He may have dirt on his upper lip, but in his mind he dons the most handsome handlebar mustache! The rocks he lobs represent smoke cannisters! It is the genius of imagination and childhood play. One day Johnny will have a job with the Coast Guard and have an actual assault weapon to fight the drug-running cartel!

Mary is no different. She is playing tea party with all her favorite guests. Mr. Frog (a stuffed animal) is seated to her left, Mr. Giraffe (a stuffed animal) to her right, and Ms. Bumblebee (a stuffed animal her mother found in the neighbor's trash) across the table. She aptly serves them their biscuits (straw and mud) and pours their Earl Grey (muddy water) into the Wedgewood (plastic plates and plastic cups). The whole time she is holding and calming her baby Elizabeth (a rag doll). The afternoon discourse is delightful as they discuss the goings-on of the community. But Mary becomes a woman, marries, owns a shop in the village and often exhibits her excellent skills as a hostess. Her children are not rag dolls, but are quite real! Childhood was made for this.

Paul used a similar picture to describe the difference between the types and symbols of the Old Covenant and the reality of the kingdom under the New Covenant. He writes,

> Now I say, as long as the heir is a child, he does not differ at all from a slave although he is owner of everything, ² but he is under guardians and managers until the date set by the father. ³ So also we, while we were children, were held in bondage under the elemental things of the world. (Gal 4:1–3)

No longer is the believer playing with stuffed animals, sticks, muddy water, and rag dolls. The reality has come! Usually these foreshadowing representatives have been called "types." But as the Abrahamic kingdom promises are realized typologically and eschatologically, it may be helpful to think of the "toy fulfillment" and the "real fulfillment." The land promised Abraham is not a little piece of property in the Middle East, but the glorified new heavens and new earth! It's the difference between a little eight-inch plastic toy house and a real palace. It is hard to compare. The little kings of the fulfillment in Israel are like little green army men in comparison to the true King of Heaven.

Abraham understood the difference between the pictures and the reality. It's like a very generous father promising his six-year-old son a Maserati. The son is excited and understands the promise. When the son turns thirteen, his father takes him down to the Maserati dealer. They go in to the show room and the father buys him the Maserati—an eighteen-inch bronze replica of a Maserati. The son likes the gift, but he looks at his dad and, with an eagerness in his eyes, says, "But when can I have the Maserati?" The father laughs and says, "Very soon!" They go home, and every day the son looks at that replica and longs for the day when he will receive what was really promised! On his sixteenth birthday, he has hardly finished opening his gifts when the dealer drives it into the driveway—the Maserati! The real promised Maserati! Abraham "rejoiced to see My day!" (John 8:56), Jesus said. All the toys of the Old Testament were instructive and pointed toward the real King and kingdom, but they could not compare.

The Old Testament gives the representative types, or toys! The reality will have a priest-king. On the toy level, there are priests and kings. The reality, the new creation, will be royal temple. But the toy level has palaces and a temple. Looking at the toys, it was hard to see how it would come together. In a sense, it was like putting together a ten-thousand-piece puzzle without the picture on the box. And if you were working on the puzzle but not getting it, and someone showed you the picture on the box top, you might say, "Oh, now it makes sense!" That's what Jesus does for the Old Testament. Now it all makes sense! After the resurrection,

Jesus explained it all to the disciples. Luke writes, "Then beginning with Moses and with all the Prophets, He explained to them the things concerning Himself in all the Scriptures" (Luke 24:27).

The distinction between the two levels, typological and real, cannot be disregarded without causing great confusion. Moses himself serves as a good example to show how essential it is to distinguish the toy from the reality. He was the mediator of the Old Covenant and led the kingdom people out Egyptian bondage, through the wilderness, to the promised land. But he was not allowed to go in! As Israel was about to enter the land of Canaan, God took Moses up on Mt. Nebo and showed him the promised land. But Moses died on that mountain in Moab. God gave Moses the reason:

> . . . because you transgressed against Me in the midst of the sons of Israel at the waters of Meribah-kadesh, in the wilderness of Zin, because you did not treat Me as holy in the midst of the sons of Israel. [52] For you will see the land at a distance, but you will not go there, into the land which I am giving the sons of Israel. (Deut 32:51–52 AT)

The reference is an event recorded in Numbers 20. They had wandered in the wilderness forty years. They came to Kadesh, in the wilderness of Zin, and they had no water. Moses and Aaron went to the door of the tabernacle, where the Glory-cloud appeared to them. God told Moses,

> Take the rod; and you and your brother Aaron assemble the congregation and speak to the rock before their eyes, that it may yield its water. You shall thus bring forth water for them out of the rock and let the congregation and their beasts drink. (Num 20:8)

But the people were angry with Moses, and Moses was angry with the people, and he disobeyed God. Moses would later write,

> So Moses took the rod from before the LORD, just as He had commanded him; [10] and Moses and Aaron gathered the assembly before the rock. And he said to them, "Listen now, you rebels; shall we bring forth water for you out of this rock?" [11] Then Moses lifted up his hand and struck the rock twice with his rod; and water came forth abundantly, and the congregation and their beasts drank. [12] But the LORD said to Moses and Aaron, "Because you have not believed Me, to treat Me as holy in the sight of the sons of Israel, therefore you shall not bring this assembly into the land which I have given them." (Num 20:9–12)

Moses had "not believed," did not treat the Lord "as holy," and "transgressed against" God. What was the transgression? He took the rod with him just as God commanded. How did he not treat God as holy? This is a unique statement about Moses' disobedience to the Lord from this one event. All sin is in some sense a disregard for the holiness of God, but what was it about this transgression that marked it out as Moses not treating God "as holy in the sight of the sons of Israel," with consequences so great that Moses was not allowed to enter the kingdom of God promised to Abraham, Isaac, and Jacob? The offense was not just Moses'. Aaron was also guilty of the offense, and died on Mt. Hor outside the promised land.[1] Both the mediator and the priest were not allowed to enter the kingdom. This offense was so significant that it is referenced multiple times. As Moses spoke to Israel before they went into the land, he reminded them of this event (Deut 1:37; 4:21; cf. Ps 106:32).

When Aaron's sons sinned, this same language is used. Leviticus 10:1–3 records,

> Now Nadab and Abihu, the sons of Aaron, took their respective firepans, and after putting fire in them, placed incense on it and offered strange fire before the Lord, which He had not commanded them. **2** And fire came out from the presence of the LORD and consumed them, and they died before the LORD. **3** Then Moses said to Aaron, "It is what the LORD spoke, saying,
> 'By those who come near Me I will be treated as holy,
> And before all the people I will be honored.'"

As priests, they had defiled their service to a holy God. God told Isaiah,

> It is the LORD of hosts whom you should regard as holy.
> And He shall be your fear,
> And He shall be your dread.
> **14** Then He shall become a sanctuary;
> But to both the houses of Israel, a stone to strike and a rock to stumble over,
> *And* a snare and a trap for the inhabitants of Jerusalem.
> **15** Many will stumble over them,
> Then they will fall and be broken;
> They will even be snared and caught. (Isa 8:13–15)

God is not merely promising a refuge; he promising to come as a holy place (*miqdash*, מִקְדָּשׁ). Isaiah is not to fear what the people fear,

---

1. Num 20:23–29.

but to fear the Lord. For God will come and dwell as a holy temple. But this temple will be a stone of stumbling. Isaiah is to "regard" the Lord as "holy." The Lord will become the temple dwelling among his people. But how does all this relate to Moses' sin? Moses' and Aaron's sin is tied to the holiness of the Lord. There is a connection to the tabernacle, the priesthood, and the holiness of God. What is the connection? And there is another question. God told Moses to take the rod, but he didn't tell Moses to strike the rock. But the text says that Moses struck the rock "twice." Unending interpreters have concluded the implication that Moses was only supposed to strike the rock once, but struck it twice and in this way disobeyed God. In a strange way, this point is right and wrong. In Numbers 20, God doesn't tell Moses to strike the rock at all, but to speak to the rock. There is no stated command to strike the rock, so it is questionable that Moses' transgression is striking the rock two times at Kadesh. But why does it refer to Moses striking the rock twice (*paam*, פַּעֲמָה) if that is not the offense?

Nahum begins his book describing the definitive judgment God will bring. He writes,

> But with an overflowing flood
> he will make a complete end of the adversaries,
> and will pursue his enemies into darkness.
> **9** What do you plot against the Lord?
> He will make a complete end;
> trouble will not rise up a second time [*paam*, פַּעֲמָה]. (Nah 1:8–9 ESV)

There will be no "second time." This translation helps when the reader translates the same word, *paam*, this way in Numbers 20:11:

> Then Moses lifted up his hand and struck the rock a second time [*paam*] with his rod; and water came forth abundantly, and the congregation and their beasts drank. (AT)

When was the first time? This was not the first time Moses struck the rock. Exodus 17 recounts the similar account at the beginning of Israel's sojourn. They had moved on from wilderness of Sin and camped at Rephidim. The people were grumbling that there was no water. Moses went to the Lord. The Lord said to Moses,

> Behold, I will stand before you there on the rock at Horeb, and you shall strike the rock, and water shall come out of it, and the people will drink. (Exod 17:6)

God commanded Moses to strike the rock, and Moses struck the rock and the people drank! That was the first time Moses struck the rock and water came forth. But now in Numbers 20 God said for Moses to speak to the rock and water would come forth. But Moses struck the rock as he had forty years earlier. In so doing, he did not honor God's holiness, did not believe, and transgressed God's command. As a result, Moses and Aaron were not allowed to enter the kingdom land. Why?

Paul writes,

> ... all drank the same spiritual drink, for they were drinking from a spiritual rock which followed them; and the rock was Christ ... (1 Cor 10:4)

Christ is the rock. The first time, Moses struck the rock, and water came forth. The second time, Moses was to speak to the rock; he struck the rock. He struck the rock twice; once before the wilderness wandering and the second after. In so doing, he violated the gospel picture. The sacrifice that brings the water of life was struck once! Moses transgressed God's command. Moses did not treat God as "holy" when he struck the rock. Moses did not believe. This is not a reference to generic unbelief. Moses failed to see the picture of Christ as the rock once to bring forth the water of life. Moses struck a rock; he didn't do so seeing what he was picturing. He did not believe. Moses did not see that he, the mediator of the Law, with Aaron the priest present, was picturing the gospel. God told Moses to talk the second time, but did not tell him to strike with the rod. The rod was representative of Moses' representative authority. Moses prayed and raised the rod and won the war. Moses raised the rod and the Red Sea divided. Moses threw down the rod and it became a snake before Pharaoh. The rod was called the "rod of God" because of this representative authority (Exod 4:20; 17:9). When Moses defiled the gospel picture, he was disallowed entrance into the kingdom.

But Moses is in heaven. At the transfiguration of Christ, Moses and Elijah were with Jesus in glory! Moses believed the gospel, though he did not see the gospel when he struck the rock the second time. On the eschatological level of the promise and fulfillment in Christ, Moses is a believer and is in heaven. But on the toy, typological level, Moses was not a believer and denied entrance into the kingdom. There are these two levels at work throughout the Old Testament. Daniel is "not my people" as he is exiled to the nations on the Old Covenant level, but Daniel is a redeemed servant of the Lord on the Abrahamic promise–New

Covenant-fulfillment level. What was promised to Abraham is fulfilled in the Old Testament on the toy level, and in the New Testament on the eschatological level.

This Abrahamic promise, typological fulfillment, and eschatological fulfillment of the kingdom of God provides the structure for the Bible. As Kline writes of Abraham,

> ... whose promises look ahead to fulfillment in two stages and at two levels under the old (Mosaic) and the new covenants. The Bible, as Old and New Testaments, was designed to provide constitutions for these old and new covenants, and in these covenants, the conferral of the kingdom-grant promised in God's covenant with Christ takes place, in typological symbol under the old and in consummate reality under the new.[2]

To confuse the two levels or two stages is to misinterpret the respective context. But to read the typological in light of the fulfillment in Christ is to turn the lights on in what otherwise would be a very dark room. The Jews who saw, as Abraham did, the coming Messiah were filled with wonderment at the promises of God. But as Paul writes,

> ... their minds were hardened; for until this very day at the reading of the old covenant the same veil remains unlifted, because it is removed in Christ. [15] But to this day whenever Moses is read, a veil lies over their heart; [16] but whenever a person turns to the Lord, the veil is taken away. [17] Now the Lord is the Spirit, and where the Spirit of the Lord is, *there* is liberty. [18] But we all, with unveiled face, beholding as in a mirror the glory of the Lord, are being transformed into the same image from glory to glory, just as from the Lord, the Spirit. (2 Cor 3:14–18)

To see Christ in the Old Covenant is to understand the Law. The Old Covenant is filled with types and shadows that point to the person and work of Christ. But the Old Covenant itself is not a covenant of grace.

COVENANT OF WORKS

The Old Testament provides the covenant document of the Old Covenant. The Law, or Torah, gives the covenant. Exodus recounts the person and work of the mediator, Moses, and the history of the covenant exodus and covenant making. The former prophets memorialize God's faithfulness

---

2. Kline, *Prologue*, 141f.

to the covenant and Israel's covenant breaking. The later prophets pronounce the covenant judgments. The wisdom literature sets forth the life and worship of the covenant-keeping wise man. To this covenant document, Genesis serves as the prologue to the Old Covenant.

There is ambiguity when someone uses the term "Old Testament." Are they referring to the actual covenant made at Sinai? Or are they referring to people and events described in the covenant prologue that took place before the covenant at Sinai? For example, one might say that Abraham is an "Old Testament believer." But this is only true if one means Abraham is discussed in the Old Testament scriptures; actually Abraham lived before the Old Testament. But who uses "Old Testament" to refer only to the covenant made at Sinai? The King James translation comes close when it translates *diatheke*[3] as "testament." Hebrews 9:15 is translated:

> And for this cause he is the mediator of the new testament, that by means of death, for the redemption of the transgressions that were under the first testament, they which are called might receive the promise of eternal inheritance. (KJV)

The "new testament" is contrasted with the "first testament." In the context of Hebrews, the "first testament" is the Mosaic Covenant, or Old Covenant. It is the "first" in the comparison of these two. The KJV translators used the common first-century meaning of *diatheke* in translating it "testament." Modern translators translate *diatheke* as "covenant" in Hebrews because *diatheke* is the word used in the Septuagint to translate the Hebrew word for "covenant." Then why is the English Bible made up of the "Old" and "New Testaments"? In the second century, a bishop in Sardis, Melito, listed the books of the Hebrew Scriptures and labeled them the "Old Covenant." When Jerome translated the Latin Vulgate in the fifth century, he translated "covenant" (*diatheke*) as *testamentum*. The Vulgate was used throughout the Middle Ages. When Wycliff translated the Bible in the fourteenth century, he translated *diatheke* as "testament." Tyndale, the Geneva Bible, and the King James translators did the same. So the English Bible is made up of the "Old Testament" and the "New Testament." The better names would be "Old Covenant" and "New Covenant Scriptures." Abraham's life is recounted in the Old Covenant scriptures, though he lived before the Old Covenant. Adam and Eve lived before the Old Covenant. The Old Covenant was made at Sinai. Following the form of the period's suzerainty treaty, Exodus 20 records the covenant.

3. διαθήκης.

The covenant starts with the historical prologue recounting the King's actions. Then the stipulations of the covenant are given. The resulting sanctions are based on obedience or disobedience to the stipulations. After the covenant stipulations are set forth in Leviticus, the sanctions are given. Leviticus promises,

> If you follow my decrees and are careful to obey my commands, **4** I will send you rain in its season, and the ground will yield its crops and the trees their fruit. **5** Your threshing will continue until grape harvest and the grape harvest will continue until planting, and you will eat all the food you want and live in safety in your land.
>
> **6** I will grant peace in the land, and you will lie down and no one will make you afraid. I will remove wild beasts from the land, and the sword will not pass through your country. **7** You will pursue your enemies, and they will fall by the sword before you. **8** Five of you will chase a hundred, and a hundred of you will chase ten thousand, and your enemies will fall by the sword before you.
>
> **9** I will look on you with favor and make you fruitful and increase your numbers, and I will keep my covenant with you. **10** You will still be eating last year's harvest when you will have to move it out to make room for the new. **11** I will put my dwelling place among you, and I will not abhor you. **12** I will walk among you and be your God, and you will be my people. **13** I am the Lord your God, who brought you out of Egypt so that you would no longer be slaves to the Egyptians; I broke the bars of your yoke and enabled you to walk with heads held high. (Lev 26:3–13 NIV)

In the same way, when Moses gives the covenant again, the sanctions are listed. Deuteronomy promises,

> If you fully obey the Lord your God and carefully follow all his commands I give you today, the Lord your God will set you high above all the nations on earth. **2** All these blessings will come on you and accompany you if you obey the Lord your God:
>
> **3** You will be blessed in the city and blessed in the country.
>
> **4** The fruit of your womb will be blessed, and the crops of your land and the young of your livestock—the calves of your herds and the lambs of your flocks.
>
> **5** Your basket and your kneading trough will be blessed.
>
> **6** You will be blessed when you come in and blessed when you go out.

> ⁷ The Lord will grant that the enemies who rise up against you will be defeated before you. They will come at you from one direction but flee from you in seven.
> ⁸ The Lord will send a blessing on your barns and on everything you put your hand to. The Lord your God will bless you in the land he is giving you.
> ⁹ The Lord will establish you as his holy people, as he promised you on oath, if you keep the commands of the Lord your God and walk in obedience to him. ¹⁰ Then all the peoples on earth will see that you are called by the name of the Lord, and they will fear you. ¹¹ The Lord will grant you abundant prosperity—in the fruit of your womb, the young of your livestock and the crops of your ground—in the land he swore to your ancestors to give you.
> ¹² The Lord will open the heavens, the storehouse of his bounty, to send rain on your land in season and to bless all the work of your hands. You will lend to many nations but will borrow from none. ¹³ The Lord will make you the head, not the tail. If you pay attention to the commands of the Lord your God that I give you this day and carefully follow them, you will always be at the top, never at the bottom. ¹⁴ Do not turn aside from any of the commands I give you today, to the right or to the left, following other gods and serving them. (Deut 28:1–14 NIV)

If they obeyed the covenant, they would be blessed in the land promised to Abraham, Isaac, and Jacob. The covenant blessing was contingent upon their keeping the covenant. But there were also curse sanctions to the Old Covenant. Leviticus threatens,

> But if you will not listen to me and carry out all these commands, ¹⁵ and if you reject my decrees and abhor my laws and fail to carry out all my commands and so violate my covenant, ¹⁶ then I will do this to you: I will bring on you sudden terror, wasting diseases and fever that will destroy your sight and sap your strength. You will plant seed in vain, because your enemies will eat it. ¹⁷ I will set my face against you so that you will be defeated by your enemies; those who hate you will rule over you, and you will flee even when no one is pursuing you.
> ¹⁸ If after all this you will not listen to me, I will punish you for your sins seven times over. ¹⁹ I will break down your stubborn pride and make the sky above you like iron and the ground beneath you like bronze. ²⁰ Your strength will be spent in vain, because your soil will not yield its crops, nor will the trees of your land yield their fruit.

> **21** If you remain hostile toward me and refuse to listen to me, I will multiply your afflictions seven times over, as your sins deserve. **22** I will send wild animals against you, and they will rob you of your children, destroy your cattle and make you so few in number that your roads will be deserted.
> **23** If in spite of these things you do not accept my correction but continue to be hostile toward me, **24** I myself will be hostile toward you and will afflict you for your sins seven times over. **25** And I will bring the sword on you to avenge the breaking of the covenant. When you withdraw into your cities, I will send a plague among you, and you will be given into enemy hands. **26** When I cut off your supply of bread, ten women will be able to bake your bread in one oven, and they will dole out the bread by weight. You will eat, but you will not be satisfied.
> **27** If in spite of this you still do not listen to me but continue to be hostile toward me, **28** then in my anger I will be hostile toward you, and I myself will punish you for your sins seven times over. **29** You will eat the flesh of your sons and the flesh of your daughters. **30** I will destroy your high places, cut down your incense altars and pile your dead bodies on the lifeless forms of your idols, and I will abhor you. **31** I will turn your cities into ruins and lay waste your sanctuaries, and I will take no delight in the pleasing aroma of your offerings. **32** I myself will lay waste the land, so that your enemies who live there will be appalled. **33** I will scatter you among the nations and will draw out my sword and pursue you. Your land will be laid waste, and your cities will lie in ruins. (Lev 26:14–33).

Deuteronomy 28:15–68 lists the curses. Moses writes,

> However, if you do not obey the Lord your God and do not carefully follow all his commands and decrees I am giving you today, all these curses will come on you and overtake you:
> **16** You will be cursed in the city and cursed in the country.
> **17** Your basket and your kneading trough will be cursed.
> **18** The fruit of your womb will be cursed, and the crops of your land, and the calves of your herds and the lambs of your flocks.
> **19** You will be cursed when you come in and cursed when you go out. (Deut 28:15–19 NIV)

This covenant was "do and live" or "disobey and die!" But there was no promise of salvation or eternity with God in heaven contained in the sanctions of the Old Covenant! There is no sanction of hell and everlasting damnation! They will live in the land innumerable as the stars, or be exiled and left few in number in bondage if they break the covenant. If they obey, they fulfill the Abrahamic Covenant. But how can this be when the fulfillment of the Abrahamic Covenant is the eternal eschatological kingdom of God? The kingdom in Canaan is typological of the eternal kingdom. The Old Covenant is a covenant made with the nation of Israel on the typological level. It is a covenant of works; if they obey, they are blessed. If they disobey, they are cursed. The promised land is typological of the new creation land. The terms of the Old Covenant do not contain any grace. It is Law!

When the covenant was made, the scene is quite different than Genesis 15. The people were not the observers watching God take the oath. Exodus 24 says,

> Then he took the book of the covenant and read it in the hearing of the people; and they said, "All that the LORD has spoken we will do, and we will be obedient!" **8** So Moses took the blood and sprinkled *it* on the people, and said, "Behold the blood of the covenant, which the LORD has made with you in accordance with all these words." (Exod 24:7-8)

Israel took the self-maledictory oath. Not God, but Israel swore that they would keep the covenant or they would take the curse of the covenant. Unlike the unconditional covenant given to Abraham by grace, this is a conditional covenant of works. Paul contrasts the two kinds of covenant. He writes,

> For Moses writes regarding the righteousness which is out of law, "The man who does these things will live in them."[4] **6** But the righteousness out of faith... (Rom 10:5-6 AT)

What is contrasted is not two ways of eternal salvation. In the context, Leviticus is promising life in the promised land based on covenant obedience. In contrast to this righteousness by keeping the covenant, Paul says that saving righteousness is through faith in the one who is the covenant keeper. On the typological level, the Old Covenant is a covenant of works.

---

4. Μωϋσῆς γὰρ γράφει τὴν δικαιοσύνην τὴν ἐκ τοῦ νόμου ὅτι ὁ ποιήσας αὐτὰ ἄνθρωπος ζήσεται ἐν αὐτοῖς. Lev 18:5; cf. Moo, *Romans*, 643f. regarding textual considerations.

THE ANGEL AND THE GLORY PRESENCE

In continuity with the patriarchal period, God is present as the Angel of the Lord. But starting with the exodus, God is also present as the Glory-cloud theophany. Far from God idly sitting in heaven waiting until Jesus would come, the Trinity is actively bringing the creation to it eschatological purpose. From beginning to end, the eschatological dwelling of God with his people is the work of the Trinity.

The Angel of the Lord

Exodus begins by describing the need for a deliverer. From their Egyptian bondage, Israel cried out to God. God heard them. Moses writes,

> So God heard their groaning; and God remembered His covenant with Abraham, Isaac, and Jacob. 25 God saw the sons of Israel, and God knew them. (Exod 2:24–25 AT)

In fulfillment of his promise to the patriarchs, God delivered the twelve tribes and formed them as his kingdom people—"God knew them." Moses continues,

> Now Moses was pasturing the flock of Jethro his father-in-law, the priest of Midian; and he led the flock to the west side of the wilderness and came to Horeb, the mountain of God. 2 The angel of the LORD appeared to him in a blazing fire from the midst of a bush; and he looked, and behold, the bush was burning with fire, yet the bush was not consumed. 3 So Moses said, "I must turn aside now and see this marvelous sight, why the bush is not burned up." 4 When the LORD saw that he turned aside to look, God called to him from the midst of the bush and said, "Moses, Moses!" And he said, "Here I am." 5 Then He said, "Do not come near here; remove your sandals from your feet, for the place on which you are standing is holy ground." 6 He said also, "I am the God of your father, the God of Abraham, the God of Isaac, and the God of Jacob." Then Moses hid his face, for he was afraid to look at God. (Exod 3:1–6)

God the Son, the Angel of the Lord, appeared from the burning bush (v. 2). The Angel is then referred to as "the Lord" (v. 4), and Moses is told that the ground is holy because God is there. Then the Angel of the Lord identifies himself as the "God of your fathers" (v. 6). Moses is afraid to look at the Angel of the Lord, who appeared because he was afraid to "look at God" (v. 6). As in Exodus 33, the Angel of the Lord is identified with God, yet distinguished from God. God the Father sits as King on the throne in heaven. God the Son is the Angel of the Lord representing the King. But as the Glory-cloud will appear as the visible Glory theophany, so the Angel of the Lord appears to Abraham as one of three men (Gen 18:1–2), and here to Moses from the midst of the burning bush.

When Israel is fleeing from Pharaoh's army, the Angel of the Lord goes with Israel. Moses writes,

> The angel of God, who had been going before the camp of Israel, moved and went behind them; and the pillar of cloud moved from before them and stood behind them. (Exod 14:19)

Contrary to Vos, the Angel is distinguished from the Glory-cloud.[5] When Israel worshiped the golden calf, God told Moses that he would send his Angel, but not his Presence (Exod 33). The Angel of the Lord would go with Israel, but not God in his Glory-cloud Presence.[6] Finally, through Moses' intercession, God agreed that his Glory-Presence would go with Israel.

From the beginning of the Mosaic Covenant, God had promised that the Angel of the Lord would bring Israel into the promised land. After the Law is given, God tells Moses,

> Behold, I am going to send an angel before you to guard you along the way and to bring you into the place which I have prepared. 21 Be on your guard before him and obey his voice; do not be rebellious toward him, for he will not pardon your transgression, since My name is in him. 22 But if you truly obey his voice and do all that I say, then I will be an enemy to your enemies and an adversary to your adversaries. 23 For My angel will go before you and bring you in *to the land of* the Amorites, the Hittites, the Perizzites, the Canaanites, the Hivites and the Jebusites; and I will completely destroy them. (Exod 23:20–23)

The Angel is the "angel of His presence" that brought Israel out of Egypt through the Red Sea (Isa 63:9). The Angel has the "name" of God in him.[7] Joshua is met by this captain of the Lord's army right before they went to conquer the promised land. Joshua 5 records the event:

---

5. Vos, *Biblical*, 122–23.
6. Kline, *Covenant Witness*, 20ff.; Kline, *Images*, 71f.
7. Kline, *Images*, 70.

The Toy Kingdom

> Now it came about when Joshua was by Jericho, that he lifted up his eyes and looked, and behold, a man was standing opposite him with his sword drawn in his hand, and Joshua went to him and said to him, "Are you for us or for our adversaries?" 14 He said, "No; rather I indeed come now *as* captain of the host of the Lord." And Joshua fell on his face to the earth, and bowed down, and said to him, "What has my lord to say to his servant?" 15 The captain of the Lord's host said to Joshua, "Remove your sandals from your feet, for the place where you are standing is holy." And Joshua did so. (Josh 5:13–15)

As the Angel of the Lord appeared to Moses, so now the Angel of Lord assured Joshua of the victory. God was with them! As they conquered the land, the Angel of the Lord was with them. Not even the king of Moab would be able to have his prophet, Balaam, pronounce curses on Israel because of the presence of the Angel of the Lord with Israel. Balaam's donkey would not go forward when he saw the Angel of the Lord standing in the way with his sword drawn. Balaam hit the donkey. They went further where there was a narrow passage. Balaam's donkey again saw the Angel of the Lord and move to the side, which pressed Balaam's foot against the wall. Balaam struck his donkey again. A third time, they went still further to a narrow place with no place to turn. The donkey saw the Angel of the Lord, and the donkey did the only thing that the donkey could do. The donkey lay down! Angry Balaam was beside himself and this time took his stick and struck his donkey. The Lord caused the donkey to say to Balaam,

> What have I done to you, that you have struck me these three times? (Num 22:28)

And Balaam responded to his donkey!

> Because you have made a mockery of me! If there had been a sword in my hand, I would have killed you by now. (Num 22:29)

To which Balaam's donkey said,

> Am I not your donkey on which you have ridden all your life to this day? Have I ever been accustomed to do so to you? (Num 22:30)

To which Balaam responded,

> No.

What a conversation! And then,

> ... the Lord opened the eyes of Balaam, and he saw the angel of the Lord standing in the way with his drawn sword in his hand; and he bowed all the way to the ground. (Num 22:31)

The Angel of the Lord spoke with Israel at Bochim (Judg 2:1). The Angel of the Lord called Gideon (Judg 6:12). Gideon knew who it was that he had seen. Judges records,

> When Gideon saw that he was the angel of the Lord, he said, "Alas, O Lord God! For now I have seen the angel of the Lord face to face." 23 The Lord said to him, "Peace to you, do not fear; you shall not die. (Judg 6:22–23)

When the Angel of the Lord came to the barren wife of Manoah to tell her that she would give birth to the Nazirite, Samson, she described him to her husband as "appearance of the angel of God, very awesome (Judg 13:6)." When the Angel came again, they prepared a burnt offering to the Lord. When Manoah asked the Angel's name, the Angel of the Lord asked why he asked, as his name is "Wonderful."[8] Then the Angel did wonders before them and finally,

> ... when the flame went up from the altar toward heaven, that the angel of the Lord ascended in the flame of the altar. When Manoah and his wife saw *this*, they fell on their faces to the ground. (Judg 13:20)

The Angel of the Lord killed 185, 000 Assyrian soldiers in their camp to save Jerusalem.[9] He is the one who leads the recognizance in Zechariah looking for the day when the righteous kingdom and temple will be established (Zech 1:12). Malachi says that the Angel of the Covenant will come, and the question will be: "who can endure the day of His coming?" (Mal 3:2). He is the consuming fire!

The answer was with Israel from the start! The one event that most often escapes the reader is the role of the Angel of the Lord in the first Passover. Not only is Jesus pictured by the sacrificial blood on the door posts at the first Passover, but he is present as the Angel of the Lord. What God told Moses is translated by the King James:

---

8. Judg 13:18; "incomprehensible," פֶּלִאי, *pili*.
9. 2 Kgs 19:35.

The Toy Kingdom

> For I will pass through the land of Egypt this night, and will smite all the firstborn in the land of Egypt, both man and beast; and against all the gods of Egypt I will execute judgment: I am the Lord.
>
> 13 And the blood shall be to you for a token upon the houses where ye are: and when I see the blood, I will pass over you, and the plague shall not be upon you to destroy you, when I smite the land of Egypt (Exod 12:12–13).

God would bring judgment on the Egyptians as he passed through the land, but would pass over the Israelite houses with the blood on the door posts. This basic idea is true, but it obscures what God actually says. God is not describing one action in these verses, but two. Traditionally, God's one action is that he will pass through the land bringing death on the firstborn Egyptians, but passing over the Israelite houses that have the blood marked entrances. But these two verses promise two actions by God. God will bring judgment on the Egyptians, and God will hover over the Israelites to protect them against the judgment. The key words translated "pass through" (*abar*, עָבַר) in verse 12 and "pass over" (*pasah*, עָבַר) in verse 13 are key to the clarification. The first, *abar* (עָבַר), means "pass through" or "pass over." God is going through the land to bring judgment. The second term, *pasah*, means "hover over."[10] A better translation would then be:

> For I will pass through the land of Egypt this night, and will strike down all the firstborn in the land of Egypt, both man and beast; and against all the gods of Egypt I will execute judgment: I am the Lord.13 And the blood will be to you for a sign upon the houses where you are: and when I see the blood, I will hover over you, and the plague will not come upon you to destroy you, when I strike the land of Egypt. (Exod 12:12–13 AT)

God is doing two things, passing through the land in judgment and hovering to protect the blood bought homes. Interestingly, Exodus 12:23 distinguishes God hovering and the destroyer bringing judgment:

> For the Lord will pass through [*abar*] to smite the Egyptians; and when He sees the blood on the lintel and on the two doorposts, the Lord will hover over [*pasah*] the door and will not allow the destroyer to come in to your houses to smite you. (AT)

The Lord passes through the land in judgment, but the Lord does not allow the destroyer to come on the Israelites. God is identified both as the

---

10. Kline, *Essential Writings*, 151ff.

destroyer who comes in judgment and as the God who hovers over their houses to protect against the destroyer. The triune God is present. God the Glory-Spirit[11] hovers over the houses marked with blood to protect them, while the destroyer brings the judgment. The destroyer is the Angel of the Lord bringing judgment on Egypt. Kline writes,

> This destroyer would be an angelic agent of God, or even the messianic Angel of the Lord himself. If the destroyer is the Angel of the Lord, the statements that God is the executor of the destructive blows (Exod 12:12, 13c, 23a, 29) find their expression in the nature of this angel as one who though distinguishable from God is identified as God.[12]

The Angel of the Lord struck down seventy thousand Israelites when David took the census. He is the executioner of covenant judgment. Malachi writes of his coming,

> For behold, the day is coming, burning like a furnace; and all the arrogant and every evildoer will be chaff; and the day that is coming will set them ablaze," says the Lord of hosts, "so that it will leave them neither root nor branch." (Mal 4:1)

His name is Jesus. John tells the reader that he is the King of kings riding the white horse, whose angels gather the nations for judgment,

> Come, assemble for the great supper of God, ^{18} so that you may eat the flesh of kings and the flesh of commanders and the flesh of mighty men and the flesh of horses and of those who sit on them and the flesh of all men, both free men and slaves, and small and great. (Rev 19:17–18)

Who will stand in the day of his coming? Those bought with his blood will stand! Jesus is judge, and he was judged for their transgressions. The Angel passes over the houses he paid for!

The Glory Presence

The theophany of God's Glory-Presence was with Israel at the exodus and led them through the wilderness into the promised kingdom land. The architecture of the tabernacle and temple replicated the royal temple in heaven. Hebrews says,

---

11. Cf. Deut 32:10–11; Isa 31:5; Exod 14:19–20.
12. Kline, *Essential Writings*, 153.

> Therefore it was necessary for the copies of the things in the heavens to be cleansed with these, but the heavenly things themselves with better sacrifices than these. **24** For Christ did not enter a holy place made with hands, a *mere* copy of the true one, but into heaven itself, now to appear in the presence of God for us. (Heb 9:23–24)[13]

The little tabernacle and temple were representative of the heavenly royal temple. The Glory-Spirit was the theophanic manifestation of that same temple. So the earthly tabernacle and temple were made in the image of the Glory-Spirit. The Glory-Spirit covered Sinai when the covenant was made. At the bottom of the mountain, the tabernacle was made to replicate God's mobile throne. The Glory of the Lord would be enthroned in the temple's holy of holies. It pictured heaven. The two golden cherubim were over the ark of the covenant. The flaming materials represented God's Glory. The two pillars of the temple represented the Glory-Spirit pillar entrance into heaven.[14]

The toy representations of the heavenly court also pictured the royal temple Adam was to build to fill the earth. The kingdom of Israel was a toy fulfillment of the promised kingdom the Second Adam would bring, which the first Adam failed to build. As Beale notes,

> . . . the Old Testament tabernacle and temples were symbolically designed to point to the cosmic eschatological reality that God's tabernacling presence, formerly limited to the holy of holies, was to extend through the whole earth. Against this background, the Revelation 21 vision is best understood as picturing the final end-time temple that will fill the entire cosmos.[15]

Beale writes, "temple was a microcosm of the entire heaven and earth."[16] As the psalmist writes,

> And He built His sanctuary like the heights,
> Like the earth which He has founded forever. (Ps 78:69)

Aaron's own priestly vestments mirrored that of the tabernacle replication of the Glory-Spirit.[17] The tabernacle and the priest were images of

---

13. See Heb 9:11.
14. Kline, *Images*, 39ff.
15. Beale, *Temple*, 25.
16. Beale, *Temple*, 31.
17. Kline, *Images*, 42ff.

the King's royal temple. The Glory-cloud descended on the throne in the tabernacle and finally in the temple.[18] On this typological toy level, the Abrahamic Covenant was fulfilled. The kingdom of God had come.

The kingdom land was conquered. The representative king ruled. The priest served in the temple. And the Glory of God filled the temple. The reality would look different, but these are the Playmobil representations of the coming kingdom. It wasn't the real kingdom. The land had not been completely cleansed of the unclean. The kings were hardly what was promised. Israel broke the covenant, and God left them. The Glory-Presence of God left the temple![19] The temple would be destroyed.

THE TOY TEMPLE AND THE REAL TEMPLE

The Wisdom and Power of God

Yes, the toy temple was rebuilt to picture the eschatological restoration. But even that temple would not last. Israel broke the Old Covenant. They would not be the everlasting kingdom of God. The Babylonians destroyed Jerusalem and the temple, and took the people captive. Where was God? He left! But what about God's promise to Abraham? Judah's fall to the Babylonians raised the question: What kind of God is Yahweh? His people are slaves, their kingdom conquered, and his temple has been turned to ruins!

Though Daniel prophesied, the book of Daniel is part of the Wisdom Literature of the Old Testament, not the Prophets. Daniel answers the question regarding God's faithfulness to his promise. The first six chapters proclaim that God's wisdom and power.

    A—Chapter 1: Daniel's dietary wisdom
    A—Chapter 2: Daniel's dream wisdom
        B—Chapter 3: Power over the fiery furnace
    A'—Chapter 4: Daniel's dream wisdom
    A'—Chapter 5: Daniel's interpretive wisdom
        B'—Chapter 6: Power over the lion's den

Daniel and his friends were faithful to the Levitical food laws. The conclusion of chapter 1 states,

18. Exod 40:34–38; 1 Kgs 8:10–11.
19. Ezek 10; cf. 11:23.

> As for every matter of wisdom and understanding about which the king consulted them, he found them ten times better than all the magicians *and* conjurers who *were* in all his realm. (Dan 1:20)

Daniel interprets the king's dream, and proclaims the eternal kingdom of God that will displace all other kingdoms. The king confesses,

> Surely your God is a God of gods and a Lord of kings and a revealer of mysteries, since you have been able to reveal this mystery. (Dan 2:47)

After God protected Shadrach, Meshach, and Abed-nego, Nebuchadnezzar witnessed to their God's power:

> Blessed be the God of Shadrach, Meshach and Abed-nego, who has sent His angel and delivered His servants who put their trust in Him, violating the king's command, and yielded up their bodies so as not to serve or worship any god except their own God. (Dan 3:28)

After none of the wise men were able to interpret his dream, the king sought the interpretation from Daniel. After the fulfillment of the horrid experience, Daniel writes the king's words:

> Now I, Nebuchadnezzar, praise, exalt and honor the King of heaven, for all His works are true and His ways just, and He is able to humble those who walk in pride. (Dan 4:37)

The next king did not learn from God's judgment on Nebuchadnezzar. Belshazzar had a feast for a thousand of his nobles. In the midst of the feast, he called for the gold and silver vessels that had been plundered from Solomon's fallen temple so that he and his wives and his nobles and concubines could drink from them. As they defiled them, offering worship to the pagan gods of gold, silver, bronze, iron, wood, and stone, they saw a hand write God's judgment on the wall. The king's knees knocked in fear and his face went pale in terror. None of his wise men could interpret the writing. The queen told the king about Daniel's extraordinary wisdom. Daniel interpreted the words of judgment on the king and the kingdom, and the king robed Daniel in purple and made him third ruler in the kingdom. That same night the king was killed (Dan 5)!

Darius the Persian conquered the Babylonians, and Daniel served his court. But Daniel was thrown in the lions den because he bowed in prayer before the King of Heaven. After God protected Daniel, the king issued a decree and acknowledged the power of Daniel's God:

> Then Darius the king wrote to all the peoples, nations and *men of every* language who were living in all the land: "May your peace abound! **26** I make a decree that in all the dominion of my kingdom men are to fear and tremble before the God of Daniel;
> For He is the living God and enduring forever,
> And His kingdom is one which will not be destroyed,
> And His dominion *will be* forever.
> **27** "He delivers and rescues and performs signs and wonders
> In heaven and on earth,
> Who has *also* delivered Daniel from the power of the lions."
> (Dan 6:25–27)

These first six chapters clearly present the wisdom and power of Yahweh. But they do not only declare attributes of God apart from his kingdom promise to Abraham. Daniel's carefulness not to be defiled by the king's unclean table, the proclamation of the kingdom that will be forever, the immunity to the fires of kings, the judgment on the proud kings of the earth, the deliverance from lions, and Gentile king confessing the living God whose kingdom will not end all directly address the kingdom promise God made Abraham. God's wisdom and power will establish his kingdom.

The temple and the Temple[20]

Central to God's kingdom is his temple. The center of the second half of Daniel addresses this part of the promise specifically. Judah was in exile seventy years. Daniel was reading Jeremiah and realized the seventy-year exile was complete![21] So, he prayed to the Lord at length. He confessed Israel's breaking of the covenant, God's justice in his judgment on Israel, and how they had not turned to the Lord even after the judgment. Yet, Daniel called for God's mercy to restore them for the sake of God's name. Daniel asked that the Glory-Spirit, the "face," fill the desolate temple again (Dan 9:17). As Daniel was praying, the angel Gabriel came to Daniel and told him that when he started praying, God gave the order to answer the prayer!

Seventy weeks are decreed (Dan 9:24). This is seventy sevens. Often this has been interpreted as 490 years. The problem is that the numbers don't work. Dispensationalists have suggested that the decree in view is Artaxerxes' decree in 445 BC, and the sixty-nine weeks ends with Christ's

---

20. See Kline, "Covenant"; Kline, *God*, 146ff.
21. Dan 9:2.

triumphal entry. Then there is a parenthesis for the Church Age, and the last week is the seven-year Great Tribulation before the Second Coming. On this reading, the first seven weeks would be from 445 to the rebuilding of the temple. But there are several obstacles for this view.

The destruction of the temple in the Babylonian siege was the result of Israel's breaking the Mosaic Covenant, the Old Covenant. God would bring restoration because of the Abrahamic Covenant (Lev 26:42). Solomon's temple and the second temple were both part of this broken covenant and could not stand. God's kingdom temple promise to Abraham must be based on an eternal foundation. Second, the years are off. The Babylonian captivity started seventy years before Daniel's prayer. Gabriel says the decree to restore the temple was given when Daniel started praying. Daniel 9:1 tells the reader that was the first year of Darius's (Cyrus) rule in 539 BC. This is a hundred years before Artaxerxes' decree to rebuild Jerusalem. Third, the decree in view is the decree that answers Daniel's prayer regarding the temple, the holy mountain (cf. Dan 9:17, 20, 24, 26). Fourth, there is nothing in the text that allows a gap from the end of the sixty-ninth week to the beginning of the seventieth week. There are seventy weeks to bring about the ultimate answer to Daniel's prayer, the anointing of a most holy place.

Gabriel told Daniel that seventy weeks were decreed for six purposes to be accomplished (Dan 9:24):

1—to finish the transgression	2—to make an end of sin
3—to make atonement for iniquity	4—to bring in everlasting righteousness
5—to seal up vision and prophecy	6- to anoint the most holy place

Within the seventy weeks, the weeks are divided into subsections: seven weeks, sixty-two weeks, and the seventieth week (Dan 9:25, 27). The promised land rested while Israel was exiled and the land was desolate (Lev 26:43). Each year of the seventy-year captivity would be seventy years of the land sabbath. Each year was a sabbath for the land. Expanded out then, the seventy years of sabbath for the land is equivalent to 490 years. This sabbatical cycle of years formed the basis for the year of Jubilee in the fiftieth year (Lev 25:13, 28; Num 36:4). Seven weeks of years would pass, and then they were to celebrate the year of Jubilee, when property was to revert to the original owner and slaves were to be given their freedom. The Old Covenant Jubilee pictured the ultimate Jubilee. So seven weeks would be forty-nine years, and would lead to the Jubilee year. Ten times seven weeks of years would be the ultimate Jubilee.

Seven weeks and the temple would be rebuilt under Cyrus. Sixty-two more weeks and the Messiah would come (Luke 4:18–19). Then the seventieth week would bring the ultimate Jubilee temple. The language of the seventy weeks is sabbatical language based on creation and Jubilee background. The first two purposes are fulfilled in the covenant judgment on Israel in 70 AD. The second two purposes are fulfilled by the Messiah on the cross. The last two purposes are fulfilled with the Second Coming. Christ is the eschatological temple that is anointed.

Gabriel details the coming of the kingdom in Christ, and the judgment on the Old Covenant kingdom people. He says,

> Then after the sixty-two weeks the Messiah will be cut off and there will not be to him,[22] and the people of the prince who is to come will destroy the city and the sanctuary. And its end will come with a flood; even to the end there will be war; desolations are determined. **27** And make a covenant prevail to the many, one week, but in the middle of the week he will put a stop to sacrifice and grain offering; and on the extremity of abominations will come one who makes desolate, even until a complete destruction, one that is decreed, is poured out on the desolate. (Dan 9:26–27 AT)

Verses 26–27 each have three parts that in parallel fashion point to the New Covenant in Christ and the covenant judgment on Israel.

Verse 26	Verse 27
A—cut New Covenant	establish the covenant
B—70 AD judgment	70 AD judgment
C—curse on Israel	curse on Israel

In verse 26, Gabriel says that after the seven and sixty-two weeks Christ will be cut off in the initiation of the New Covenant. Israel did not give Christ the honor due him. Christ, through the Roman soldiers, destroyed Jerusalem and the temple in 70 AD. Israel broke the Old Covenant, and so they would receive the covenant curse and be no more. Verse 27

---

22. אֵין לוֹ; see Kline, *God*, 150.

parallels verse 26. Whereas the Old Covenant did not yield blessing, in the midst of the seventieth week, Christ would cause covenant blessings to prevail to the many. Making the Old Covenant obsolete, Christ would put an end to the Old Covenant sacrifices. Christ the Lord, exalted to the right hand of the Father, would bring covenant judgment on the temple, the "abomination of desolations." Christ would bring complete and total desolation on the toy temple. Christ is the temple who brings the true eschatological temple. He would leave desolate the temple Israel filled with abominations in their covenant breaking. At the beginning and end of Christ's ministry, he cleared the toy temple that the Jews had filled with abominations. Christ, the temple, stood in contrast to the Old Covenant filthy toy! The toy would be destroyed!

The same contrast is the center of Stephen's witness to the Sanhedrin. Like Moses, whose face shone in glory when he came down from meeting with God, Stephen's face "shone like an angel" (Acts 6:15). After he recounted the covenant with Abraham, and Israel's idolatrous history, he focused on the tabernacle and the temple. The pivot point to confronting them with their hard heartedness is in Acts 7:48–50:

> However, the Most High does not dwell in *houses* made by *human hands*; as the prophet says:
> 49 "Heaven is My throne,
> And earth is the footstool of My feet;
> What kind of house will you build for Me?" says the Lord,
> "Or what place is there for My repose?
> 50 Was it not My hand which made all these things?"

God doesn't live in something made by man! Stephen then proclaimed they had killed the prophets God sent, and finally Christ! As they stoned Stephen, he continued the conclusion of his testimony:

> Behold, I see the heavens opened up and the Son of Man standing at the right hand of God. (Acts 7:56)

Here is the contrast. The temple of heaven, where Christ is seated as Lord at the right hand of the Father, is contrasted with the toy tabernacle and temple that were temporarily given to instruct Israel. But they were only toys! God doesn't dwell in temples made by man. Christ made the Old Covenant obsolete.[23]

---

23. Heb 8:13.

7

The King and The Kingdom
(The New Covenant)

THE KINGDOM OF THE LORD JESUS

Administration of the New Covenant

THE NEW COVENANT IS the administration of the kingdom by the Lord Jesus. During the Last Supper Jesus gave them the meal and said,

> "... for I say to you, I will not drink of the fruit of the vine from now on until the kingdom of God comes." [19] And when He had taken *some* bread *and* given thanks, He broke it and gave it to them, saying, "This is My body which is given for you; do this in remembrance of Me." [20] And in the same way *He took* the cup after they had eaten, saying, "This cup which is poured out for you is the new covenant in My blood." (Luke 22:18–20)

Looking forward to the full realization of the kingdom of God, he gave them the sacrament of the New Covenant. Afterwards, he told the disciples,

> And I covenant to you, just as my Father covenanted to me the kingdom, [30] that you may eat and drink at My table in My kingdom, and you will sit on thrones judging the twelve tribes of Israel." (Luke 22:29–30 AT)

By his obedience to the Pactum Salutis, Jesus has crown rights to the kingdom. So, as Lord of the kingdom, he has covenanted the kingdom to the church. Because of his covenant faithfulness as the servant in the Pactum Salutis, he now, as Lord, bestows on his disciples the kingdom blessing. Because of his covenant obedience, they will sit enthroned in glory. The Pactum Salutis is the covenant-of-works basis for the disciples receiving the kingdom by grace under the New Covenant. In this regard the New Covenant is quite different than the Old Covenant. Christ is the mediator of the New Covenant as Moses was the mediator of the Old Covenant. But the New Covenant blessing is based on Christ's covenant faithfulness under the Pactum Salutis, whereas the blessing sanction of the Old Covenant depended on Israel's obedience to the covenant.

Jesus is the faithful vassal son who obeyed the Pactum Salutis and so merited the covenant blessing. Hebrews 3 contrasts Jesus and Moses when it says,

> Now Moses was faithful in all His house as a servant, for a testimony of those things which were to be spoken later; **6** but Christ *was faithful* as a Son over His house . . . (Heb 3:5–6)

Moses was not the vassal party to the Old Covenant; Israel was. So Israel is the vassal covenant son.[1] Both were covenants of works: the Old on the typological level, the Pactum Salutis on the eschatological. Israel broke the covenant and was judged. The Lord Jesus obeyed, even to damnation on the cross, and merited the seat in the glory of heaven. The New Covenant administers to his disciples those blessings the Lord Jesus merited.

The Lord Jesus is the faithful Second Adam who passed the probation of the Pactum Salutis; so now he confirms to his disciples the kingdom in the New Covenant. The kingdom is his, so it is theirs. This is the promise God gave Abraham. His seed would receive the kingdom, so Abraham would receive the kingdom. On the typological level, his seed received the kingdom. But that was but a toy and temporary. Now the seed has come and with him the kingdom. By his blood, the kingdom has been established. He has cut the covenant with his own blood. His blood is at once the basis of the Lord Jesus' enthronement under the blessing sanction of Pactum Salutis, and at the same time it is the inauguration of the New Covenant. Kline writes,

> Therefore the Father had now bestowed on him the promised and merited reward, enthronement at the Father's right hand, the dignity of lordship in administering the new covenant . . .[2]

1. Hos 11:1; Exod 4:22.
2. Kline, *Glory*, 168.

Understanding the juncture of the Pactum Salutis and the New Covenant provides the context for the Gospels.³ The Gospel writers provide the person and work of the Second Adam as federal head of the kingdom of God. At the same time, this same account presents the covenant mediator in the inauguration of the kingdom through the New Covenant. He mediates to believers the covenant blessing he secured as the Second Adam.

Received by Faith

The kingdom of God has come through the obedient servant, Jesus Christ, the Lord. All who receive him by faith have citizenship in his kingdom. John writes that while Israel rejected their King,

> But as many as received Him, to them He gave the right to become children of God, *even* to those who believe in His name. (John 1:12)

John is saying more than that Jesus' work takes away sin and restores the believer to God. Through this first chapter of John's Gospel is the eschatological proclamation that the kingdom has come in Christ. He is the Creator (John 1:3) who became a man who was the temple image of the King (John 1:14). He was the servant of Isaiah (John 1:23) who took away the sin of the world (John 1:29). He is the Son of Man who gives access to the King of Heaven (John 1:49–51). The kingdom is his (Dan 7:14, 27). All who receive him have rights to the kingdom. Jesus' priestly work is not just the passive obedience of atoning for sin, but the active obedience that merited eschatological glory. The author of Hebrews writes,

> For this reason He is the mediator of a new covenant, so that, since a death has taken place for the redemption of the transgressions that were *committed* under the first covenant, those who have been called may receive the promise of the eternal inheritance. (Heb 9:15)

Through his death, the called receive the eternal inheritance. They are "heirs of the promise" (Heb 6:17). They are the "partakers of a heavenly calling" (Heb 3:1). As F. F. Bruce notes,

> And now that this redemptive death has taken place, the "promise of the eternal inheritance" has been made good to those "that

---

3. Kline, *Structure*, 172ff.

have been called"; the new covenant, and everything that the grace of God provides under it, is forever theirs.[4]

The kingdom promised Abraham (Heb 6:13) has become the kingdom of all who believe through the New Covenant in Christ. Jesus has made the way (Heb 10:19–22; John 10:7, 9; 11:25;14:6;).

KINGDOM OF PRIESTS

Adam was to produce a kingdom of priests, but instead he produced a world filled with defiled despots. But now the Second Adam sits as Lord on the throne at the right hand of the King of Heaven until his enemies are made a footstool for his feet. Hebrews quotes Psalm 110:1:

> . . . having offered one sacrifice for sins for all time, SAT DOWN AT THE RIGHT HAND OF GOD, [13] waiting from that time onward UNTIL HIS ENEMIES BE MADE A FOOTSTOOL FOR HIS FEET. (Heb 10:12–13)

This Adam takes defiled enemies and makes them his faithful subjects. This Adam is filling the earth with a kingdom of priests (Rev 1:6; 1 Pet 2:9). He is recreating them in his Glory image.

Image of the Lord

Jesus, the faithful priest-king, has been glorified and is clothed with the Glory-Spirit. John sees the Lord at the beginning of Revelation. He is the glorified Son of Man described in the likeness of the Father and Spirit. He is the king who images the King. As such, he is dressed as a priest. John writes,

> Then I turned to see the voice that was speaking with me. And having turned I saw seven golden lampstands; [13] and in the middle of the lampstands *I saw* one like a son of man, clothed in a robe reaching to the feet, and girded across His chest with a golden sash. [14] His head and His hair were white like white wool, like snow; and His eyes were like a flame of fire. [15] His feet *were* like burnished bronze, when it has been made to glow in a furnace, and His voice *was* like the sound of many waters. [16] In His right hand He held seven stars, and out of His mouth came

---

4. Bruce, *Hebrews*, 209.

a sharp two-edged sword; and His face was like the sun shining in its strength. (Rev 1:12–16)

He is the priest standing in the midst of the temple lampstands, the church. He has the priest keys (Rev 1:18; Isa 22:22). He wears the long robe, the ephod, and breast piece.[5] At the end of Revelation, the Lord's bride is dressed in priestly and temple garb to image the Lord. Like the priest, she is adorned with twelve stones (Rev 21:19–21). She is clothed in priestly linen (Rev 19:7–9).

The Law was not able to produce a kingdom of priests to image the King. What the Law could not do, Christ has done. Paul writes,

> But their minds were hardened . . . [17] Now the Lord is the Spirit, and where the Spirit of the Lord is, *there* is liberty. [18] But we all, with unveiled face, beholding as in a mirror the glory of the Lord, are being transformed into the same image from glory to glory, just as from the Lord, the Spirit. (2 Cor 3:14, 17–18)

The redeemed are transformed by the Glory of the Lord. This is a significant difference between the Old and New Covenants. Jeremiah writes of the New Covenant,

> I will put My law within them and on their heart I will write it; and I will be their God, and they shall be My people. (Jer 31:33)

Whereas the Law was written on stone and brought condemnation, the New Covenant is transformative. The Lord's Spirit writes the righteousness of God on the hearts of his people. They are given new hearts and live as image bearers of the King.

Kingdom Righteousness

The Lord's Spirit does not enable the redeemed to obey the Mosaic Law. The King's righteousness is infinitely greater than the Law given at Sinai. Jesus is quick to disavow any notion that he settles for a lower standard. Jesus says,

> Do not think that I came to abolish the Law or the Prophets; I did not come to abolish but to fulfill. [18] For truly I say to you, until heaven and earth pass away, not the smallest letter or stroke shall pass from the Law until all is accomplished. (Matt 5:17–18)

---

5. Kline, *Images*, 48f.

Far from Jesus dismissing the righteousness required by the Law, Jesus has come to bring about ultimate kingdom righteousness. But it is a kingdom righteousness that surpasses the Law given at Sinai (Matt 5:20). The Law said,

> "You shall not commit murder" and "Whoever commits murder shall be liable to the court" (Matt 5:21; cf. Exod 20:13).

But on this mountain, King Jesus says,

> ... everyone who is angry with his brother shall be guilty before the court; and whoever says to his brother, "You good-for-nothing," shall be guilty before the supreme court; and whoever says, "You fool," shall be guilty *enough* to go into the fiery hell. (Matt 5:22)

Six times Jesus contrasts what the Law required with the greater righteousness. The six references to the Law are chiastically arranged in three pairs:

A—You shall not commit murder (Matt 5:21)
   B—You shall not commit adultery (Matt 5:27)
      C—Give her a certificate of divorce (Matt 5:31)
      C'—You shall not make false vows (Matt 5:33)
   B'—An eye for an eye and tooth for a tooth (Matt 5:38)
A'—You shall love your neighbor and hate your enemy (Matt 5:43)

The C and C' discuss the marriage vow and false vows respectively. The B and B' are textually linked by the "eye" (Matt 5:29, 38). The A and A' share hatred. But the three pairs share more than verbal similarities. Jesus answers the A sections with a righteousness that requires humility. He says,

> Therefore if you are presenting your offering at the altar, and there remember that your brother has something against you, ²⁴ leave your offering there before the altar and go; first be reconciled to your brother, and then come and present your offering. ²⁵ Make friends quickly with your opponent at law while you are with him on the way. (Matt 5:23-25)

And again,

> But I say to you, love your enemies and pray for those who persecute you, ⁴⁵ so that you may be sons of your Father who is in heaven; for He causes His sun to rise on *the* evil and *the* good,

> and sends rain on *the* righteous and *the* unrighteous. (Matt 5:44–45)

In both of these sections, Jesus requires humility before God. Before making the offering, the offender is to humble himself and seek reconciliation. In the light of God's kindness, they are required to be as their Father in heaven and love and pray for their enemies.

The B sections are concerned with justice. Jesus says,

> If your right eye makes you stumble, tear it out and throw it from you; for it is better for you to lose one of the parts of your body, than for your whole body to be thrown into hell. (Matt 5:29)

And,

> ... whoever slaps you on your right cheek, turn the other to him also. (Matt 5:39)

The King requires a righteousness that does not show mercy to harbor one's own sin. But it is a righteousness that extends mercy to the injustice of others.

The C sections focus on faithfulness to vows. Jesus says,

> I say to you that everyone who divorces his wife, except for the reason of unchastity, makes her commit adultery; and whoever marries a divorced woman commits adultery. (Matt 5:32)

And again,

> ... let your statement be, "Yes, yes" or "No, no"; anything beyond these is of evil. (Matt 5:37)

Jesus requires faithfulness.

What is notable is the focus on humility, justice, and covenant faithfulness. They echo Micah's answer to the question, "With what shall I come to the Lord And bow myself before the God on high?" (Mic 6:6). God was faithful to his covenant with Israel in the days of Balak. What did the Law require of Israel? Micah writes,

> He has told you, O man, what is good; And what does the Lord require of you But to do justice, to love faithfulness, And to walk humbly with your God? (Mic 6:8 AT)

God required justice, covenant faithfulness, and humility before God. Israel broke the covenant and the toy kingdom was judged. But now, Jesus, the king of the kingdom of God, has come bringing righteous rule and obedience before God.

Jesus concludes the six contrasts between the Law and the righteousness he brings,

> Therefore, you will be perfect, as your Father who is in heaven is perfect. (Matt 5:48 AT)[6]

This kingdom righteousness is not a greater law to keep to obtain the blessings of the kingdom. This greater righteousness is the kingdom Jesus brings to those who are already confirmed in the blessings of the kingdom. Many commentators cannot let Jesus say what he says, and they translate the indicative "you will be perfect" into an imperative "be perfect." But that is exactly what Jesus is not saying. Jesus is promising the eschatological glorification. This New Covenant kingdom righteousness is the result of the obedience of Christ to the Pactum Salutis. He does not pronounce the kingdom righteousness as a condition for believers to receive the blessing. Because of his own obedience, he now fulfills all righteousness. He kept the stipulation to obtain the blessing. He sent the Spirit to apply both the blessing and transformational righteousness to believers. Like the Abrahamic promise, so is the New Covenant fulfillment: both are unconditional covenants based on the meritorious obedience of the Lord Jesus under the Pactum Salutis. The New Covenant blessings are received by faith, not covenant obedience. He starts by pronouncing those blessings.

Jesus' words do not start with covenant stipulations followed by covenant sanctions of curse and blessing. Jesus starts immediately with the blessing sanctions:

> Blessed are the poor in spirit . . .
> Blessed are those who mourn . . .
> Blessed are the gentle . . .
> Blessed are those who hunger and thirsts for righteousness.
> Blessed are the merciful . . .
> Blessed are the pure in heart . . .
> Blessed are the peacemakers . . .
> Blessed are those who have been persecuted . . . (Matt 5:3–10)

Jesus does not give any curse sanctions. He speaks to the redeemed. They are the salt of the earth, the light of the world. He starts with their standing

---

6. Ἔσεσθε οὖν ὑμεῖς τέλειοι ὡς ὁ πατὴρ ὑμῶν ὁ οὐράνιος τέλειός ἐστιν.

in the kingdom by the New Covenant. They are blessed. The judgment is adjudicated based on his obedience, and the covenant blessing is theirs. Someone may argue that the parallel passage is found in Luke 6, and that there are both blessings and curses:

> Blessed *are* you who are poor . . .
> Blessed *are* you who are hungry . . .
> Blessed *are* you who weep now . . .
> Blessed *are* you when men hate you . . .
> Woe to you who are rich . . .
> Woe to you who are well fed now . . .
> Woe *to you* who laugh now . . .
> Woe *to you* when speak well of you . . . (Luke 6:20–26)

But on closer examination, these are not blessing-and-curse sanctions of one covenant, but the blessings that belong to the redeemed under the New Covenant and the curses that belong to the unbeliever under the Covenant of Works in Adam.[7] But, in contrast to Sinai, there are no curses set before the redeemed. These are the blessings of being in Christ. Jesus starts his message,

> . . . for theirs is the kingdom of heaven.
> . . . for they shall be comforted.
> . . . for they shall inherit the earth.
> . . . for they shall be satisfied.
> . . . for they shall receive mercy.
> . . . for they shall see God.
> . . . for they shall be called sons of God.
> . . . for theirs is the kingdom of heaven (Matt 5:3–10)

The covenant blessings are theirs. And they will be a holy nation by the transforming grace of the Lord Jesus' Spirit.

TEMPLE BUILDER

The church is the holy nation, but the church is also the temple. The Lord Jesus sits at the right hand of the Father until he enemies are made to be a footstool for his feet. This footstool language immediately references the temple. Isaiah writes,

---

7. Cf. Isa 65:13–15; Jas 5:1–6.

> Thus says the LORD, "Heaven is My throne and the earth is My footstool. Where then is a house you could build for Me? And where is a place that I may rest? (Isa 66:1)

Jesus is seated at the right hand of the Father while he is building the eschatological temple-bride. The seven churches in Revelation are the seven lampstands of the temple. The Lord promises,

> He who overcomes, I will make him a pillar in the temple of My God, and he will not go out from it anymore; and I will write upon him the name of My God, and the name of the city of My God, the new Jerusalem, which comes down out of heaven from My God, and My new name. (Rev 3:12)

Jesus is the temple builder. God gave Ezekiel visions of the temple builder and the eschatological temple. Ezekiel writes,

> ... there was a man whose appearance was like the appearance of bronze, with a line of flax and a measuring rod in his hand. (Ezek 40:3)

His appearance is like the theophany of the Lord in Daniel. He is the builder.[8] He showed Ezekiel the inner and outer courts, the pillars, the area for sacrifices, and the altar. But this is not another little temple that would be built in Canaan. This is the eschatological royal temple of the Lord Jesus and his bride seen in Revelation 21. This is not the toy;[9] this temple is the church. Ezekiel describes this coming temple as like a "city" (Ezek 40:2). But the Glory of God will fill the entirety of this temple-city, not just the holy of holies (Ezek 40:35; cf. Jer 3:16–17). The dimensions of Ezekiel's temple dwarf anything built before. Using the toy to describe the reality, the temple is the same size as the city, roughly a square mile. The water trickles out of the temple and becomes a large river that brings life even to the Dead Sea (Ezek 47:10).

The Lord Jesus fills the earth with the temple. Seated at the right hand of the Father, all authority is his. Before he ascends, he tells the disciples,

> All authority has been given to Me in heaven and on earth. **19** Go therefore and make disciples of all the nations, baptizing them in the name of the Father and the Son and the Holy Spirit, **20** teaching them to observe all that I commanded you; and lo, I am with you always, even to the end of the age. (Matt 28:18–20)

---

8. Zech 2:1; Rev 11:1.
9. Beale, *Temple*, 340ff.

He commissions them to fill the earth with his temple-bride. Their commission is not the basis of their blessing. Their blessing is the basis of their commission. As Kline writes,

> But Jesus does not summon the church to earn the eternal kingdom by obedience to the demands of the new covenant. Rather, it is as the one who, by the active and passive obedience of his life and death, has already merited salvation and the glory of the kingdom for his church that Jesus addresses to his disciples the great commission.[10]

When the Lord Jesus ascended to the Father, he sent his Glory-Spirit to fill the bride-temple at Pentecost for witness to the nations.

PUTTING ON CHRIST

Historia Salutis and the *Ordo Salutis*

Theologians have used the Latin *historia salutis* ("history of salvation") to denote the actual historical events in God's redemptive work. God made a promise to Abraham, delivered Israel in the exodus, and made a promise to King David. Jesus was incarnated in a virgin, was proclaimed to be God's Son at his baptism, faced Satan in the temptation in the wilderness, proclaimed the kingdom, died on the cross, was resurrected, and ascended to the Father. In distinction, the *ordo salutis*, the order of salvation, refers to the application of redemption in the believer. God issues a general call of salvation, the Spirit gives the sinner a new heart that results in faith, and the believer is justified, becomes the child of God, and is sanctified and glorified.

Paul often uses the words "in Christ" to reference the union the believer has with Christ. At root, the union references Christ's legal federal headship to the elect. All who were represented by Adam were "in Adam," and all who are represented by Christ are "in Christ" (1 Cor 15:22). This legal union is the basis for the manifestation in the believer's life. The Lord Jesus' obedience to the Pactum Salutis and consequential enthronement is the legal obedience of the believer and enthronement at the right hand of the Father (Eph 2:6). What Jesus did as federal head in the *historia salutis* is the basis for the application to the believer in the *ordo salutis*. What is legally true "in Christ" becomes experientially true in the believer's redemption.

---

10. Kline, *Glory*, 169.

Justification

There is a popular little quip that defines justification as "just as if I had never sinned." But Christ's sacrificial death does more than take the sinner back to the sinless state. Christ's work was not only to suffer in passive obedience to the Father, but he also yielded an active obedience to the stipulations of the Pactum Salutis. The righteousness required for eschatological glory is not sinlessness, but perfect obedience. Paul writes,

> ... the doers of the Law will be justified. (Rom 2:13)

This is the righteousness that issues forth in "glory and honor and peace to everyone who does good" (Rom 2:10). This is a blessing given "according to his deeds" (Rom 2:6). But, as noted earlier, this blessing is given in the context of a works covenant, for God was not required to make a world in which this blessing was given in recompense for doing good. But in the Covenant of Works with Adam and the Pactum Salutis with the Second Adam, this is the blessing sanction given to the covenant obedience required by the covenant. Covenant righteousness is required to receive glory.

The Lord Jesus was "appointed"[11] to be the Son of God by the resurrection. This is not a denial of the deity of the Second Person of the Trinity, the Son of God. But within the context of the Pactum Salutis, Jesus was appointed to be the Son of God by the resurrection. Referring to the resurrection, the psalmist writes, "today I have begotten Thee" (Ps 2:7; cf. Acts 13:33; Heb 1:5). Because of his obedience, the Father exalted him. Paul writes,

> Being found in appearance as a man, He humbled Himself by becoming obedient to the point of death, even death on a cross.
> 9 For this reason also, God highly exalted Him. (Phil 2:8–9)

The resurrection is the Father's "justification"[12] of Jesus as the obedient covenant son. In the resurrection, Jesus is declared righteous to the stipulations of the Pactum Salutis. His righteousness is not just sinlessness; it is perfect covenant obedience, even to undergo the wrath of God. This is his active obedience: not to actively obey in his passive obedience, but to

---

11. ὁρισθέντος *horizo*; Rom 1:4.
12. Declared to be righteous.

actively obey the covenant requirements. So he merited the glory and was exalted to the right hand of the Father.[13]

Paul connects Jesus' resurrection and the believer's justification when he writes,

> ... who was delivered over because of our transgressions,
> and was raised because of our justification. (Rom 4:25)

Adam's sin left mankind with a twofold condition that prohibited its eschatological blessing. Sinners have broken the covenant and are justly condemned, and they have failed to keep the covenant stipulations. The Second Adam has addressed both. He suffered the damnation due to the transgression, and he merited the eschatological blessing by his covenant-keeping righteousness. He went to the cross because of "transgressions," and he was resurrected because of "justification." His atoning sacrifice removed sin; his covenant-keeping righteousness attested to by his resurrection merits the blessing for the elect. His justification, declaration to be the covenant-keeping righteous son, is the basis for declaring the believer to be the righteous covenant keeper. God's justification of the believer is the legal application of the federal head's covenant-keeping righteousness. The believer is legally accounted to have kept the covenant because Jesus kept the covenant. So, by faith the believer is declared to be "righteous" based on the imputed righteousness of Christ. When the believer believes the gospel, he puts on the righteousness of Christ in justification.

Adoption

Justification is the declaration that the believer has fulfilled the righteous demands of the covenant. In the context of the Pactum Salutis, this is concurrently a legal declaration that the believer is child of God. The Second Adam kept the stipulations and so is exalted to Glory as righteous son. In Christ, the elect receive by faith the sanctioned blessing of the Pactum Salutis. So the believer is declared to be the covenant-keeping child of God. Adoption is not some second act of God when a believer trusts in Christ. Both justification and adoption are applications of the believer's covenantal union in Christ under the Pactum Salutis. Christ is the righteous son who kept the covenant stipulations. He is declared so. So, the

---

13. John 17:4–5.

believer is also declared the righteous son of God who legally kept the covenant stipulations in Christ. Adoption is the believer's new citizenship.

This covenant application is the fruition under the New Covenant of the kingdom secured by the obedience of the Second Adam under the Pactum Salutis. If Adam had obeyed the Covenant of Works and passed the probation, he and all he represented as federal head would have been confirmed in covenant-keeping righteousness though their kingdom work of filling the earth with the family of God and building what was to be the eschatological temple still laid before them. So, the Second Adam kept the Pactum Salutis and has secured the outcome, the eschatological temple. He is seated at the right hand of the Father, and believers, legally in him, are confirmed in righteousness (Eph 2:6). Now he is turning enemies into citizens of his kingdom.

When Jesus' biological family came to take him away, Jesus said,

> "Who are My mother and My brothers?" ^{34} Looking about at those who were sitting around Him, He said, "Behold My mother and My brothers! ^{35} For whoever does the will of God, he is My brother and sister and mother." (Mark 3:33–35)

The redeemed community is the eschatological kingdom family. John writes,

> But as many as received Him, to them He gave the right to become children of God, *even* to those who believe in His name . . . (John 1:12)

So Hebrews says,

> . . . He is not ashamed to call them brethren . . . (Heb 2:11)

Paul calls them the "sons of God" (Rom 8:19).

Adam was commissioned to multiply and fill the earth with the kingdom people who would ultimately be the glorified temple humanity. God said, "Be fruitful and multiply, and fill the earth, and subdue it" (Gen 1:28). But the earth became the graveyard instead of the kingdom. The genealogies in Genesis 5 and 11 record Adam's failure. But the seed of Eve will fill the earth with the kingdom people (Gen 3:15). Abraham is promised that the kingdom is his in the seed, which is Christ (Gal 3:16). This promise is not fulfilled in the twelve toy tribes, which Paul says are the children of Sinai and are slaves like Hagar. The seed is Christ, and the children of the kingdom are from "the Jerusalem above is free; she is our mother" (Gal 4:26).

Sanctification

The believer is confirmed in the covenant-keeping righteousness of the Second Adam and accounted now to be the child of God seated in Christ at the right hand of God. The believer has become member of the holy nation, the kingdom of priests. The transformation of the believer to be in the image of the Lord Jesus is sanctification. Paul is clear that the elect are saved to be "conformed to the image of His Son, that he might be the firstborn among many brethren" (Rom 8:29). The Second Adam is the first of the many sons of the kingdom. His sonship is theirs, and they are conformed to his image that the kingdom would be filled with those bearing his holiness. Paul writes the Ephesians, "put on the new man, the one created according to God in righteousness and holiness of the truth" (Eph 4:24 AT).

He is the Lord of Glory, the temple of the Glory-Spirit. The redeemed are his body, the temple filled with the Spirit. This truth is the basis for the unity of the church.

> For He Himself is our peace, who made both groups into one and broke down the barrier of the dividing wall ... [19] So then you are no longer strangers and aliens, but you are fellow citizens with the saints, and are of God's household, [20] having been built on the foundation of the apostles and prophets, Christ Jesus Himself being the corner stone, [21] in whom the whole building, being fitted together, is growing into a holy temple in the Lord, [22] in whom you also are being built together into a dwelling of God in the Spirit. (Eph 2:14, 19–22)

Because the believer is the dwelling of the Spirit, he is called to walk in righteousness. Paul writes,

> Or do you not know that your body is a temple of the Holy Spirit who is in you, whom you have from God, and that you are not your own? [20] For you have been bought with a price: therefore glorify God in your body. (1 Cor 6:19–20)

The believer is not transformed by standing before the Law of Moses, but as he lives in the presence of the Lord Jesus. Moses' face shone after being in the presence of the Glory-cloud, but the covenant brought only condemnation because it did not have the power to transform the Israelites. In contrast, the New Covenant is a ministry that brings life. Paul writes,

> For if the ministry of condemnation has glory, much more does the ministry of righteousness abound in glory. (2 Cor 3:9)

It is not a ministry of righteousness because the Spirit now enables the elect to keep the stipulations of the covenant and thus receive the sanctioned blessing Israel failed to obtain. That would be another covenant of works. The New Covenant is a ministry of righteousness because it is the application of the merited blessings of the Pactum Salutis. The believer stands in the finished covenant-keeping righteousness of Jesus and in him is now exalted to the right hand of the Father. He is the glorified Lord, and his Spirit now applies the benefits of his finished work to the believer. The Spirit of Christ gives a living heart and faith as the believer is declared righteous by the righteousness that completely found in Christ. The Lord's Spirit is given to the believer "the Spirit of adoption" (Rom 8:15). And the Lord's Spirit brings transformation to renew the believer in the image of the Lord Jesus.

As the Lord Jesus is the image of God, so the Spirit of the Lord transforms the believer into the likeness of the Lord Jesus that the new family of God bear the image of God in Christ. Moses' face shone, but the glory faded and Israel was condemned. Jesus' face shines as the Lord of Glory at the right hand of the King of Heaven with an unfading glory, and his Glory-Spirit now brings freedom from the Law of sin and death.[14]

> Now the Lord is the Spirit, and where the Spirit of the Lord is, there is liberty. **18** But we all, with unveiled face, beholding as in a mirror the glory of the Lord, are being transformed into the same image from glory to glory, just as from the Lord, the Spirit. (2 Cor 3:17–18)

The believer is being transformed into the image of the Lord as he beholds the Lord of Glory.

Glorification

Sabbath glory was the sanctioned blessing promised Adam in the Covenant of Works. Abraham was promised the kingdom from heaven (Heb 11:6). Moses looked to the eschatological kingdom, which made

---

14. Rom 8:2.

the reproach of Christ "greater riches than the treasures of Egypt" (Heb 11:26). The believer has not been brought again to stand before Sinai. The believer has been given citizenship in heaven.[15] Paul writes,

> For our citizenship is in heaven, from which also we eagerly wait for a Savior, the Lord Jesus Christ; **21** who will transform the body of our humble state into conformity with the body of His glory, by the exertion of the power that He has even to subject all things to Himself. (Phil 3:20–21)

When he comes, the Lord Jesus will bring his people body and soul to Glory.[16] Adam brought many sons to shame and damnation, but the Second Adam's obedience has brought the believer to legal claim on heaven. Hebrews says,

> But you have come to Mount Zion and to the city of the living God, the heavenly Jerusalem, and to myriads of angels, **23** to the general assembly and church of the firstborn who are enrolled in heaven, and to God, the Judge of all, and to the spirits of *the* righteous made perfect, **24** and to Jesus, the mediator of a new covenant. (Heb 12:22–24)

In Christ, the believer has already come legally to the heavenly Jerusalem. And as the Lord's Spirit is the earnest[17] of the Glory-Spirit, the believer now is already participating in the heavenly city. The New Covenant is not a covenant to keep; it is the application of covenant blessings merited by the covenant kept by Christ in the Pactum Salutis.

THE GOSPEL

Paul's letter to the Romans is perhaps the clearest articulation of the juxtaposition of the Second Adam's meriting the kingdom in the Pactum Salutis and the reception of the kingdom by grace through faith in the New Covenant. If Adam had passed the probation of the Covenant of Works, all his offspring would have been confirmed in covenant righteousness and been assured of the eschatological sabbath glory. So too, now the kingdom the Second Adam merited in the Pactum Salutis is confirmed to the believer in the New Covenant. For many, this will seem like a strange

---

15. Eph 2:19.
16. Heb 2:10: "bring many sons to *Glory.*"
17. Eph 1:13–14.

thesis. Where does Romans talk about the kingdom of God, the Pactum Salutis, or even the New Covenant?

Generally, Protestants have read Romans with an eye on the elements of the *ordo salutis*, the "order of salvation." The focus has been on what Romans says about the believer's justification, the atonement for his sin, sanctification, adoption, glorification, or free will and predestination. The closest Protestants have usually come to seeing the bigger picture of redemptive history has been the discussion of the Jew-and-Gentile problem in Romans 9–11. Evangelicals have generally thought of Romans as developing the need for the gospel in chapters 1–3, setting forth the atoning work of Christ in chapter 3, defending justification through faith in chapter 4, briefly referencing the work of Christ in contrast to the sin of Adam in chapter 5, discussing the believer's sanctification in chapters 6–8, digressing to discuss God's gospel purpose for the Jews and Gentiles in 9–11, and applying the gospel in chapters 12–16. Certainly Romans does have much to say regarding the *ordo salutis*.

However, in recent years an argument has been made among Protestants that the focus of Romans is not so much on the elements of the *ordo salutis*, but rather the history of redemption is center stage with its primary focus on the Jew-Gentile problem. This mono-covenantal approach, known as the "New Perspective on Paul," has argued that Paul's primary concern in Romans is the inclusion of the Gentiles into the church. While a full critique is beyond the scope of this book, this nomistic reading is strongly condemned by Paul in Galatians! Yes, Paul is focused on the history of redemption and is very concerned with the Jew-Gentile problem. But the gospel proclaimed in Romans is more cosmic and depends on the essential contrast of meritorious works and the faith that receives by grace!

The Second Adam is Victorious

Paul immediately provides the reader with Romans' thesis. Christ Jesus the Lord has been enthroned Son of God and has brought the eschatological age of the Spirit.[18] Paul writes,

> ... concerning His Son, who was born of a seed of David according to the flesh, ⁴ who was declared the Son of God with

---

18. Moo, *Romans*, 47–50.

> power by the resurrection from the dead, according to the Spirit of holiness, Jesus Christ our Lord. (Rom 1:3–4 AT)

The eternal Son of God became the incarnate Second Adam. Now, through his covenant-keeping obedience, the Second Adam has been enthroned Son of God, the Lord. He is the king pictured by and promised to David. He is the king who brings the kingdom filled with image-bearing obedient Gentiles. God promised Abraham he would be a father of many nations. Now the kingdom has come, which does not just fill the borders of Palestine but fills the earth. Paul writes,

> ... through whom we have received grace and apostleship to bring about *the* obedience of faith among all the Gentiles for His name's sake ... (Rom 1:5)

Adam was to multiply and fill the earth with the citizens of the kingdom of God. He did not. But the king has come, and already his kingdom redemption is reaching to the ends of the earth. Paul writes,

> First, I thank my God through Jesus Christ for you all, because your faith is being proclaimed throughout the whole world. (Rom 1:8)

This is the gospel, the power of God to save Jew and Gentile. Paul writes,

> For I am not ashamed of the gospel, for it is the power of God for salvation to everyone who believes, to the Jew first and also to the Greek. [17] For in it *the* righteousness of God is revealed from faith to faith; as it is written, "But the righteous man shall live by faith." (Rom 1:16–17)

What Adam did not do, the Second Adam has done. Christ Jesus is the vassal king Adam failed to be.

Paul then turns to consequences of Adam's disobedience to the Covenant of Works. He did not obey and obtain the sabbath glory as federal head. His disobedience brought the wrath of God on all men. Paul writes,

> For the wrath of God is revealed from heaven against all ungodliness and unrighteousness of men who suppress the truth in unrighteousness ... (Rom 1:18)

They have exchanged the Glory of God for idols (Rom 1:23). They dishonored the Creator and embraced "the lie" (Rom 1:25). Adam had been offered the eternal eschatological Glory, but when Eve offered him an apple, he ate! The resulting universal ruin is ever present.

The Law-keeping Jew has not escaped Adam's guilt and God's condemnation. Paul continues,

> Therefore you have no excuse, everyone of you who passes judgment, for in that which you judge another, you condemn yourself; for you who judge practice the same things. (Rom 2:1)

Though they had the Law of God, they did the very same things they condemned. Paul writes,

> But because of your stubbornness and your unrepentant heart, you are storing up wrath against yourself for the day of God's wrath, when his righteous judgment will be revealed. (Rom 2:5)

Paul then sets before them the covenant sanctions of the Covenant of Works that remain to be adjudicated, but hang over them with condemnation. All who are found to be righteous by the terms of the covenant will received "glory, honor and immortality ... eternal life" (Rom 2:7; see 2:10). But those who have embraced the lie and evil will receive "wrath and anger" (Rom 2:8). It doesn't matter whether you are a Jew or a Gentile (2:9–10); the sanctions of the Covenant of Works with Adam are universal. Adam sinned; all sinned. All are covenant breakers. There is none righteous before the King of Heaven (3:9ff.). All are under the power of sin.

The Law revealed the righteousness of God, but it did not provide righteousness. Rather, Jew and Gentile alike are condemned by it. But the Law did point to the righteousness from heaven. Paul writes,

> But now apart from the Law the righteousness of God has been manifested, to which the Law and the Prophets testify. (Rom 3:21 AT)

The righteousness that comes through faith was known before Christ, but in the work of Christ the righteousness of God is seen. Christ obeyed the righteous requirements of God in the Pactum Salutis. His passive obedience on the cross propitiated the wrath of God for sin committed under the Covenant of Works (Rom 3:25). Too, in his active obedience, he merited the blessing under the Pactum Salutis. So God is just. He has punished sin, and rewarded Christ's covenant righteousness. Christ has brought redemption (Rom 3:24). Christ has paid the price. Though believers receive the gift purely by grace, their reception of the righteousness of Christ is purely a matter of legal reciprocity.

For Paul to speak of justification is not merely removal of sin. To be justified by faith is to be legally righteous through faith. This righteousness is not absence of sin, but active covenant obedience. Paul concluded in Romans 3:10ff. that there is none who is righteous. As Paul delineated in Romans 2, God will judge every man according to his works. To those who "obey unrighteousness, wrath and indignation" (Rom 2:8). They are those who do "evil" (Rom 2:9). But to the one who does good, "glory and honor" (Rom 2:7). They are those who do good (Rom 2:10). They are recompensed with "glory and honor" (Rom 2:10). The covenant blessing to the righteous is "ACCORDING TO HIS DEEDS" (Rom 2:6) and covenant judgment is repaid to the unrighteous.

So how can those who are condemned be counted as covenant keepers? In Adam, there is only condemnation. But in Christ, the believer is legally the righteous covenant keeper. Imputed righteousness is the legal accounting that the righteous record of Christ, the Second Adam federal head, has become the legal record of the believer through faith. So God is just and justifies those who believe.

Righteousness is legal obedience to the covenant Law. Joseph was a righteous man in relationship to the Mosaic Law (Matt 1:19). Daniel is presented as a righteous servant of God through the first six chapters of Daniel. But in Daniel 9:5 he confessed his own unrighteousness before God. Righteousness is never a matter of the creature before the Creator outside a covenant context. There is no human history outside man's covenant relationship with God in Adam or in Christ.

The legal merit of Christ is given by grace to all who believe. God is just—it is a matter of law and righteousness. Sinners are counted covenantally righteous through faith by grace. Paul then turns to the promise made to Abraham. Abraham did not earn rights to the kingdom. Abraham through faith became heir of the kingdom. He became heir because he was righteous, but the righteousness was not his but the righteousness of Christ made his through faith (Rom 4:13). Paul concludes with the twofold work of Christ. He was "delivered over because of our transgressions, and was raised because of our justification" (Rom 4:25). In the cross he took the curse of the Covenant of Works, and in the cross he fulfilled the righteous stipulation of the Pactum Salutis. The resurrection declared his righteousness, and through faith the believer is counted righteous, "justified."

Paul immediately moves to the sanctioned blessing and writes,

> Therefore, having been justified by faith, we have peace with God through our Lord Jesus Christ, 2 through whom also we

> have obtained our introduction by faith into this grace in which
> we stand; and we exult in hope of the glory of God. (Rom 5:1-2)

Now that the believer has been counted righteous, he has "peace" with God. The "peace" is not just a reference to relationship of the believer with God, but is derived from the *shalom* of the Old Testament. It is "God's eschatological intervention."[19] Jeremiah promises,

> "For I know the plans that I have for you," declares the LORD, "plans for peace [*shalom*] and not for calamity to give you a future and a hope." (Jer 29:11 AT)

The benediction of Numbers 6:26 is that "The LORD lift up His countenance on you and give you peace."[20] This is not the promise of an inner feeling, but the blessing of the covenant. In the context of the Covenant of Works, it is "eternal life" (Rom 2:7, 10). It is the eschatological blessing of "glory and honor." The eschatological blessing belongs to the righteous through faith. So the believer exults in the "hope of the glory of God" (Rom 5:2). In Adam's sin, all "fall short of the glory of God" (Rom 3:23). But now, in the righteousness of Christ through faith, the believer is assured of that eschatological blessing.

Though Paul has been discussing the contrast between the Second Adam and the first Adam throughout the first four and a half chapters of Romans, Paul deliberately lays out the contrast between the reign of death that came on all in the disobedience of Adam with the reign of eschatological kingdom life that has now come through the covenant obedience of the Second Adam to all who believe (Rom 5:12-21).

Paul then articulates the transition of the believer from death in Adam to resurrection life in Christ in chapter 6. The discussion of the old man, the "flesh," is a reference to all who are in Adam. Parenthetically, then Paul discusses the inability of the Law to bring freedom from sin (Rom 7). Paul continues the Adamic contrast in chapter 8. Paul declares that in contrast to Adam and in contrast to the Law's inability to bring deliverance, Christ has brought the freedom of kingdom righteousness. Paul writes,

> Therefore there is now no condemnation for those who are in Christ Jesus. **2** For the law of the Spirit of life in Christ Jesus has set you free from the law of sin and of death. (Rom 8:1-2)

---

19. Moo, *Romans*, 139.
20. *shalom.*

Though Paul digressed to discuss the inability of the Law to bring kingdom righteousness, Paul is still contrasting those in Adam and those in Christ. Paul declares that the believer in no longer under the wrath of God for breaking the covenant in Adam. Paul reaches back to chapter 5 and uses *katakrima*, "condemnation," which is only used in the New Testament in Romans 8:1 and 5:15, 18. The believer's sin has been atoned for. But that does not leave them as members of the old world "without sin" in Adam. They are now in Christ, citizens of the eschatological kingdom. They have been set free by the "law of the Spirit of life in Christ Jesus." Those in Christ are no longer under the authority of the Law, which resulted in sin and death in Adam. The law of the Spirit resulting in life through the obedience of Christ has freed the believer, in Christ.

Romans 8 is full of references to the Spirit. The kingdom has come. Whereas the Spirit created Adam in the image of the King of Heaven, and Adam's offspring images where to fill the earth as temple images of the King, the result of Adam's transgression of the Covenant of Works was a world filled with sin and graves. But now the faithful vassal king, the Second Adam, has come and is enthroned victorious. He is robed in the Spirit-Glory of the King of Heaven; he is image of the King. The Spirit of the Lord Jesus now applies the victory of the Second Adam to believers. The Spirit gives freedom from the penalty of sin. The Spirit transforms the believer into the image of the righteous Lord Jesus. Being in Christ means the believer is in the Spirit (Rom 8:9) and has a new mind, a mind set on the things of the Spirit. The Spirit that brought death and condemnation to all in Adam is now life to those in Christ. For in Christ they are counted righteous (Rom 8:10; see 5:21). The Spirit of the enthroned Christ will ultimately bring resurrection Glory to the believer's body. Those who are in Christ are putting to death the deeds of the body by the Spirit. Theirs is life. They are the citizens of the kingdom, the royal humanity, the sons of God (Rom 8:14). The Spirit that created Adam to fill the kingdom with a royal humanity is the Spirit of the Lord Jesus now filling the kingdom with the sons of God (Rom 8:15). As sons, in the enthroned Lord Jesus Christ, believers are fellow heirs with Christ to the Glory (Rom 8:17). As Abraham was promised the kingdom in his seed, so now believers receive the kingdom in the seed, Christ. The Lord Jesus' Spirit will bring them to glory. He leads and intercedes for the believer. Chapter 8 is not so much a call for believers to cooperate in sanctification as it is descriptive of the powerful victorious work of the enthroned Second Adam's Spirit. He contrasts the frustration that came on creation through the transgression of Adam with the Glory that belongs to the believer (Rom 8:18ff.). Paul concludes,

> But in all these things we overwhelmingly conquer through Him who loved us. 38 For I am convinced that neither death, nor life, nor angels, nor principalities, nor things present, nor things to come, nor powers, 39 nor height, nor depth, nor any other created thing, will be able to separate us from the love of God, which is in Christ Jesus our Lord. (Rom 8:37-39)

Paul then turns to address the Jew-Gentile question. Though chapters 9-11 specifically address this issue, Paul continues to address the question in the context of the Lord Jesus as Second Adam. Paul started the letter with the bold declaration that Isaiah's promise that God would come and bring salvation "to everyone who believes, to the Jew first and also to the Greek" (Rom 1:16) has been fulfilled in the Lord Jesus Christ. Throughout the section, Isaiah is the prominent Old Testament background. Isaiah promised that God would come and bring salvation to the Jews and to the Gentiles. Paul references the Isaiah promises throughout (Rom 9:27-29, 33; 10:11, 15-16, 20-21; 11:8, 26-27, 34; 12:11; 15:12, 21). Like the Gospel writers, Paul proclaims clearly that the Pactum Salutis promised in Isaiah has been fulfilled in the exalted Second Adam, the Lord Jesus Christ. His Spirit now applies the blessings of that covenant to the redeemed, Jew and Gentile alike. A central hallmark to the promise of the Pactum Salutis in Isaiah is the salvation that brings the Gentiles from the ends of the earth into the kingdom of God. Paul sees his own ministry to the Gentiles as the proclamation of the blessing secured by the work of Christ applied by the Spirit of the enthroned Lord Jesus to build the temple[21] of God (Rom 15:14-21).

Heirs by Faith

Paul's gospel declaration to the Romans that Jesus has received the kingdom as the obedient Second Adam in the Pactum Salutis, as Isaiah foretold, is matched in clarity by his bold proclamation that the kingdom the Lord Jesus merited is received by grace through faith alone in the New Covenant. Jesus referred to both covenants when he told the disciples,

---

21. Rom 9:33; 15:20.

And I covenant to you, just as my Father covenanted to me the kingdom, **30** that you may eat and drink at My table in My kingdom." (Luke 22:29–30 AT)

Though Paul doesn't use the term, he is very clear that he is talking about the New Covenant. In Romans 11:26–27, Paul quotes Isaiah:

> THE DELIVERER WILL COME FROM ZION,
> HE WILL REMOVE UNGODLINESS FROM JACOB.
> **27** THIS IS MY COVENANT WITH THEM,
> WHEN I TAKE AWAY THEIR SINS.

This covenant is in the context of the Abrahamic Covenant (Rom 9:5–9). It is actually the fulfillment of the Abrahamic Covenant (Rom 4:1ff., 13; 11:1, 15ff., 28). Isaiah writes,

> "A Redeemer will come to Zion,
> And to those who turn from transgression in Jacob," declares the LORD.
> **21** "As for Me, this is My covenant with them," says the LORD: "My Spirit which is upon you, and My words which I have put in your mouth shall not depart from your mouth, nor from the mouth of your offspring, nor from the mouth of your offspring's offspring," says the Lord, "from now and forever." (Isa 59:20–21)

In contrast to the covenant with the redeemer, the servant of the Lord, here God's covenant is with the redeemed. Isaiah says that God saw the injustice and oppression by the enemies of his people. There was no man to interceded for his people (Isa 59:16). God clothed himself for war to repay his adversaries "according to *their* deeds," to bring "recompense to His enemies" (Isa 59:18). But in faithfulness to his promises to Abraham, God would redeem his kingdom people. Christ the Lord, vassal king of God, has now been exalted to the heavenly Zion (see Heb 12:22–23). The kingdom blessings he secured are covenanted with the redeemed. The Spirit of the King of Heaven now clothes the Redeemer, the Lord Jesus. Applied to the redeemed, they now are the holy people of the kingdom. The Spirit and the word of God will never depart from them.

Like Abraham, the redeemed are heirs to the kingdom by grace through faith alone (Rom 4:1ff., 13). The death sanction due them under the Covenant of Works has been satisfied (Rom 3:25; 8:1). Through faith they have received the meritorious righteous record of the Lord Jesus (Rom 4:25; 5:12ff.). They are transformed into the image of the Lord Jesus by his Spirit (Rom 6; 8:29), and are the kingdom family of God (Rom

8:15–23). And theirs is the kingdom Glory (Rom 8:30). God's Spirit and word will forever be theirs. They look forward, as coheirs of the Lord Jesus, to the day when the eschatological sabbath *shalom* will come. Paul encourages his readers, "the God of peace will soon crush Satan under your feet" (Rom 16:20). The Lord Jesus has crushed his head; so too, believers are victorious!

Section Three

The Reward

8

The New Covenant Blessing

THE REWARD

THE COVENANT BLESSINGS OF the New Covenant are received by the believer by grace through faith. All the blessings the believer receives were merited by the Lord Jesus under the terms of the Pactum Salutis. This singular source of all the blessings has been obfuscated by the use of "reward" in translating words in the Old and New Testament. There is an equivocation between the older meaning of "reward," which is representative of underlying Hebrew or Greek terms, and the current usage of the term. This has encouraged a bifurcation in which salvation is received by grace and additional rewards are granted according to the believer's works. There is no basis for this division in the term itself in the Old or New Testament usage.

The Linguistic Background

The word "reward" is actually a slippery term. A brief glance at the *Oxford English Dictionary* shows a range of use through the years. In the fourteenth century, "reward" could refer to "regard, consideration, or heed; estimation or worth." This use is obsolete. "Reward" could also mean "recompense or retribution for wrongdoing." It is still used for getting the punishment deserved. J. Irving wrote in 1980, "Ronkers was very sympathetic to his venereal patients and did not make them feel steeped in sin or wallowing in their just rewards." Though it is rare now, it can also refer to the remuneration or pay given for work done. E. Marshall wrote in 1904, "An equitable reward should be given to the menhadener for towing a ship."[1] More commonly, it means, "recompense ... for some service, merit, or favour, or for hardship endured." Familiar is the use for "money offered for information leading to the solving of a crime."[2] Psychology has a technical use for the term in behavioral theory. Businesses like to use the term to refer to an incentive for repeat patronage. The definition has changed over time with usage, and is now rarely used to denote pay for work done. Rather, today's general use is

> ... something that is given in return for good or evil done or received or that is offered or given for some service or attainment.[3]

A preschooler who was good for the day may receive a sticker as a reward. An employee who works overtime finishing a significant project may be rewarded to acknowledge their work. But a worker who picks up his paycheck at the end of the pay period is not receiving a reward. He worked for it; they paid him. The employer is obligated to pay his wages.[4] Reward is not part of the picture. A reward is an extra, a bonus recognition for service or attainment.

Though both the rare meaning of recompense or pay for work done and the common usage for recompense or recognition for service, merit, or favor both share the idea of something received in consequence of something done, there is a crucial distinction between the two definitions. When the employer pays the employee, there is a legal necessity to pay what is owed. But when the teacher gives the preschooler a sticker to reward good behavior, the teacher is under no such obligation to recompense. It is not obligated payment for work done. A survey of the words translated "reward" in the English Bible demonstrate that just payment for work done is in view instead of the more common notion of "recompense" or recognition for something done.

---

1. Marshall, *Middle Wall*, 447.
2. *OED*, s.v. "reward."
3. *Merriam-Webster.com Dictionary*, s.v. "reward," https://www.merriam-webster.com/dictionary/reward.
4. Rom 4:4.

There is a spectrum of views among those who argue that God "rewards" believers for the good works they do. Some come very close to saying that the believer is saved by grace and rewarded for their works—paid for their works done! Others shy away from this, sensing the tension between grace and payment earned for works done. They often say that the believer is saved by grace and receives rewards corresponding to their works, by grace. Some will even say that God "rewards" believers to recognize the works they did that he enabled. But nonetheless, each of these make "reward" something additional to the salvation and kingdom received by every believer.

The Bible does not have a category for "reward" outside of the blessing offered in the covenant. The English translation equivocates on "reward." The terms translated "reward" in both the Old and New Testament refer to payment or just recompense for work done. But the common meaning of "reward" causes the reader to import a meaning of an additional recompense or recognition beyond the covenant blessing of salvation and kingdom received by every believer. This common-use meaning for "reward" is absent from the Bible.

Both the Old and New Testaments use words that have been often translated "reward." Psalm 19:11 promises the Law keeper,

> ... by them your servant is warned;
> in keeping them there is great reward [*eqeb*, עֵקֶב].

This word translated "reward" is also translated "consequence."[5] In Isaiah 5:23, *eqeb* is translated, "Who justify the wicked in consequence of a bribe" (AT). Psalm 40:15 reads, "Let those be appalled according to the consequence of their shame" (AT). In light of this meaning, *eqeb* is used as a conjunction translated "because."[6] Numbers 14:24 says,

> But My servant Caleb, because [*eqeb*] he has had a different
> spirit and has followed Me fully, I will bring into the land which
> he entered, and his seed shall take possession of it. (AT)

God would bless Caleb for his faithful obedience. He would enter the promised land with his descendants because he followed the Lord fully. Caleb would be blessed in consequence, because (*eqeb*) he followed God. Is this a "reward"? As the psalmist acknowledged the "great consequence" of keeping the Law, the "reward" is the sanctioned blessing under the

---

5. Brown, *Hebrew*, 784.
6. Brown, *Hebrew*, 784.

Mosaic Covenant. The "reward" is the legal consequence under the Old Covenant. So Caleb following God fully means he is a covenant keeper who enjoys the legal consequence under the Law. This same covenant blessing is expressed in Proverbs. Proverbs 22:4 says, "Because [*eqeb*] of humility and the fear of Yahweh, riches, honor and life" (AT). Deuteronomy 7:12–13 makes explicit the consequence of covenant blessing to covenant obedience. Moses writes,

> Then it shall come about, because (*eqeb*) you listen to these judgments and keep and do them, that the Lord your God will keep with you the covenant and the lovingkindness which He swore to your forefathers. ¹³ He will love you and bless you and multiply you; He will also bless the fruit of your womb and the fruit of your ground, your grain and your new wine and your oil, the increase of your herd and the young of your flock, in the land which He swore to your forefathers to give you.

The translation of *eqeb* as "reward" does not align with the modern use of "reward." There is a legal, covenantal relationship between the obedience and the consequential blessing. This use of *eqeb* is also found in Genesis 22:18 and 26:5. Because (*eqeb*) Abraham obeyed God, God would bless. In each case, though *eqeb* may imply the consequential blessing, *eqeb* does not necessarily indicate a positive "reward." The consequence (*eqeb*) may actually be shame (Ps 40:15) or judgment (2 Sam 12:6).

Another word that is sometimes translated "reward" is *seker*. Proverbs 11:18 says,

> The wicked earns deceptive wages,
> But he who sows righteousness *gets* a true reward [*seker*, שָׂכָר].

The wicked earn wages that promise one thing and deliver another. Waltke writes, "Pharaoh threw the boy babies into the river (Exod 1:22), but God drowned his entire army in the Red Sea (Exod 14:28)."[7] The wicked think they are working for life, but are recompensed with destruction. In contrast, the righteous is like a farmer who scatters the seed to plant the crop, and receives true pay (*seker*) for his work. Isaiah 19:10 declares the coming judgment on Egypt:

> The foundations will be broken,
> All who make wages [*seker*] will be troubled of soul. (AT)

---

7. Waltke, *Proverbs*, 501.

Leah boasts that God gave her a "reward" (*sakar*, שָׂכָר) because she had given her maidservant to Jacob. She said, "God has rewarded me" (Gen 30:18 NIV). But the "reward" is really just "wages." Genesis 30:16–18 says,

> When Jacob came in from the field in the evening, then Leah went out to meet him and said, "You must come in to me, for I have surely hired [*sakar*] you with my son's mandrakes." So he lay with her that night. ¹⁷ God gave heed to Leah, and she conceived and bore Jacob a fifth son. ¹⁸ Then Leah said, "God has given me my wages [*sakar*] because I gave my maid to my husband."

Leah was jealous of her sister Rachel, so she gave her handmaid to Jacob. Now she sold the mandrakes to Rachel for the access to sleep with her husband Jacob. It is a sad tale, but God hears Leah and she conceives a son. But in her guilt she self-righteously says God was paying her back for giving her handmaid to Jacob. Laban paid wages (*sakar*) to Jacob for his labor (Gen 30:28).

David uses another word that has been translated "reward" (*gamal*, גָּמַל) when he writes,

> The LORD has rewarded [*gamal*] me according to my righteousness;
> According to the cleanness of my hands He has recompensed me.
> ²¹ For I have kept the ways of the LORD,
> And have not wickedly departed from my God.
> ²² For all His ordinances were before me,
> And I did not put away His statutes from me.
> ²³ I was also blameless with Him,
> And I kept myself from my iniquity.
> ²⁴ Therefore the LORD has recompensed me according to my righteousness,
> According to the cleanness of my hands in His eyes. (Ps 18:20–24)

The parallel in verse 24, "recompensed," is synonymous with *gamal* in verse 20.

When David was mourning the death of Absalom, Barzillai requested that he be allowed to cross over the Jordan with the king to return to his home city rather than go to Jerusalem with the king. The wealthy eighty-year-old had faithfully provided earlier for David in his time of need. David said he would take him to Jerusalem and take care of him there. Barzillai says just crossing the Jordan and going home would be *gamal* enough. He says,

> Why should the king compensate me *with* this reward [*gamal*]?
> ³⁷ Please let your servant return, that I may die in my own city near the grave of my father and my mother. (2 Sam 19:36–37)

The *gamal* is a recompense, a compensation, a repayment for the good Barzillai had done David before. This was not just relational payback. Barzillai had done good to God's anointed, and David was recompensing him accordingly.

The Hebrew words that have been translated "reward" contain within them a payment or just recompense for something done. The same is true of the Greek words used in the LXX that have been translated "reward." A word meaning "recompense" (*antapodosis*, ἀνταπόδοσις) is used in Psalm 19:11. More common is the word μισθός (*misthos*). It is the faithful wage the farmer reaps (Prov 11:18). It is the wage Laban paid Jacob.[8] It is the wage Pharaoh's daughter paid Moses mother for caring for him.[9] In Ecclesiastes, it is the better return of wages to two laborers.[10] It is the wage Leah said God paid her.[11] When Abraham returned from rescuing Lot, he refused to be paid the war booty by the local suzerain, and proclaimed that Yahweh alone was his suzerain. So God told Abraham,

> Do not fear, Abram,
> I am a shield to you;
> Your reward [*misthos*] shall be very great. (Gen 15:1)

Abraham had just demonstrated his covenant obedience and allegiance to God. So God would repay him. God would give him an heir and a kingdom through his twelve sons. This language of recompense is seen again after Abraham offers up Isaac. Because of Abraham's obedience, God will give him the kingdom (Gen 22:6; see 26:5). The *misthos* of Genesis 15:1 is recompense for obeying God.

This meaning of "wage" for *misthos* is common in classical Greek. Homer uses *misthos* for the stated or agreed wage for work under Laomedon.[12] Herodotus uses it for the "bribe" paid to Themistocles to help defend Euobea.[13] Thucydides uses *misthos* for soldiers' pay.[14] The mean-

---

8. Gen 29:15; 30:28, 32f.; 31:7–8.
9. Exod 2:9.
10. Eccl 4:9.
11. Gen 30:18.
12. Homer, *Illiad*, 440 (II.21.445); μισθῷ ἔπι ῥητῷ.
13. Herodotus, *Histories*, 4 (8.4.2); πείθουσι Θεμιστοκλέα ἐπὶ μισθῷ.
14. Thucydadies, *Thucydides*, 84 (1.143.2); ὀλίγων ἡμερῶν ἕνεκα μεγάλου μισθοῦ.

ing of "wage" is seen in the translation of *misthos* in the New Testament. Jesus instructs the disciples to stay in the house that receives their gospel message. He says, "the laborer is worthy of his wages [*misthos*]" (Luke 10:7). James warns the oppressors that the "pay [*misthos*] of the laborers" cries out against them (Jas 5:4). Judas bought a field with the "price" (*misthos*) for betraying Jesus (Acts 1:18). The rarely used definition for "reward" of "remuneration or pay given for work done"[15] is the use present in these examples from antiquity. What is absent is a "reward" that is a bonus recognition not required for works done.

The Sanctioned Blessing

If Adam had kept the stipulations of the Covenant of Works, he would have been "recompensed" or "rewarded" with the eschatological kingdom in glory. Within the terms of the covenant, he would have merited the sanctioned blessing. Abraham portrays, on the typological level (the toy level), covenant obedience that merits the kingdom. As Paul makes clear in Galatians, Abraham's obedience is only meritorious of the kingdom on the typological level. But it prefigures the seed of Abraham whose covenant obedience merits the eschatological kingdom.

The covenant blessings of the Mosaic Covenant are the "reward." Obedience is basis for the covenant blessing of "riches, honor, and life." Proverbs 22:4 says,

> Because [*eqeb*] of humility *and* the fear of Yahweh
> Are riches, honor and life. (AT)

The humility that yields the reward is the same as the fear of the Lord. Likewise, the blessings are the same as those promised in recompense to covenant obedience. First Kings 3:12–14 records God's promise to Solomon:

> Behold, I have given you a wise and discerning heart, so that there has been no one like you before you, nor shall one like you arise after you. [13] I have also given you what you have not asked, both riches and honor, so that there will not be any among the kings like you all your days. [14] If you walk in My ways, keeping My statutes and commandments, as your father David walked, then I will prolong your days.

---

15. OED.

Covenant reward would be given Solomon for covenant obedience. As Waltke notes,

> The wages of pure religion are *riches* [see 3:16] and with it *honor* (*kābôd*; see 3:16; 15:33; 18:12) *and* bringing the compound predicate to its fitting climax, *life* . . . but conditioned prolonging his days (see 3:2) on his continued obedience to the covenant.[16]

The reward was the covenant blessing, even under the toy kingdom. The psalmist extols the covenant Law and confesses,

> The law of the Lord is perfect . . .
> Moreover, by them Your servant is warned;
> In keeping them there is great reward [*eqeb*]. (Ps 19:7, 11)

The reward is not additional to the covenant blessing; it is the covenant blessing. King David praises God in Psalm 18:20 for recompensing him according to his righteousness. As king of the typological kingdom of God, the blessing is the Mosaic Covenant blessing. He keeps the Law, and God blesses. When Saul hunted David, David did not take Saul's life when he had the opportunity. David voices his faith that God will repay David according to his righteousness. First Samuel 26:23–24 says,

> The Lord rewards[17] everyone for their righteousness and faithfulness. The Lord delivered you into my hands today, but I would not lay a hand on the Lord's anointed. **24** As surely as I valued your life today, so may the Lord value my life and deliver me from all trouble. (NIV)

Samuel had anointed David to be the king that would replace Saul. David speaks, as the rising king of the covenant people, of the blessings of the Mosaic Covenant on those who keep the Law. It is not an add-on, bonus "reward." Rather, under the Law, blessing is promised as recompense for righteous obedience to the covenant Law. The Old Testament lacks examples of believers who are saved by faith and yet will receive eternal rewards according to their works. The modern use of "reward" does not serve well to translate the actual Greek and Hebrew words that have been translated "reward." The Greek and Hebrew words are unyieldingly linked to the idea of recompense or payback for something done. The words in themselves do not carry with them the modern notion of recognition of the quality of the deed done. The idea of a bonus for the

---

16. Waltke, *Proverbs*, 2:202.
17. יָשׁוּב, *yashub*, "return."

way something is done is absent. This Old Testament use informs the use found in the New Testament.

Jesus, in the same way, promises "reward" as synonymous with the kingdom of God. Throughout the Sermon on the Mount, Jesus contrasts the righteousness of the Pharisee with the righteousness of the kingdom of God. He states the contrast in Matthew 5:20:

> For I say to you that unless your righteousness surpasses *that* of the scribes and Pharisees, you will not enter the kingdom of heaven.

The blessings of the Beatitudes belong to the believers: the poor in spirit, those who mourn, the persecuted. Their reward in heaven is great (Matt 5:12). For theirs is the kingdom (Matt 5:3, 10). They will see God (Matt 5:8). They are the sons of God (Matt 5:9). The reward is not an add-on; it is the kingdom inheritance.

After Jesus contrasts the righteousness required by the Law with the righteousness of the kingdom of heaven, Jesus calls the believers to live in faith looking for that kingdom. They are not to pray for the show of man like the Pharisees, who have no kingdom reward, but to pray to their Father in expectation of the kingdom blessing (Matt 6:5–6). They are not to give to the poor for the honor of men, but to give secretly, expecting God's kingdom blessing (Matt 6:2–4). They are not to fast to be noticed by men, but to fast to the Father (Matt 6:16–18). This is all about the kingdom that the Pharisees have no part in. The kingdom focus of the Lord's Prayer in the middle of this section demonstrates the context. The "righteous" of this world have no place in the kingdom of God. But those who believe and follow Jesus are transformed by his Spirit and bear the fruit of that faith. Later in the sermon, Jesus says,

> Watch out for false prophets. They come to you in sheep's clothing, but inwardly they are ferocious wolves. [16] By their fruit you will recognize them. Do people pick grapes from thornbushes, or figs from thistles? [17] Likewise, every good tree bears good fruit, but a bad tree bears bad fruit. [18] A good tree cannot bear bad fruit, and a bad tree cannot bear good fruit. [19] Every tree that does not bear good fruit is cut down and thrown into the fire. [20] Thus, by their fruit you will recognize them. (Matt 7:15–20 NIV)

In each case—alms, prayer, fasting—the Pharisee has no lasting reward in the kingdom. But the believer is promised that God's kingdom reward is theirs. They are to live in this eschatological reality. Hebrews says regarding Moses,

> ... considering the reproach of Christ greater riches than the treasures of Egypt; for he was looking to the reward. (Heb 11:26)

So Jesus calls for believers to live as citizens of heaven. He is not offering bonus points to the obedient believer when he says,

> Do not store up for yourselves treasures on earth, where moths and vermin destroy, and where thieves break in and steal. [20] But store up for yourselves treasures in heaven, where moths and vermin do not destroy, and where thieves do not break in and steal. [21] For where your treasure is, there your heart will be also. [22] The eye is the lamp of the body. If your eyes are healthy, your whole body will be full of light. [23] But if your eyes are unhealthy, your whole body will be full of darkness. If then the light within you is darkness, how great is that darkness!
> [24] No one can serve two masters. Either you will hate the one and love the other, or you will be devoted to the one and despise the other. You cannot serve both God and money. (Matt 6:19–24)

Jesus is calling believers to live as those who are heirs of the kingdom. Those who believe look for the day; those who do not believe live for the present. This is not a question of additional rewards, but rather the promise of kingdom blessing to those who by faith live for the kingdom of God. Those who by faith seek that kingdom will receive the reward merited by Christ.

Jesus' promise to the disciples demonstrates the equality of rewards promised believers. Jesus says,

> He who receives you receives Me, and he who receives Me receives Him who sent Me. [41] He who receives a prophet in *the name of a prophet* shall receive a prophet's reward; and he who receives a righteous man in the name of a righteous man shall receive a righteous man's reward. [42] And whoever in the name of a disciple gives to one of these little ones even a cup of cold water to drink, truly I say to you, he shall not lose his reward. (Matt 10:40–42)

The key to the passage is the opening. To receive those sent by Jesus is to receive Jesus, and to receive Jesus is to receive the Father. The kingdom belongs to these! Jesus then states the same promise in various ways. The person who receives the messenger from God will receive the same reward as the messenger. The one who receives the righteous followers of Jesus will receive the same reward. The one who gives hospitality to "little ones" the world scorns will receive their reward. Three times Jesus says the same thing. Whether one receives Jesus, or his messenger, or those seeking his kingdom righteousness, or the believers counted as nothing by the world, the reward of the kingdom is promised. What is clearly not present in these words is some notion that great rewards are to be gained through welcoming a prophet, average rewards from receiving a disciple, and lower rewards from receiving the insignificant!

Paul exhorts believing slaves to reflect their eternal hope in their daily labors,

> Whatever you do, do your work heartily, as for the Lord rather than for men, **24** knowing that from the Lord you will receive the reward (ἀνταπόδοσιν *antapodosis*)[18] of the inheritance. (Col 3:23–24)

Their recompense is not the wage that perishes, but their recompense is inheritance of the kingdom of God!

Second John 1:8 is another passage that shows the reward is the kingdom blessing. John writes,

> Watch yourselves, that you do not lose what we have accomplished, but that you may receive a full reward.

What is a "full reward"? Is there a possibility they would get less than a "full reward"? John's contrast is not between a "full reward" and a partial reward. John is warning them against receiving the false teacher. He writes,

> For many deceivers have gone out into the world, those who do not acknowledge Jesus Christ *as* coming in the flesh. This is the deceiver and the antichrist. **8** Watch yourselves, that you do not lose what we have accomplished, but that you may receive a full reward. **9** Anyone who goes on ahead and does not abide in the teaching of Christ, does not have God; the one who abides in the teaching, he has both the Father and the Son. (2 John 1:7–9 AT)

The danger is not that they will have a diminished reward, but that they will have no reward. There are those who first professed gospel faith but now claim to have more knowledge. The have moved "on ahead" and did not "abide in the teaching of Christ." John is saying, "There is nothing

---

18. Recompense; Isa 59:18 LXX.

more!" Those who have the gospel have the Father and the Son, the full reward! There is no gray scale of rewards in view. There are only two groups: those who abide in the gospel and those that don't.

Received by Persevering Faith

Jesus warned the religious that there would be those who would stand condemned on Judgment Day:

> Not everyone who says to me, "Lord, Lord," will enter the kingdom of heaven, but the one who is doing the will of my Father who is in heaven. (Matt 7:21 AT)

When Jesus sent out the twelve disciples, he taught them that there would various responses to the gospel message—some spurious, some genuine:

> The sower sows the word. [15] These are the ones who are beside the road where the word is sown; and when they hear, immediately Satan comes and takes away the word which has been sown in them. [16] In a similar way these are the ones on whom seed was sown on the rocky *places*, who, when they hear the word, immediately receive it with joy; [17] and they have no *firm* root in themselves, but are *only* temporary; then, when affliction or persecution arises because of the word, immediately they fall away. [18] And others are the ones on whom seed was sown among the thorns; these are the ones who have heard the word, [19] but the worries of the world, and the deceitfulness of riches, and the desires for other things enter in and choke the word, and it becomes unfruitful. [20] And those are the ones on whom seed was sown on the good soil; and they hear the word and accept it and bear fruit, thirty, sixty, and a hundredfold." (Mark 4:14–20)

Among some, the initial responses would be indistinguishable. But those with real faith would persevere in the face of Satan's efforts to the contrary. They would persevere as the roots deepened in the face of persecution. They would persevere in the face of the momentary afflictions and seductions of this world. Those who do truly believe bear fruit! Those with genuine faith are like the disciples, who were often confused and embarrassingly obtuse. John says as the crowds were leaving Jesus, he asked the disciples, "You do not want to go away also, do you?" (John 6:67). Because he believed, Peter said, "Lord, to whom shall we go? You have words of eternal life" (John 6:68). Believers know they have nowhere else to go. Jesus is their only hope.

In Revelation 1-3, Jesus, the Lord of Glory, calls the churches to persevere in gospel faith as he prepares the eschatological temple bride for the great wedding day. He calls them to turn from the idolatry and immorality of the world and serve the Lord. Five of the churches are in some degree of danger. He warns the church at Ephesus that they have lost their "first love." The gospel love of Jesus has been lost and they no longer do the deeds of those energized by the love of Christ! They are in danger of the lampstand no longer standing in their midst. The church is part of the temple the Lord Jesus is building. They are a lampstand in that temple, but if the gospel is gone, the church will not be part of the temple (Rev 2:5).

He warns the church at Pergamum that they have in their midst those who are involved in idolatry and immorality. Jesus will come and make war against them (Rev 2:16). Then he warns the church at Thyatira. They tolerate a false prophetess who has brought idolatry and immorality. Jesus will come in judgment on her and her followers (Rev 2:22-23). Then Jesus warns the church at Sardis. They have a history of gospel life, but now they are spiritually dead (Rev 3:1). Finally, Jesus warns the church at Laodicea. They have no need of Jesus! They say, "I am rich, and have become wealthy, and have need of nothing" (Rev 3:17). Jesus says,

> ... and you do not know that you are wretched and miserable and poor and blind and naked, **18** I advise you to buy from Me gold refined by fire so that you may become rich, and white garments so that you may clothe yourself, and *that* the shame of your nakedness will not be revealed; and eye salve to anoint your eyes so that you may see. (Rev 3:17-18)

What is notable is that in each of these five instances, Jesus is not warning that believers will have their rewards reduced, but that churches will no longer be the churches of the Lord Jesus, that professing believers will be revealed for what they really are! In contrast, the promises to the seven churches all speak of the eschatological hope of every believer!

Jesus promises the Ephesian believers to eat of the "tree of life." He promises the believers at Smyrna the "crown of life." He promises the believers at Pergamum

> ... hidden manna, and I will give him a white stone, and a new name written on the stone which no one knows but he who receives it. (Rev 2:17)

They will eat the bread of life from heaven (cf. John 6:31–35). To him is the acquittal stone, which provides admittance to the final kingdom. To the believers at Thyatira, Jesus promises,

> ... AUTHORITY OVER THE NATIONS; 27 AND HE SHALL RULE THEM WITH A ROD OF IRON, AS THE VESSELS OF THE POTTER ARE BROKEN TO PIECES, as I also have received authority from My Father. (Rev 2:26–27)

As the Lord Jesus sits enthroned in Glory, so those will who persevere in gospel faith to the end. Jesus promises the believers in Sardis that they will walk with him in white and he will acknowledge them before the Father. Jesus promises the church at Philadelphia that they will be part of the final temple. Finally, to the Laodicean church, Jesus promises,

> ... I will grant to him to sit down with Me on My throne, as I also overcame and sat down with My Father on His throne. (Rev 3:21)

In contrast to the warnings against apostasy, Jesus promises the blessings of eschatological kingdom. To the persevering believer is the kingdom, the throne, and the crown. Theirs is to dwell with the Lord Jesus in the eschatological temple of the Father forever.

There are not multiple houses in heaven that differ in size and delightfulness awarded in proportion to the believer's works. This erroneous view is garishly portrayed by Eli's song "That's All the Lumber."[19] A man comes to the gates of heaven. Peter takes the new arrival to the house he built during his life. The man is excited as they pass by stone mansions. But as they continue, the houses keep getting smaller and smaller. They get to the man's heavenly abode, and it is a two-room shack. Peter says he hopes the man is happy. The man can't believe that is all there is. Then the chorus explains that the size of the house is based on the amount of lumber the man sent through his good works. The man can't believe it. He asks Peter if that is what he deserves, and Peter tells him he should have done more. The man asks if Peter can send him back, assuring him he will do better. But it's too late.

---

19. Thanks to Sarah Thomas for bringing this song to my attention! From *Things I Prayed For* (1998).

The New Covenant Blessing

Jesus is encouraging the disciples as they face the coming troubles. As they believe in God, Jesus exhorts them to believe in himself. Jesus says,

> Do not let your hearts be troubled. You believe in God; believe also in me. **2** My Father's house has many rooms; if that were not so, would I have told you that I am going there to prepare a place for you? (John 14:1–2 NIV)[20]

The notion that the Father's "house" is heaven and there are many "mansions" there came from the Vulgate, which had "mansiones" ("lodging-places").[21] The word translated "mansions" or, as the NIV translates, "rooms" is a simple word for dwelling place. In this house there are many of these. There are plenty of rooms! Jesus is not comforting the disciples in their trouble with thoughts of the size and elaborateness of the "mansions" or even "rooms" they can have depending on how good their works are on Judgment Day! He comforts them that the reason he will leave them and go to the cross is so they too can live with him in the Father's house! They are not at home, but he leaves them so that they will be!

To the one who perseveres in faith will be given the unfading victor's crown. Paul's faith was not a dead lifeless faith, but a faith that evidenced itself in daily life. Two things are at once true about this living faith. Paul had bold confidence in the assurance of his own salvation. In the midst of his suffering, Paul writes Timothy,

> ... I know whom I have believed and I am convinced that He is able to guard what I have entrusted to Him until that day. (2 Tim 1:12)

He was assured of his salvation! But at the same time, Paul knew he had no hope other than in Christ. His was a persevering faith. He writes,

> ... I have become all things to all men, so that I may by all means save some. **23** I do all things for the sake of the gospel, so that I may become a fellow partaker of it. **24** Do you not know that those who run in a race all run, but *only* one receives the prize? Run in such a way that you may win. **25** Everyone who competes in the games exercises self-control in all things. They then *do it* to receive a perishable wreath, but we an imperishable. **26** Therefore I run in such a way, as not without aim; I box

---

20. Μὴ ταρασσέσθω ὑμῶν ἡ καρδία· πιστεύετε εἰς τὸν θεόν, καὶ εἰς ἐμὲ πιστεύετε. 2 ἐν τῇ οἰκίᾳ τοῦ πατρός μου μοναὶ πολλαί εἰσιν· εἰ δὲ μή, εἶπον ἂν ὑμῖν ὅτι πορεύομαι ἑτοιμάσαι τόπον ὑμῖν.

21. Morris, *John*, 638 n. 6.

> in such a way, as not beating the air; **27** but I discipline my body and make it my slave, so that, after I have preached to others, I myself will not be disqualified. (1 Cor 9:22-27)

Paul is not talking about additional rewards that may be lost. In verses 22-23, Paul writes the Corinthians that the gospel compels him to sacrifice his own rights for the sake of the gospel! Persevering faith requires discipline. This is not new to Paul. Jesus said,

> If anyone wishes to come after Me, let him deny himself, and take up his cross daily, and follow Me. For whosoever wishes to save his life shall lose it, but whoever loses his life for My sake, he is the one will save it. (Luke 9:23-24)

Paul uses an analogy to illustrate the point. Just as the athlete disciplines himself for the prize, so the believer pushes on for the promised day. Faith perseveres, but the warning is real to those who would start the race and not finish. There is this double truth. Believers have assurance, but believers are aware that those who apostatize are disqualified. Paul calls the Corinthians to the same persevering faith that he lives each day. The chapter may end with verse 27, but the argument continues into the next chapter. Israel's unbelief is a warning to the Corinthians, who may turn to idolatry rather than continuing in the faith (1 Cor 10:1-12).

The glory, the enthronement, belongs to the persevering believer. Paul writes,

> For who is our hope or joy or crown of exultation? Is it not even you, in the presence of our Lord Jesus at His coming? **20** For you are our glory and joy. (1 Thess 2:19-20)

Craig Blomberg explains the "crown of exultation." He writes,

> It appears in synonymous parallelism with the "hope" and "joy" of eternal life itself, the pleasure of unending fellowship with other believers whom we have played some role in helping nurture.[22]

As Blomberg notes, the crown of joy is not unique to a soul winner; it is the joy promised to all believers. All believers participate in kingdom work in this life and will enjoy the exultation when they are enthroned in glory. The thief who turned to Jesus on the cross lived a short life on earth, but he will rejoice at the thousands of people who are in heaven because

---

22. Blomberg, "Degrees," 163.

his story was read and preached. The unknown beggar who turned to Jesus and shortly entered heaven thereafter will rejoice and exult that he was part of the kingdom on earth. Joy, hope, and exultation are the crowning glory of all believers.

Paul writes about the "the crown of righteousness,"

> . . . in the future there is laid up for me the crown of righteousness, which the Lord, the righteous Judge, will award to me on that day; and not only to me, but also to all who have loved His appearing. (2 Tim 4:8)

All believers receive the "crown of righteousness." The "crown of righteousness" is righteousness, just as the "crown of life" is eternal life. James assures those who persevere under trial,

> Blessed is a man who perseveres under trial; for once he has been approved, he will receive the crown of life which *the Lord* has promised to those who love Him. (Jas 1:12)

This is the hope and confidence of all believers. Faithful elders are not promised super rewards. Their hope is the same as all believers. Peter writes,

> And when the Chief Shepherd appears, you will receive the unfading crown of glory. (1 Pet 5:4)

All of these crowns speak of the victorious glorification of believers. Isaiah writes of the glory that is the believer's because of Christ:

> In that day the Lord of hosts will become a beautiful crown
> And a glorious diadem to the remnant of His people. (Isa 28:5)

Motyer writes, "It is a mark of the people of the Messianic day that they see the Lord himself as their adornment."[23]

TALENTS AND MINAS

Jesus contrasts the living faith of believers with the unbelief of nominal Christians in the Parable of the Minas in Luke 19, and the Parable of the Talents in Matthew 25. Though the details are different, the central point is the same in each. In Luke 19, Jesus says,

---

23. Motyer, *Prophecy of Isaiah*, 230.

A man of noble birth went to a distant country to have himself appointed king and then to return. ¹³ So he called ten of his servants and gave them ten minas. "Put this money to work," he said, "until I come back."

¹⁴ But his subjects hated him and sent a delegation after him to say, "We don't want this man to be our king."

¹⁵ He was made king, however, and returned home. Then he sent for the servants to whom he had given the money, in order to find out what they had gained with it.

¹⁶ The first one came and said, "Sir, your mina has earned ten more."

¹⁷ "Well done, my good servant!" his master replied. "Because you have been trustworthy in a very small matter, take charge of ten cities."

¹⁸ The second came and said, "Sir, your mina has earned five more."

¹⁹ His master answered, "You take charge of five cities."

²⁰ Then another servant came and said, "Sir, here is your mina; I have kept it laid away in a piece of cloth. ²¹ I was afraid of you, because you are a hard man. You take out what you did not put in and reap what you did not sow."

²² His master replied, "I will judge you by your own words, you wicked servant! You knew, did you, that I am a hard man, taking out what I did not put in, and reaping what I did not sow? ²³ Why then didn't you put my money on deposit, so that when I came back, I could have collected it with interest?"

²⁴ Then he said to those standing by, "Take his mina away from him and give it to the one who has ten minas."

²⁵ "Sir," they said, "he already has ten!"

²⁶ He replied, "I tell you that to everyone who has, more will be given, but as for the one who has nothing, even what they have will be taken away. ²⁷ But those enemies of mine who did not want me to be king over them–bring them here and kill them in front of me." (Luke 19:13–27 NIV)

In the story, a noble leaves to receive his throne. But he would return. He gives a mina to each of his ten servants to steward while he is away. His own subjects reject him. When he returns, he gathers his servants. The first reports that he has gained a 900-percent increase on the mina. The master gives him ten cities to govern. The second earns a 400-percent increase, and he is given five cities to rule over. Another servant returns the original mina. He was afraid of the master and knew the master was a "hard man" who took what was not his. This wicked servant who did nothing for his master is stripped of the one mina and killed along with the other subjects who rejected the master.

The parallel is found in Matthew 25. Jesus says,

> Again, it will be like a man going on a journey, who called his servants and entrusted his wealth to them. [15] To one he gave five bags of gold, to another two bags, and to another one bag, each according to his ability. Then he went on his journey. [16] The man who had received five bags of gold went at once and put his money to work and gained five bags more. [17] So also, the one with two bags of gold gained two more. [18] But the man who had received one bag went off, dug a hole in the ground and hid his master's money.
>
> [19] After a long time the master of those servants returned and settled accounts with them. [20] The man who had received five bags of gold brought the other five. "Master," he said, "you entrusted me with five bags of gold. See, I have gained five more."
>
> [21] His master replied, "Well done, good and faithful servant! You have been faithful with a few things; I will put you in charge of many things. Come and share your master's happiness!"
>
> [22] The man with two bags of gold also came. "Master," he said, "you entrusted me with two bags of gold; see, I have gained two more."
>
> [23] His master replied, "Well done, good and faithful servant! You have been faithful with a few things; I will put you in charge of many things. Come and share your master's happiness!"
>
> [24] Then the man who had received one bag of gold came. "Master," he said, "I knew that you are a hard man, harvesting where you have not sown and gathering where you have not scattered seed. [25] So I was afraid and went out and hid your gold in the ground. See, here is what belongs to you."
>
> [26] His master replied, "You wicked, lazy servant! So you knew that I harvest where I have not sown and gather where I have not scattered seed? [27] Well then, you should have put my money on deposit with the bankers, so that when I returned I would have received it back with interest.
>
> [28] "So take the bag of gold from him and give it to the one who has ten bags. [29] For whoever has will be given more, and they will have an abundance. Whoever does not have, even what they have will be taken from them. [30] And throw that worthless servant outside, into the darkness, where there will be weeping and gnashing of teeth." (Matt 25:14–30 NIV)

Again, a master entrusts wealth to his slaves before leaving on a journey. When he returns, he finds the first servant has doubled the money. The master praises him and welcomes him into "the joy of your master." The second, though starting with less, has doubled the money. The master praises him and welcomes him into "the joy of your master." But the third slave returns the original money, which he had not done anything with. He was afraid of the master, whom he believed took what did belong to him. The wicked slave is stripped of the talent and thrown into "outer darkness," where there is "weeping and gnashing of teeth."

There are differences in the details between the two parables. There are ten servants in one, three in the other. There is a noble in one, a master in the other. A mina was worth far less than a talent. In the first story, the first and second servants produce different rates of return on their stewardship, but in the second story, they both double what they started with. In the first story, they both start with a mina, but in the second, they start with different amounts. The differences actually function to focus on the similarities. In both parables there is a master who entrusts wealth to servants. Two of the servants are praised and rewarded when the master returns. In both the third servant is unfaithful and does not receive a reward.

The "outer darkness" makes clear the third servant is not a believer. Matthew 8:12 says,

> ... the sons of the kingdom will be cast out into the outer darkness; in that place there will be weeping and gnashing of teeth.

Matthew 13:41–42 says,

> The Son of Man will send forth His angels, and they will gather out of His kingdom all stumbling blocks, and those who commit lawlessness, **42** and will throw them into the furnace of fire; in that place there will be weeping and gnashing of teeth.

It is clear that "outer darkness" is hell. Matthew 13:49–50 says,

> So it will be at the end of the age; the angels will come forth and take out the wicked from among the righteous, **50** and will throw them into the furnace of fire; in that place there will be weeping and gnashing of teeth.

Jesus uses the same language for the wedding guest who is not dressed for the wedding. Matthew 22:11–14 says,

The New Covenant Blessing

> But when the king came in to look over the dinner guests, he saw a man there who was not dressed in wedding clothes, 12 and he said to him, "Friend, how did you come in here without wedding clothes?" And the man was speechless. 13 Then the king said to the servants, "Bind him hand and foot, and throw him into the outer darkness; in that place there will be weeping and gnashing of teeth." 14 For many are called, but few *are* chosen.

He professed, but he did not possess—was not "chosen." This same thing happens to the unfaithful servant who beats his fellow servants. Jesus says,

> ... the master of that slave will come on a day when he does not expect him and at an hour which he does not know, 51 and will cut him in pieces and assign him a place with the hypocrites; in that place there will be weeping and gnashing of teeth. (Matt 24:50–51)

In the story, the master doesn't "cut him in pieces" with his rebuke! The master dismembers the wicked slave when he cuts him in pieces! He is not a true servant; he is assigned a place with those who professed but were not real believers. He is a hypocrite. The first point to note about both parables, then, is the contrast is between faithful servants and the unfaithful servant who did not use the mina or talent for the master! Second, in the Parable of the Talents, the master's response to the faithful servants is the same with commendation. But the reward is not specified. The unfaithful servant is thrown into outer darkness, where there is weeping and gnashing of teeth. Both the faithful servants receive the reward, the same commendation, and the unfaithful servant is consigned to hellfire.

Third, in the Parable of the Minas, seven of the servants are not even listed when giving the account to the master. The lack of commendation to the second servant is an ellipsis. Like the seven, who are not the point of the story, so the lack of commendation is not the point. In the Parable of the Talents, the servants start with different amounts, illustrative of the different amounts of opportunity, abilities, and resources entrusted to believers. This difference in servants is not the source of rebuke or diminished final blessing. So too, with the servants and the minas, servants produce different amounts of results. But this is not a reference to faithfulness or half-hearted service. Rather, as Jesus teaches, the fruit will "produce a crop—some thirty, some sixty, some a hundred times what was sown" (Mark 4:20 NIV). There is another ellipsis in the Parable of the Minas. The unfaithful servant is stripped of his minas. He receives no reward, no further stewardship. Implied is the fact that though he lived for a while with the servants of the master's house, he belongs to the enemies of the master. There are not three groups, but two: the faithful servants and the enemies of the master. When the master returns, he will say to those who were unfaithful servants, "I never knew you!" Both parables, with different details, teach the same point. The faithful servants of the Lord will be blessed when he comes, and the unfaithful servants will be shown for what they are—hypocrites—and cast into hell. Charles Spurgeon got the Lord's point when he preached on the Parable of the Talents:

> As to whether there are degrees or not, I know not; but this I know, he that doeth his Lord's will, shall have said to him, "Well done, good and faithful servant."[24]

WHAT JESUS SAID ABOUT DEGREES OF REWARD

Jesus did teach regarding degrees of reward when the disciples asked about them. There are two occasions where Jesus clearly is responding to the disciples' question about degrees of reward. They follow each other and underline the disciples' lack of understanding.

What Will We Get?

A rich young ruler approached Jesus and asked, "Teacher, what good thing shall I do that I may obtain eternal life?" (Matt 19:16). The question started in ignorance. The ruler didn't know who Jesus was, and he didn't know who he himself was. He thought Jesus was just a teacher, and he thought he himself could do something to obtain eternal life. He didn't know he stood in the presence of the Son of Man. He didn't know he was a sinner incapable of doing any truly good work to obtain eternal life. Jesus corrects both his errors. First, he asks the man why he addressed Jesus as "good" since only God is "good." Hint, hint. Second, Jesus directs him to the Mosaic Law, not to suggest a way for the man to obtain eternal life, but that the man might know his need of Christ. The man responds that he knows and has kept the Law. Jesus tells him to sell all his

---

24. Spurgeon, "Two Talents."

possessions and give it all to the poor. The man leaves in grief, for he has much property.

Then Jesus turns to the disciples and says it is easier for a camel to go through the eye of a needle[25] than for a rich man to enter the kingdom of God. The disciples get the point. They ask, if a rich man can't be saved, then who can? After all, riches were the blessing of obedience to the Law. So if a rich man blessed by God couldn't get into the kingdom, no one could! Jesus tells them that what is not possible for man is possible for God. Even the rich could be saved.

This is all too much for Peter to pass up. Peter and the disciples have sold what they have and followed Jesus. He asks, "Behold, we have left everything and followed You; what then will there be for us?" (Matt 19:27). Peter is asking what "treasure in heaven" they will have (see Matt 19:21). Peter is in fact asking the "degrees of reward" question, "How much will I get?" Peter had left family and friends and his vocation to follow Jesus. How much can Peter expect in return? The rich young ruler asked about obtaining eternal life, but Jesus promised treasure in heaven! Peter latches onto that promise and asks, "How much for what we've done?" Peter is not asking if they will have eternal life; he is way past that! He asks, "What will our reward be?"

Jesus answers Peter's question about degrees of reward. There is no clearer answer about what God says on the subject of degrees of reward for believers in all of Scripture. And the disciples then and disciples now still do not have ears to hear what Jesus says. Jesus says,

> Truly I say to you, that you who have followed Me, in the regeneration when the Son of Man will sit on His glorious throne, you also shall sit upon twelve thrones, judging the twelve tribes of Israel. **29** And everyone who has left houses or brothers or sisters or father or mother or children or farms for My name's sake, will receive many times as much, and will inherit eternal life. (Matt 19:28–29)

Jesus promises his disciples that they will be enthroned when he comes on his glorious throne! In fact, all believers will receive much more than they gave up to follow Jesus and will inherit eternal life. Jesus flips the answer on Peter! Peter thinks, "We get eternal life and treasures on top depending on what we've done. How much do we get for what we've

---

25. "There is no solid historical evidence to support the legend that a narrow gate in the Jerusalem wall was called the Needle's Eye . . ." Blomberg, *Matthew*, 299.

done?" Peter is thinking of eternal life as the base line, "in the kingdom," but what "rewards" will we have? Jesus turns it upside down: "All believers[26] will be blessed beyond measure and have eternal life!"

Jesus is not promising the twelve disciples a special place in the kingdom. In fact one of the twelve will not even be there! Jesus uses the imagery of the toy, Israel under the Law, to describe the eschatological glory of the kingdom. The disciples are asking how much they will get. Their question demonstrates their ignorance! It is like a three-year-old asking about Disneyland before going for the first time, "Will there be swings and slides?" Mom smiles and chuckles a bit as she replies, "Yes, there will be swings and slides." But the child asks, "Will it be fun?" Unable to explain what is coming, Mom says, "Yes, you will have lots of fun."

Jesus says in effect, "You are thinking about how much you will get because of what you have done. You don't get it. You are thinking like the rich young ruler, 'reward for good things I did.' You've got to get way past that thinking. All believers get much more than they left! All believers get eternal life! Because the treasure is not based on what you did, but on grace." Jesus says, "But many *who are* first will be last; and *the* last, first (Matt 19:30). There are many, like the rich young ruler, who are first in the way the world works, but will be last.

Then Jesus tells a parable to bring the point home:

> For the kingdom of heaven is like a landowner who went out early in the morning to hire laborers for his vineyard. ² When he had agreed with the laborers for a denarius for the day, he sent them into his vineyard. ³ And he went out about the third hour and saw others standing idle in the market place; ⁴ and to those he said, 'You also go into the vineyard, and whatever is right I will give you.' And so they went. ⁵ Again he went out about the sixth and the ninth hour, and did the same thing. ⁶ And about the eleventh hour he went out and found others standing around; and he said to them, 'Why have you been standing here idle all day long?' ⁷ They said to him, 'Because no one hired us.' He said to them, 'You go into the vineyard too.'
>   ⁸ When evening came, the owner of the vineyard said to his foreman, 'Call the laborers and pay them their wages, beginning with the last *group* to the first.' ⁹ When those *hired* about the eleventh hour came, each one received a denarius. ¹⁰ When those *hired* first came, they thought that they would receive more; but each of them also received a denarius. ¹¹ When they received it,

---

26. Disciples are those who have left all to follow Jesus; Luke 14:25–35.

> they grumbled at the landowner, ¹² saying, 'These last men have worked *only* one hour, and you have made them equal to us who have borne the burden and the scorching heat of the day.' ¹³ But he answered and said to one of them, 'Friend, I am doing you no wrong; did you not agree with me for a denarius? ¹⁴ Take what is yours and go, but I wish to give to this last man the same as to you. ¹⁵ Is it not lawful for me to do what I wish with what is my own? Or is your eye envious because I am generous?' ¹⁶ So the last shall be first, and the first last (Matt 20:1–16).

They all get the same pay at the end of the day! Jesus is not teaching that believers are paid the same for their works, but he is saying that believers all get the same reward in the kingdom. Billy Graham and the thief on the cross, the apostle Paul and Lot, Daniel and the adulterer in Corinth who repented—all get the same reward! Some don't remember a day when they did not know and serve Jesus and they go to him when they are a hundred. Some live a life of wickedness and moments before death find him to be their Savior. All believers are the same in the eternal kingdom. Jesus says, "Is it not lawful for me to do what I wish with what is my own? Or is your eye envious because I am generous?" It is his to give. The kingdom is his because he is the faithful Son of Man who gave his life as a ransom for many and now is seated at the right hand of the Father. Who are you to say he cannot give equally in his grace to every believer? This is not the way of this world, but it is the way of the King of Glory. So the last shall be first!

There is no separation of discussion of salvation and degrees of reward here. The rich young ruler asked about salvation. Jesus promised treasure and eternal life. The disciples asked about rewards, and Jesus answered. It is all one package purchased by the Lord Jesus.

On Your Right and On Your Left?

The second passage is found starting in Matthew 20:20:

> Then the mother of the sons of Zebedee came to Jesus with her sons, bowing down and making a request of Him. ²¹ And He said to her, "What do you wish?" She said to Him, "Command that in Your kingdom these two sons of mine may sit one on Your right and one on Your left." ²² But Jesus answered, "You do not know what you are asking. Are you able to drink the cup that I am about to drink?" They said to Him, "We are able."

> ²³ He said to them, "My cup you shall drink; but to sit on My right and on *My* left, this is not Mine to give, but it is for those for whom it has been prepared by My Father."
> ²⁴ And hearing *this*, the ten became indignant with the two brothers. ²⁵ But Jesus called them to Himself and said, "You know that the rulers of the Gentiles lord it over them, and *their* great men exercise authority over them. ²⁶ It is not this way among you, but whoever wishes to become great among you shall be your servant, ²⁷ and whoever wishes to be first among you shall be your slave; ²⁸ just as the Son of Man did not come to be served, but to serve, and to give His life a ransom for many."
> (Matt 20:20–28)

John and James' mother comes to Jesus and requests positions of prominence for them in his kingdom. They and their mother are clearly thinking about greatness in the kingdom. The other disciples are offended when they hear about their request. What have John and James done to receive great positions in the kingdom? This is such a teaching moment for Jesus to explain positions in the kingdom! He can explain to them that if they do great and faithful good works in their lives, then he will reward them accordingly! But if they slack off and don't do much, they will be in the kingdom but they won't have much in the way of rewards! The disciples are clearly thinking about levels of reward, responsibly, and kingdom blessing! If they do well, surely they will gain much. This is the reason they are upset with James and John. If James and John are asking for the places of honor, they must think they have done more than the other disciples!

But Jesus corrects the foundational assumptions. They are thinking the way the Gentile rulers think, the way the world assesses kingdom service. The world is filled with levels. The world outside the kingdom of God runs on who has authority over whom, who is closer to the top! It is all about merit—who works harder, who cheats better, who is smarter, who works the system better, who knows whom, who is richer, who is prettier. It's all about getting status and reward. But this is not the kingdom of God. The kingdom of God is radically different. For the sons of the kingdom, it is not about *getting* but about *giving*. Grace upends everything. The children of the kingdom don't work to *get*. They work because they *have*. They are compelled by the love of Christ to serve. Jesus rebukes the disciples. They have no idea what they are really asking. There will be two men on his right and left, but it is not what the disciples think. On the cross, Jesus shows greatness in his kingdom. The Son of Man lays down his life to ransom many.

The disciples had already asked about degrees of reward (levels of blessing) before, and Jesus had just given them a vividly scandalous parable to explain the answer. But they were deaf and didn't understand a word he said.

This whole block of Matthew 19:16—20:28 is focused on the grace of the kingdom Jesus brings through his death on the cross (see Matt 20:18–19). When his death is seen for what it is, there is no place left for the way the world thinks. Jesus' death doesn't just take away original sin, or even just take away all sin for the believer! Jesus' death is the one act of obedience that puts him on his glorious throne and all disciples with him! All the reward is in Christ Jesus the Lord.

9

The Judgment According to Works

THE JUDGMENT

THERE MAY BE MANY points of doctrine that can be debated, but one of the clearest truths is that there is a coming Judgment Day in which all will give account. This fact is the great leveler. The rich, the poor, male, female, slave, free, successful, ordinary, moral, immoral, religious, secular—no matter the time lived in history or manner of passing, all will stand before the judge to give account. Scripture does not allow an exemption to avoid appearing before the Great Assize. Paul writes,

> For we must all appear before the judgment seat of Christ, so that each one may be recompensed for his deeds in the body, according to what he has done, whether good or bad. (2 Cor 5:10)

Paul appeals to this coming judgment when he writes to the church in Rome,

> For we will all stand before the judgment seat of God. 11 For it is written,
> "As I LIVE, SAYS THE Lord, EVERY KNEE SHALL BOW TO ME,
> AND EVERY TONGUE SHALL GIVE PRAISE TO GOD."
> 12 So then each one of us will give an account of himself to God. (Rom 14:10–12)

John writes of this ominous day,

> Then I saw a great white throne and Him who sat upon it, from whose presence earth and heaven fled away, and no place was found for them. **12** And I saw the dead, the great and the small, standing before the throne. (Rev 20:11–12)

This is the great day that makes the nations tremble. John writes,

> Then the kings of the earth and the great men and the commanders and the rich and the strong and every slave and free man hid themselves in the caves and among the rocks of the mountains; **16** and they said to the mountains and to the rocks, "Fall on us and hide us from the presence of Him who sits on the throne, and from the wrath of the Lamb; **17** for the great day of their wrath has come, and who is able to stand?" (Rev 6:15–17)

There will be no place to hide. No king or president will be immune. No general or billionaire will influence the halls of power to avoid this court. All are subject to its jurisdiction and condemnation.

According to Works

Not only is it universal to include all people, but the Final Judgment is comprehensive to include the total specific details of a person's life. The Final Judgment is not a summary evaluation of a life lived. The day of judicial accounting evaluates every thought, word, and deed. Jesus leaves no doubt regarding the judgment's specificity when he says,

> But I tell you that every careless word that people speak, they shall give an accounting for it in the day of judgment. (Matt 12:36)

There is not a word that was spoken that will not be reviewed by the Final Judgment. Paul writes,

> Therefore do not go on passing judgment before the time, *but* wait until the Lord comes who will both bring to light the things hidden in the darkness and disclose the motives of *men's* hearts. (1 Cor 4:5)

The very thoughts and motives of a person's heart will be laid bare before the judge. The Final Judgment is all-inclusive. The judgment according to one's works is pervasive in Scripture.

Many have succumbed to the erroneous teaching that man will be judged in summary of a life lived. "I'm pretty good. I'm better than my neighbor." God's grace and the general life lived will see the believer through. Like the Judaizers, they fail to see the typological nature of the Law of Moses and the eschatologically higher righteousness required by Jesus. As James says, "For whoever keeps the whole law and yet stumbles in one *point*, he has become guilty of all" (Jas 2:10). There is no one born of Adam who is not culpable. Paul concludes, "THERE IS NONE RIGHTEOUS, NOT EVEN ONE . . ." (Rom 3:10). Who can stand?

Protestants have generally tried to separate the believer's judgment "according to works" from the unbeliever's judgment "according to works." In so doing, they have argued that believers are save by grace, but judged according to their works to determine their rewards. Some even make two judgments: the "Great White Throne Judgment," where the unbeliever is judged according to his works and condemned, and the "Bema Seat of Christ," where believers' lives are evaluated by the Lord according to works to determine their rewards. Others just make these two aspects of the same judgment.

John Murray tries to maintain the distinction between salvation by grace and reward according to works when he writes,

> We must maintain therefore, justification complete and irrevocable by grace through faith and apart from works, and at the same time, future reward according to works.[1]

In this view, the unbeliever is judicially recompensed for his sin "according to works." But since the believer's sins have been atoned for by the death of Christ, the judgment for the believer only determines his rewards "according to works." The problem is, that this shift is usage requires an equivocation on "according to works." When the unbeliever is condemned for his sin, the "according to works" is the legal and judicial ground for punishment, but the believer is not rewarded based on the judicial ground of his works.

Protestants have argued that the unbeliever is justly condemned. The sinner lied; he is judged. He lusted; he is judged. He coveted; he is judged. Sin by sin, he is accountable for every idle thought as he stands before the judge. For every moment he lived and did not honor God as God, but worshiped the creation, he will be judged. Every breath he received in rebellion and unbelief he stored up for the day of wrath. He will be judged for every demerit, every sin. Every good work he did that was not out of a heart of faith will be judged. "According to works" is the judicial basis of his condemnation. But when the believer is considered,

---

1. Murray, "Justification," 221.

it is argued, "according to works" does not refer to the legal criteria. Protestants have not wanted to say that as the unbeliever's sin legally merits punishment, the believer's works legally merit the proportionate reward. In order to protect grace, Protestants then change the meaning of "according to works" when applied to the believer. It does not refer to the judicial basis of judgment and reward, but rather is evidence of faith and is rewarded proportional to the works done. This equivocation on "according to works" is untenable when the biblical use is examined.

To say that the basis of reward is different than the basis of condemnation does not accord with the common use of "according to works" for both. The biblical usage does not allow a bifurcated meaning: one the juridical grounds for punishment, the other the evidential basis for proportional reward. Throughout Scripture, "according to works" is used as just recompense for deeds done.

Under the Old Covenant, the typological level, this same judicial meaning is used when the psalmist praises God,

> And covenant faithfulness [*chesed*, חֶסֶד] is Yours, O Lord, For
> You recompense a man according to his work. (Ps 62:12 AT)

David's hope is in God's covenant faithfulness. Though he is the object of treachery, his trust is in God, who will deliver him according to the promises of the covenant. In the scales of God's justice, the wicked are found to be nothing (Ps 62:9–10). But David's confidence is that he will be recompensed by God. David's choice of words is revealing. The word translated "recompense" is *shalem* (תְשַׁלֵּם). The recompense David looks for is just. G. L. Carr explains the meaning of the word:

> . . . peace being restored through payment (of tribute to a conqueror, Josh 10:1), restitution (to one wronged, Exod 21:36), or simply payment and completion (of a business transaction, II Kgs 4:7). The payment of a vow (Ps 50:14) completes an agreement so that both parties are in a state of *shālôm*. Closely linked with this concept is the eschatological motif in some uses of the term.[2]

First, this recompense is the just recompense. David looks to the restitution owed, like the payment owed a conqueror, like the payment of a vow made, or like a payment in a business transaction. There is no grace here. David's hope is in God's covenant justice to repay. Second, this repayment

---

2. Carr, "שָׁלַם (*shalem*)," 931.

brings a completion or wholeness that brings a state of *shalom*, peace. Though usage determines meaning, it is not accidental that the word David uses, *shalam*, is the verbal form of the word *shalom*. God's recompense to the wicked and the righteous brings the *shalom*. Implicit is the justice of God who repays. The justice that condemns the wicked according to their deeds is the same justice that rewards the righteous according to their deeds. The relationship of the evil deeds to condemnation is the same as the relationship of the righteous deeds to the reward. The judge is impartial and just, and his covenant adjudication is based on works. That is David's hope.

Proverbs 24:11–12 also illustrates the righteousness of the recompense according to works. Solomon writes,

> Deliver those who are being taken away to death,
> And those who are staggering to slaughter, Oh hold *them* back.
> ¹² If you say, "See, we did not know this,"
> Does He not consider *it* who weighs the hearts?
> And does He not know *it* who keeps your soul?
> And will He not render to man according to his work?

The proverb warns those who would fail to protect the innocent. They may plead ignorance, but God, who weighs the heart, knows. God is just and will judge based on justice according to works. He will "render" (*shub*, הֵשִׁיב) accordingly. Again, there is only just recompense; there is no mercy or grace in view. God will give retribution. He protects the soul of those warned; he will repay in like kind. Waltke writes, "If the son turns a blind eye to helping victims and does nothing to help them, the Protector of Life will turn a blind eye to him in his crisis. Count on it!"[3]

Scripture uses "according to works" to reference the legal basis of condemnation and blessing. The judge is impartial. The relationship of the works to the condemnation is the same as the relationship of the works to the blessing. In both directions, it is a matter of strict covenant justice. In the court of God, in neither case is it used to refer as evidence of another basis for condemnation or blessing. The works are the legal basis, good or bad.

Throughout the Old Testament, God's covenant justice is affirmed. Hosea declares the coming sanction for Judah's covenant disobedience:

> The LORD also has a dispute with Judah,
> And will punish Jacob according to his ways;

---

3. Waltke, *Proverbs*, 278.

He will repay him according to his deeds. (Hos 12:2)

The Writings contain the same language. God will repay the wicked "according to" their deeds. The psalmist writes,

> Requite them according to their work and according to the evil of their practices;
> Requite them according to the deeds of their hands;
> Repay them their recompense. (Ps 28:4)

Elihu speaks of the justice of God:

> For He pays a man according to his work,
> And makes him find it according to his way.
> ¹² Surely, God will not act wickedly,
> And the Almighty will not pervert justice. (Job 34:11–12)

Ezekiel proclaims the just judgment of God "according to" Israel's disobedience when he writes,

> Therefore I will judge you, O house of Israel, each according to his conduct. (Ezek 18:30)

And again,

> I, the Lord, have spoken; it is coming and I will act. I will not relent, and I will not pity and I will not be sorry; according to your ways and according to your deeds I will judge you," declares the LORD God. (Ezek 24:14)

Israel accuses God of unrighteousness, but God in his justice will judge. God says,

> Yet you say, "The way of the Lord is not right." O house of Israel, I will judge each of you according to his ways. (Ezek 33:20)

The point of dispute is focused exactly on the judicial righteousness of God. Israel says God is not right. But God will demonstrate his righteousness in judging "according to his ways." God will justly recompense for disobedience.

Revelation's climatic description of the judgment on the harlot Babylon uses the same language, where he quotes the psalmist. The psalmist writes,

> O daughter of Babylon, you devastated one,
> How blessed will be the one who repays you
> With the recompense with which you have repaid us. (Ps 137:8)

So Jeremiah writes,

> Summon many against Babylon,
> All those who bend the bow:
> Encamp against her on every side,
> Let there be no escape.
> Repay her according to her work;
> According to all that she has done, *so* do to her. (Jer 50:29)[4]

God used Babylon to bring covenant recompense on Israel. So God would bring recompense on Babylon for her wickedness. The legal recompense of the judgment on Israel under the Mosaic Covenant and judgment on Babylon demonstrates the strict legal adjudication based on works in both cases. As God judged Israel, so God will judge Babylon! John echoes this earlier judgment on Babylon when he writes of the Final Judgment on the harlot Babylon:

> Pay her back even as she has paid, and give back to her the equivalent according to her deeds; in the cup which she has mixed, mix the equivalent for her. [7] To the degree that she glorified herself and lived sensuously, to the same degree give her torment and mourning. (Rev 18:6–7 AT)

The common English translations "to give back double" and to "mix double" pose a problem for justice and a contradiction to verse 7: "to the degree that she ... to the same degree." Kline's article "Double Trouble" explains that "double" is not twice as much, but "equivalent" or "duplicate." Beale concurs with Kline:

> But Kline has demonstrated convincingly that the almost unanimous translation "double" in the English versions is inaccurate ... Kline especially establishes the meaning "duplicate/equivalent" in texts to which Revelation 18:6 may allude ...[5]

Revelation 18:6 does not say that the Harlot Babylon will receive twice as much punishment as her wickedness deserves! The judgment will "double," will repay in kind, her sins. So verse 7: "to the degree that she ... to the same degree." There is no mercy in the strict covenant justice of God.

The demon-possessed harlot Babylon (Rev 18:2) has ensnared the nations in her immorality. Her sins are as "high as the heavens" (Rev 18:5). She exalts herself as the queen in her luxurious wealth (Rev 18:7,

---

4. Cf. Jer 51:24; 50:15.
5. Beale, *Book of Revelation*, 901.

11ff.) as she kills the people of God (Rev 18:24). So will her recompense be. Every injustice, every sin, every act of wickedness, every act of sorcery, every economic transaction will be repaid by the unending wrath of God. According to her deeds, she will be repaid—to the same degree.

Adjudication of the Covenant of Works

The Final Judgment looms over the opening chapters of Romans as the backdrop for the gospel. Paul proclaims that the gospel is the power of God for Jew and Gentile alike. He writes,

> For I am not ashamed of the gospel, for it is the power of God for salvation to everyone who believes, to the Jew first and also to the Greek. (Rom 1:16)

Both Jew and Gentile stand in need of God's salvation. Paul then works backwards, starting with the Gentiles, to show the universal condition of man outside Christ. He immediately references the judgment that hangs over all men born of Adam. He writes,

> For the wrath of God is revealed from heaven against all ungodliness and unrighteousness of men who suppress the truth in unrighteousness ... (Rom 1:18)

This is the wrath that has been delayed since the fall at creation (see Rom 1:20). Paul then describes at length the universal rebellion of the Gentiles against the King. They knew him and did not honor him (Rom 1:21). But the Jew is no different. The Gentiles have no excuse. So too, Paul starts his discussion of the Jews, "Therefore you have no excuse" (Rom 2:1). The Jews, just as the Gentiles, are "storing up wrath" for themselves for the Final Judgment. Paul writes,

> But because of your stubbornness and unrepentant heart you are storing up wrath for yourself in the day of wrath and revelation of the righteous judgment of God, ⁶ who WILL RENDER TO EACH PERSON ACCORDING TO HIS DEEDS: ⁷ to those who by perseverance in doing good seek for glory and honor and immortality, eternal life; ⁸ but to those who are selfishly ambitious and do not obey the truth, but obey unrighteousness, wrath and indignation. ⁹ *There will be* tribulation and distress for every soul of man who does evil, of the Jew first and also of the Greek, ¹⁰ but glory and honor and peace to everyone who does good, to the Jew first and also to the Greek. ¹¹ For there is no partiality with God. ¹² For

> all who have sinned without the Law will also perish without the Law, and all who have sinned under the Law will be judged by the Law; **13** for *it is* not the hearers of the Law *who* are just before God, but the doers of the Law will be justified. (Rom 2:5-13)

Paul is not writing of hypotheticals here. Paul is not writing about believers who obey versus unbelievers who do not obey. Paul is writing about the universal condition of Jew and Gentile, who will face the "revelation of the righteous judgment of God" (Rom 2:5). The context of that wrath is very significant and important to understand. Paul is not writing about some generic judgment for man's sin. The wrath that is coming is the adjudication of the Covenant of Works with Adam. This is the context for the book as a whole. Jesus is the faithful Second Adam (Rom 1:3-4). Since the fall, the Gentiles have been in rebellion (Rom 1:19ff.). In Adam, all have sinned (Rom 5:12ff.). So there is none righteous (Rom 3:10). The "old man" in Romans 6:6 is reference to the federal headship of Adam. The contrast of the "flesh" and the "Spirit" in Romans 8 is a contrast of life in Adam and life in Christ, not a contrast between the material and immaterial. The subjugation of creation to death in chapter 8 is in the context of Adam's sin. The references to Abraham (Abrahamic Covenant) and David (Davidic Covenant) culminate in the fulfillment in the gospel of Jesus Christ. He is the promised king. But all this is in the context of the kingdom of God in the Covenant of Works with Adam, and the Pactum Salutis of the Second Adam.

As discussed earlier, there is no context prior in time or logic to the Covenant of Works with Adam. There was no natural state prior to the Covenant. There was no creation before the Covenant of Works with Adam. There was no theological sublayer of the Creator and creature prior to the Covenant of Works. God, the King of Heaven, created Adam to be his image bearer in the Covenant of Works to establish his kingdom on earth. Earth itself was created as the kingdom of God that Adam was to subdue. The starting point on earth is not something prior to this Covenant of Works. The Covenant of Works is the starting point. Any other conjecture does not recognize Moses' account in Genesis 1 and 2. So the Final Judgment is in the context of this kingdom and covenant. There is no general Final Judgment outside the context of the Covenant of Works with Adam. The Final Judgment is the adjudication of the Covenant of Works with Adam.

God told Adam that on the day he ate of the tree of the knowledge of good and evil he would die. But when Adam sinned and God came as the Spirit of the Day (of Judgment), God delayed the judgment. There would be curses common to mankind, but the final sanction of death and damnation was delayed. Adam would live and work; Eve would give birth to children. God would save sinners. But man has been on death row since Adam sinned. While God has fed and clothed man, man has piled up sins for the Judgment Day. But the Judgment Day is coming, and it is the judgment due all in Adam that has been delayed so long.

This specific context is evident from the criteria and sanctions. When the Judgment Day comes and the wrath is revealed, God's impartial justice will be seen. He will ". . . RENDER TO EACH PERSON ACCORDING TO HIS DEEDS" (Rom 2:6). Man will receive recompense for what he has done. He has not persevered in "doing good" for the King, but rather has lived in selfish ambition and unrighteousness, and suppressed the truth. He has lived a lie. His disobedience will be repaid in justice according to his deeds. If Adam had obeyed, if there were any righteous in accord with the requirements of the Covenant of Works, they would have received glory, honor, and eternal life. The basis of judgment is obedience to the righteous requirements of God under the Covenant of Works. Adam disobeyed, and all in him disobeyed. There is none that will escape the judgment sanction.

The sanctions also make clear that the coming judgment is the adjudication of the Covenant of Works. As noted previously, the promise of glory, honor, and eternal life is the sanctioned sabbath promise given to Adam under the covenant. There is nothing in the just nature of God that requires him to create a creature whom he would bless with sabbath glory for obeying him. It is the promise of the Covenant of Works. In covenant justice, God promised obedience would merit eschatological sabbath glory.

The covenantal nature of the Final Judgment is also evidenced by Paul's subsequent reasoning. The Jew boasts that he is the covenant people of God in the Old Covenant (see Rom 2:23). Not only did that Law condemn the Jews in their disobedience to the typological covenant narrowly, but that Law more broadly testified to the eternal righteousness of God, and specifically to those created in the Covenant of Works as the image bearer of the righteous King. So the Law of Israel condemned all. Paul writes,

> Now we know that whatever the Law says, it speaks to those who are under the Law, so that every mouth may be closed and all the world may become accountable to God ... (Rom 3:19)

Both the Jew and the Greek will stand before the same impartial judge (Rom 3:10–11). The Gentile, knowing the righteousness of God by nature (Rom 1:19–21), will be condemned even though he did not receive the Mosaic Law. The Jew, even though he was in covenant with God under the Law, will by that same Law be shown to be a sinner. All will be "judged by the Law." For it is the "doers of the Law" who will be judged righteous. Both the Gentile, who never stood under the Mosaic Covenant, and the Jew, who stood in Old Covenant, are condemned by this same judgment to recompense sinners with wrath and the righteous with glory and eternal life. For both Jew and Gentile stand condemned under the Covenant of Works in Adam. Whether guilty in Adam as fellow image bearers who by nature knew the righteousness of God as Gentiles, or Jews who lived under the published Law of God, both stand together guilty in the face of the Covenant of Works in Adam.

Paul presents the two outcomes when he writes,

> ... to those who by perseverance in doing good seek for glory and honor and immortality, eternal life; **8** but to those who are selfishly ambitious and do not obey the truth, but obey unrighteousness, wrath and indignation. (Rom 2:7–8)

These are not two alternatives set before the Romans. These were the two outcomes set forth in the Covenant of Works with Adam. In Adam, there has been only one outcome—all died. All are under the covenant condemnation. There is no hypothetical offer to some anonymous person that he can obtain eternal life if he does good, seeking glory and honor and immortality. All enter this world already under the judgment of condemnation in Adam. Paul is not presenting a hypothetical, but the historic sanctions set forth to Adam. And all are condemned in sin. This is the urgent state of affairs that compels Paul. Paul exhorts the Corinthians,

> For we must all appear before the judgment seat of Christ, so that each one may be recompensed for his deeds in the body, according to what he has done, whether good or bad. (2 Cor 5:10)

Paul affirms the seriousness of man's condition. All must appear before the judgment. Some want to limit this judgment to believers before Christ to receive rewards in accordance with their good works. Paul knows no such limitation here. He says "all" must appear. In the next verse he says that it is the expectation of this ominous judgment that motivates him to proclaim the gospel. He says, "knowing the fear of the Lord, we persuade men" (2 Cor 5:11). He concludes,

> Therefore, we are ambassadors for Christ, as though God were making an appeal through us; we beg you on behalf of Christ, be reconciled to God. (2 Cor 5:20)

Paul has in view the great day of just judgment and unending condemnation and punishment.

This same day of accounting is the basis for his rebuke of those in the church who name themselves as servants of Christ, but whose lives do not accord with his grace. He writes,

> For we will all stand before the judgment seat of God. ¹¹ For it is written,
> "As I live, says the Lord, every knee shall bow to Me,
> And every tongue shall give praise to God."
> ¹² So then each one of us will give an account of himself to God. (Rom 14:10–12)

Paul reminds them that believers belong to the Lord Jesus (Rom 14:8). They have no place judging the servant of the Lord. It is to the Lord that believers are accountable. He then affirms the coming Final Judgment. All are answerable to this court. In the broad context of Scripture, there is an implicit warning against the professing believer who would be the cause of believers' spiritual ruin. Paul warns, "determine this—not to put an obstacle or a stumbling block in a brother's way" (Rom 14:13). And again, "Do not destroy with your food him for whom Christ died" (Rom 14:15). Jesus had warned the unfaithful servant,

> But if that slave says in his heart, "My master will be a long time in coming," and begins to beat the slaves, *both* men and women, and to eat and drink and get drunk; ⁴⁶ the master of that slave will come on a day when he does not expect *him* and at an hour he does not know, and will cut him in pieces, and assign him a place with the unbelievers. (Luke 12:45–46)

Though Paul does not spell out the full extent of warning, he certainly implies the seriousness of judging a fellow believer. Jesus left no room for ambiguity when he said,

> ... whoever causes one of these little ones who believe in Me to stumble, it would be better for him to have a heavy millstone hung around his neck, and to be drowned in the depth of the sea. ⁷ Woe to the world because of its stumbling blocks! For it is inevitable that stumbling blocks come; but woe to that man through whom the stumbling block comes! ⁹ It is better for you to enter life with one eye, than to have two eyes and be cast into the fiery hell. (Matt 18:6–9)

Paul is not talking about degrees of reward, but the general judgment of all men. Then the true servants of the Lord and the false servants will be manifest.

There is no equivocation by Paul or any other writer of Scripture. The phrase "according to works" means just recompense based on the merit or demerit of deeds done. As the phrase is used of the Final Judgment, it always references the final execution of the death sanction of the Covenant of Works. God is impartial, and whether Gentile created in the image of God or Jew under the Old Covenant, all in Adam have sinned and will be condemned. Then who can be saved?

THE JUDGE

Jesus the Lord

The best news in the cosmos is that Jesus will come as the judge. This is the most glorious and amazing detail on Judgment Day. The seat of God's judgment (Rom 14:10) is the seat of the Son of Man, the Second Adam, Jesus. He is Lord (2 Cor 5:10). There is a man who is judge on the final Judgment Day! Jesus says,

> For the Son of Man is going to come in the glory of His Father with His angels, and WILL THEN REPAY EVERY MAN ACCORDING TO HIS DEEDS. (Matt 16:27)

Likewise, Paul writes,

> ... because He has fixed a day in which He will judge the world in righteousness through a Man whom He has appointed, having furnished proof to all men by raising Him from the dead. (Acts 17:31)

And again,

> For after all it is *only* just for God to repay with affliction those who afflict you, 7 and *to give* relief to you who are afflicted and to us as well when the Lord Jesus will be revealed from heaven with His mighty angels in flaming fire, 8 dealing out retribution to those who do not know God and to those who do not obey the gospel of our Lord Jesus. 9 These will pay the penalty of eternal destruction, away from the presence of the Lord and from the glory of His power, 10 when He comes to be glorified in His saints on that day, and to be marveled at among all who have believed—for our testimony to you was believed. (2 Thess 1:6-10)

Jesus said,

> ... He gave Him authority to execute judgment, because He is *the* Son of Man. (John 5:27)

The one righteous man, the Lord Jesus, will adjudicate the sanction of death on all who sinned in Adam.

Believers are too quick to say, "Of course Jesus is the judge; he is God." While it is certainly true and essential to the faith to believe in the full deity of the Lord Jesus, that is not the reason he is the judge on the final day. The Lord Jesus as exalted vassal in Glory is seated as judge because he kept the Pactum Salutis as Second Adam. He is the Son of Man enthroned. He is the Son of Man and judges as representative of the King of Heaven.

He is the one who holds the seven stars in his right hand, who walks among the lampstands (Rev 2:1). He is the one who was dead and came to life (Rev 2:8). He has the sharp two-edged sword (Rev 2:12). He is the one who is the Son of God and has eyes like a flame of fire and feet like burnished bronze (Rev 2:18). He is the one has the seven spirits of God (Rev 3:1). He has the key of David (Rev 3:7). He is the faithful and true witness (Rev 3:14). These self-identifying statements are the claims of the Son of Man, who has victoriously defeated Satan. He is building the eschatological temple, the church. He is the obedient servant of the King of Heaven. He is the image bearer exalted in Glory. His is the Spirit's power and authority. He is the king that was promised to David. To him authority is given to exercise final judgment on Satan and all his hosts. As resurrected Lord, he has the keys of life and death to throw Satan into the lake of fire (Rev 1:18; 20:1-2, 10). Jesus is judge!

His Reward

Judicial recompense "according to works" is actually the basis of the gospel hope of the believer. Isaiah proclaims the gospel promise in Isaiah 40:

> "Comfort, O comfort My people," says your God.
> 2 "Speak kindly to Jerusalem;
> And call out to her, that her labor[6] has ended,
> That her iniquity has been removed,
> That she has received of the Lord's hand
> The equivalent for all her sins." (Isa 40:1–2 AT)

God did not repay Israel twice what her sins deserved, but equivalent to what her sins deserved. Her debt has been paid. Israel's seventy-year captivity has paid the debt for her covenant disobedience. Kline draws the connections to the background in Leviticus:

> It is this covenant curse of the determined period of exile predictively threatened in Leviticus 26 that is the underlying, unifying image of Isa 40:2 as a whole. And Lev 26:41 is clearly the primary source of the language in the second of the statements in that verse, which may be translated: "The debt of her iniquity has been paid."[7]

This payment for Israel's iniquity under the Old Covenant is the background for the full payment for sin in the suffering servant described in Isaiah 52:13—53:12. This servant of the King is the faithful one, who in obedience to the Father, took the wrath belonging to the elect under the Covenant of Works in Adam and merited as their federal head the sabbath glory under the Pactum Salutis. The comfort Isaiah proclaims rests on the strict judicial nature of both of these covenants. Isaiah promises the covenant blessing:

> Behold, the Lord God will come with might,
> With His arm ruling for Him.
> Behold, His reward is with Him
> And His recompense before Him.
> 11 Like a shepherd He will tend His flock,
> In His arm He will gather the lambs
> And carry *them* in His bosom;
> He will gently lead the nursing *ewes*. (Isa 40:10–11)

---

6. צְבָאָהּ, *tsaba*; Job 7:1; 10:17; 14:14; Num 4:23.

7. Kline, "Double," 173.

The Judgment According to Works

Jesus, God incarnate, has earned the reward. The Shepherd's reward is his sheep. This is the gospel hope Jesus repeats in Revelation 22. The crescendo of promise is usually missed because of mistranslation. Most English versions translate Jesus' words,

> Behold, I am coming quickly, and My reward *is* with Me, to render to every man according to what he has done. (Rev 22:12)

It's like the old joke: "What do cows drink?" "Milk!" "No, water!" The mind automatically goes a certain direction, even when it is incorrect. Throughout the Bible, the phrase is "according to works" or "deeds." So it is understandable that translators would jump to the conclusion that the same thought is present in verse 12. But look at the actual wording. Even if you don't know Greek, you can see the difference.

> "according to his deeds" (Matt 16:27)
> κατὰ τὴν πρᾶξιν αὐτοῦ
>
> "according to his deeds" (Rom 2:6)
> κατὰ τὰ ἔργα αὐτοῦ
>
> "according to their deeds" (Rev 20:12)
> κατὰ τὰ ἔργα αὐτῶν
>
> "according to his deeds" (2 Tim 4:14)
> κατὰ τὰ ἔργα αὐτοῦ

The same language is in the Septuagint.

> "according to his ways" (Jer 17:10)
> κατὰ τὰς ὁδοὺς αὐτοῦ
>
> "according to his works" (Ps 62:12)
> κατὰ τὰ ἔργα αὐτοῦ
>
> "according to his works" (Prov 24:12)
> κατὰ τὰ ἔργα αὐτοῦ

But in contrast, look at what Jesus actually says.

> "as the work is his" (Rev 22:12)
> ὡς τὸ ἔργον ἐστὶν αὐτοῦ

The question is: who is the "his"? Does it refer to the person judged as in the examples above? Or does it refer to Jesus? The answer is found in understanding the reference to Isaiah 40:10 and 62:11. Isaiah writes,

> Behold, the Lord comes ... His reward is with him, the recompense before Him.

As Beale notes, "The last clause in Isaiah concerning 'the work' defines 'reward.'"[8] As noted before, the reward is the covenant blessing merited by the servant of the Lord. The shift to the third-person "the work is his" is an intentional reference to the words in Isaiah. Beale further observes,

> That "reward" and "work" focus on salvation is apparent in that Isa 40:10 gives the content of the "good news" announced ... in 40:9 ... Similarly, "reward" and "work" in Isa 62:11 are further descriptions of the announcement to Israel that "your salvation comes."[9]

When Isaiah's words were heard, there would have been no comfort in the notion that God was coming to give recompense based on the good works the hearer did! That was exactly why Israel had faced covenant judgment! The comfort is found in God who comes having merited the blessing for the hearer! This is the work Jesus fulfilled when he merited the reward. Hear now the crescendo of Jesus' words:

> Behold, I am coming quickly, and My reward [μισθός *misthos*] is with Me, to give to each as the work is His. [13] I am the Alpha and the Omega, the first and the last, the beginning and the end. (Rev 22:12–13 AT)

Jesus puts his work and reward in the ultimate context. He is God! He says,

> I am the Alpha and the Omega, the first and the last, the beginning and the end. (Rev 22:13)

Jesus is affirming that he is the fulfillment of the promises of Isaiah. He is the God who fulfilled the eternal intra-Trinitarian covenant, the Pactum Salutis. Isaiah writes, "Behold, the Lord God will come with might" (Isa 40:10). God would come, and God would merit the blessing. Jesus is coming with the blessing (reward, *misthos*), because he is the God who has fulfilled the Pactum Salutis. He comes with his reward, his people, his sheep, his bride! His is the glory on that day.

---

8. Beale, *Book of Revelation*, 1136.
9. Beale, *Book of Revelation*, 1136.

When the Lord Jesus comes with "His mighty angels in flaming fire" to give recompense under the covenant curse, he comes with his reward to be "glorified in His saints on that day, and to be marveled at among all who have believed" (2 Thess 1:10). Beale notes that "Behold, I am coming quickly, and My reward is with Me" (Rev 22:12) references the Isaiah background. Beale writes,

> Jesus' second assertion in v 12 is an allusion to Isa 40:10 and 62:11 . . . What is prophesied of the Lord in Isaiah is now prophesied by Jesus to be fulfilled in himself . . .[10]

Jesus has come as God incarnate, the Son of Man, and merited as Second Adam the eschatological blessing, his temple bride in glory.

THE JUSTIFIED

The Protestant Problem

Since the Reformation, Protestants have struggled with how to give proper credence to the reward given "according to works" and at the same time protect justification by faith alone. The common solution has been to say that sin keeps one from heaven and rewards are proportionate to good works. So Jesus' death removes the sin problem, and the believer gains entrance into heaven by grace alone through faith alone. However, the rest of the picture is that once in heaven, the believer's eternal destiny is rewarded by degrees according to works done while on earth. This presents a significant problem that is universally acknowledged even by the very Protestants that argue it is not insuperable.

J. I. Packer asks, "How can these two statements be fitted together? How does free forgiveness and justification by faith square with judgment according to works?"[11] Josep Ton confesses, "Hence, Protestants have perpetually questioned how one can coherently talk of rewards. If everything is given by God by grace, then speaking about rewards seems to be nonsense."[12] This dilemma was immediately present after the Reformation embraced justification through faith by grace alone. Emma Disley chronicles the theological tension among Protestants:

---

10. Beale, *Revelation*, 1136.
11. Packer, *Knowing*, 132.
12. Ton, *Suffering*, xiv.

The Protestant rejection of the doctrine of Purgatory, and the concomitant affirmation of the existence of "only two places" after death, raised questions concerning the intricate Dantean gradations of rewards and punishments envisaged by medieval scholasticism. If works played no part in justification, Protestants would surely find difficulty in speaking in terms of specific or individual rewards after death.[13]

Protestants were immediately confronted by the untenable combination of a justification by grace and rewards according to works. Some have rejected the degrees-of-reward view as a repudiation of grace. Jean Vernon (sixteenth-century pastor) writes,

> Sith that God in geving us unto life everlasting, doeth not respect or regard the dignitie of our good workes; howe can the doctrine of them stande, which do appoint degrees of joye and felicitie in heaven affirming that we shal there excel one an other in glorye?[14]

Vernon found it inconceivable that the saving grace of God, which does not regard in any sense the believer's works when considering eternal life, would evaporate when the believer's everlasting happiness and blessing is established by works. How could the leveling grace that saves be upended by degrees of joy based on one's works? The seventeenth-century professor John Cameron wrote to refute fifteen arguments set forth for degrees of reward.[15]

Generally, Protestants have not relinquished holding to both salvation by grace and reward according to works. The popular author Randy Alcorn speaks for many when he writes, "Salvation is a matter of God's work for man. Reward is a matter of man's work for God."[16] Representative of many Evangelicals is John Stott's comment,

> The whole New Testament teaches this; although we sinners can be 'justified' only by faith in Christ, yet we shall be 'judged' by our works. This is not a contradiction. It is because good works of love are the only available public evidence of our faith. Our faith in Jesus Christ is secret, hidden in our hearts. But if it is genuine, it will manifest itself visibly in good works. As James

---

13. Disley, "Degrees," 77–78.
14. Disley, "Degrees," 86.
15. Disley, "Degrees," 87, cites John Cameron, *Praelectiones* (1632).
16. Alcorn, "Believer's."

put it, 'I will show you my faith by what I do ... faith without deeds is useless.' (James 2:18,20). Since the judgment day will be a public occasion, it will be necessary for public evidence to be produced, namely the outworking of our faith in compassionate action. Jesus himself taught this many times. For example: 'The Son of man is going to come in his Father's glory with his angels, and then he will reward each person according to what he has done' (Matt 16:27). It is not our salvation, but our judgment, which will be according to our works.[17]

Even to the present, this Gordian knot remains at the heart of Evangelical scholarship. Dane Ortland notes fourteen ways to resolve this important question of the relationship of justification by grace with judgment according to works.[18] Some have sought to maintain grace while giving serious weight to an evaluation of the believer's works at the Final Judgment. Erwin Lutzer, senior pastor of The Moody Church in Chicago, Illinois (1980–2016), writes,

> If we think of heaven as a theme park, we must emphasize that the entrance ticket is free ... But if we want to go on some of the rides, if we want to be rewarded and not be embarrassed at the sadness we cause Christ, we must be faithful on earth. The entrance is free, but some additional benefits are based on merit.[19]

The starkness of the incongruousness of salvation by grace and rewards according to works is clear. Lutzer concludes,

> What we do know is that Paul taught clearly that we will receive the consequences of our wrongs at the judgment ... Even if our sins are represented as forgiven, we cannot escape the conclusion that our lifestyle is under judicial review, with appropriate rewards and penalties. We will suffer for our "wrongdoing."[20]

Charles Stanley goes so far as to say that the servant who has not been faithful is saved, but will be in the outer corridors of heaven weeping and wailing at his loss of reward! Stanley writes,

> We cannot conceive of the agony and frustration we would feel if we were to undergo such an ordeal; the realization that our

---

17. Stott, *Life*, 327.
18. Ortland, "Justified," 324.
19. Lutzer, *Your*, 60.
20. Lutzer, *Your*, 63.

unfaithfulness had cost us eternally would be devastating. And so it will be for many believers.[21]

While Stanley acknowledges the gnashing will not be forever, the difference in rewards will be.

Some have tried to soften the difference by suggesting that the rewards are proportional to works done, but not merited by works done. Augustine writes, "God crowns in us the gifts of His own mercy."[22] As the believer's works are the manifestation of God's grace in the believer, so too the rewards are his crowning gifts. Protestants, however, tend to read Augustine as though he were a Protestant. He wasn't, and it is misrepresentative to read his reference to gifts to us as though he were.

Bavinck too tries to harmonize grace and good works when he writes,

> The eternal blessedness and glory he received was, for him, the reward for his perfect obedience. But when he confers this righteousness of his on his people through faith and unites eternal life with it, the two, both the righteousness conferred and future blessedness, are the gifts of his grace, a reality that utterly excludes all merit on the part of believers ... God crowns his own work, not only in conferring eternal life on everyone who believes but also in distributing different degrees of glory to those who, motivated by that faith, have produced good works.[23]

Bavinck here tries to have it both ways. The salvation and reward is merited by Christ, who freely gives by grace future blessedness, but also distributes degrees of glory proportional to the good works done. Though this separates the grace that justifies from the works of sanctification, it conjoins them when eternal blessedness is considered. So while it theoretically protects justification from works, it soaks glorification in those same works! It is not significantly different, ultimately, than the infused righteousness of Catholicism. In by grace, but rewarded according to the righteous works of the believer. Blomberg notes,

> Ironically, those who most want to preserve the biblical doctrine of grace often unwittingly allow works a greater prominence in determining believers' destinies than do those who stress lordship salvation. As one of my students once put it, much conservative Christianity reminded him of an exclusive country club

---

21. Stanley, *Eternal*, 127.
22. Augustine, *Homilies on John*, 22.
23. Bavinck, *Reformed Dogmatics*, 729.

trying to attract a broader clientele. The club, therefore, advertised that membership for the first year would be absolutely free. But after that, you paid through the nose.[24]

How can grace be maintained when the righteousness that is rewarded is the righteousness of the believer? It is at this very point that some give a full-throated defense that even the works that the believer does are through the grace of God. No less than the Catholics have for years made the same argument! Here the Protestant is caught on the horns of the dilemma. If the defender of grace so emphasizes the gracious work of God that he crowns by degree of reward, then the exhortation and warning based on those same passages lack their impetus. For ultimately, in that view, the degrees of reward merely indicate the differences of grace at work in believer's lives. But the very power of the warning that the believer will be rewarded according to his works lies in the responsibility and eternal consequences that are thereby attained. It is this blending of grace and works that annihilates any grace professed by Catholicism. The genius of the Reformation doctrine of justification is not limited to a salvation that merely obtains entrance to heaven but leaves the believer immediately confronted with an eternity based on the works done in life. In addition, there is unresolved question: What is the baseline of grace? How good will heaven be for the worker in 1 Corinthians 3:15, who will be saved, but will have no reward? Or how do the rewards of the thief on the cross compare to the octogenarian martyr who has faithfully and at great personal cost served the Lord Jesus? Grace, by definition, ceases to be grace once works are added.

Other have suggested that the rewards are a greater capacity to enjoy the blessing given the believer by grace. Thiselton writes,

> an amateur musician who has slaved over a piece of music may subsequently derive "more" from hearing the same music played by a top-rank professional than a child invited to the same performance.[25]

But capacity is not limited to the believer's growth in obedient faith. Capacity as a person is shaped by a multitude of factors. And if all believers will enjoy heaven at their full capacity, how again is that a warning to the unfaithful believer?

---

24. Blomberg, *1 Corinthians*, 84.
25. Thiselton, *First Corinthians*, 305.

Others have asked if the rewards and losses even last for eternity, or whether Paul speaking of either blessings and losses in this life or some temporary blessing or loss felt when Christ comes. Craig Blomberg acknowledges that Paul is teaching degrees of reward in 1 Corinthians 3, but he denies that these are for eternity. Blomberg writes,

> Doubtless all will have varying degrees of praise and blame from Christ on Judgment Day, but nothing in this passage even remotely suggests that such differing responses are somehow perpetuated throughout all eternity.[26]

But truly, if the passages used to support degrees of reward according to works support such, it is difficult to maintain that they are temporary. As the believer is faced with the Final Judgment and his eternal state, it is hardly convincing that he is offered temporary rewards in heaven to motivate him.

Closer to the point, Blomberg's honesty is refreshing when he writes,

> The idea that our eternal happiness is all contingent on performance in this life should be fundamentally depressing for all who are honest about their level of maturity or growth in the faith.[27]

Far too little weight is placed on the meritorious obedience of the Lord Jesus, and a ludicrous degree of attention given the flawed obedience of believers.

But here is the problem: "reward" is not used in Scripture with the modern definition of a bonus for doing something good. In fact, the word often translated "reward" both in the Old and New Testaments is the word for "recompense" or "wage." Second, "according to works" is never used in Scripture to indicate something evidentiary; it is the just basis for recompense, for good or bad. Most Protestants have tried to separate the reward from the meritorious basis in order to protect grace and recognize reward based on works. But in separating these, they actually disregard both the grace given believers and the very meritorious basis for the eschatological blessing. How one puts Jesus and Paul together will either turn off all the lights and leave one looking for the exit or illuminate the world with the Light of the World. How do you put together that Jesus said to the believers in the Sermon on the Mount, "great is your reward [*misthos*, wage] in heaven" (Matt 5:12) with Paul's words, "Now to the one

---

26. Blomberg, *1 Corinthians*, 80.
27. Blomberg, *1 Corinthians*, 80.

who works, the wage (*misthos*) is not credited as grace, but according to what is owed" (Rom 4:4 AT)? Don't just read past that! If you cannot see the apparent conflict between Paul and Jesus here, you are not reading or thinking or both! Jesus says it is wages the believer receives; Paul says it is not wages or it would not be grace! And, contrary to the writers on Matthew who become agnostics as to what is meant by "reward," Scripture is full of the background that explains the "wage" the believer looks for in Christ. But here is the crux of the cross: it is the place where justice and law meet with grace. Seeing that juncture and the bigger relationship of the grace of salvation is in perfect harmony with the eschatological wage that is promised the believer.

One Justification

Justification through faith alone is at the heart of the Reformation. Luther understood this article and wrote, "if that article stands, the church stands; if it falls, the church falls."[28] Calvin called justification through faith the "main hinge." The Reformers were so passionate to protect justification from commingling with the works of the believer. But what was ardently guarded against at the front door has come through the wide-open back door! By abstracting justification from kingdom and covenant roots, Protestants have made the believer's works the basis on which his eternal condition rests! He thought he was marrying Rachel, but he married Leah! And Protestants have been trying to justify the unholy arrangement ever since: saved by grace, rewarded by works after a final justification according to those works on Judgment Day! In trying to separate justification from the rewards according to works, they have reduced justification to entrance into heaven and left the extent of bliss to be determined by the believer's works. Scripture does not allow this separation between justification and the rewarded blessing.

When the Lord Jesus comes in judgment, the books are opened to judge each person according to his works (Rev 20:13). But there is also another book, the Book of Life. John writes,

> . . . another book was opened, which is *the book* of life . . . And if anyone's name was not found written in the book of life, he was thrown into the lake of fire." (Rev 20:12, 15)

---

28. McGrath, *Iustitia*, vii n. 1.

The background for this description is found in Daniel 7 and 12. Daniel 7 describes God, the Ancient of Days, seated in judgment. The books are opened (Dan 7:10). The judgment is made. The kingdom is given to the Son of Man. Daniel writes,

> One like a Son of Man was coming,
> And He came up to the Ancient of Days
> And was presented before Him.
> 14 And to Him was given dominion,
> Glory and a kingdom,
> That all the peoples, nations and *men of every* language
> Might serve Him.
> His dominion is an everlasting dominion
> Which will not pass away;
> And His kingdom is one
> Which will not be destroyed. (Dan 7:13–14)

The bestial kingdoms of the earth lose their power, and the persecutor of the people of God is thrown into the lake of fire. Daniel recounts the angel's explanation:

> But the court will sit *for judgment*, and his dominion will be taken away, annihilated and destroyed forever. 27 Then the sovereignty, the dominion and the greatness of *all* the kingdoms under the whole heaven will be given to the people of the saints of the Highest One; His kingdom *will be* an everlasting kingdom, and all the dominions will serve and obey Him. (Dan 7:26–27)

The Son of Man receives the kingdom as representative of the people of God. The kingdom given him is the kingdom given them. Daniel writes that it is at the climax of the persecution of the nations against the people of God that the Lord Jesus will come and rescue the believers. Daniel writes, "everyone who is found written in the book, will be rescued" (Dan 12:1).

What is important to see is the integral relationship of the eschatological deliverance and blessing to the exaltation of the Lord Jesus and his reception of the kingdom. This then is connected to the Book of Life, which has recorded the names of those saved!

When the Lord Jesus comes, he comes as the Lord of Glory (1 Cor 2:8), who as Son of Man has been exalted to the right hand of the King of Heaven. He judges as the recipient of the kingdom exalted in eschatological dominion and glory. He judges on behalf of the Father. He is the faithful Second Adam, priest-king, who reigns in glory and brings judgment on all the enemies of the kingdom. As Adam was to guard Eden as a holy priest and crush the enemies of the King, so the Lord Jesus brings judgment to protect the holiness of the kingdom. John writes,

> And the beast was seized, and with him the false prophet who performed the signs in his presence, by which he deceived those who had received the mark of the beast and those who worshiped his image; these two were thrown alive into the lake of fire which burns with brimstone. (Rev 19:20)

The beast and the false prophet are thrown into the lake of fire. Those who are judged according to their works, whose names are not written in the Book of Life, are thrown into the lake of fire (Rev 20:15). The devil, the dragon, is thrown into the lake of fire (Rev 20:10).

The Lord Jesus is the victorious warrior because he was the faithful servant of the King. When the Son of Man ascends to the Ancient of Days and receives the kingdom, it is because he fulfilled the stipulations of the Pactum Salutis with the King of Heaven. While obedience to the stipulations of the Pactum Salutis overlaps with the Covenant of Works with Adam, and while Jesus does what Adam failed to do, the Lord Jesus does more under the Pactum Salutis than was required of Adam under the Covenant of Works. They are two separate covenants. Jesus was required by the stipulations of the Pactum Salutis to bear the sanction of damnation under the Covenant of Works with Adam for the elect. His active obedience was not merely actively taking their place under the wrath of God, but actively obeying the Pactum stipulation that required his death under the wrath of God for the elect. The cross is the intersect of the Covenant of Works with Adam and the Pactum Salutis with the Lord Jesus. On the cross he bore the sanction of the Covenant of Works for the elect. In his obedience, he fulfilled the stipulation of the Pactum Salutis and merited the eschatological blessing. His ascension and exaltation is as the obedient covenant keeper of the Pactum Salutis. In his resurrection, ascension, and exaltation, he is crowned the righteous servant. His righteousness, then, was earned. His covenant blessing was attained through keeping the covenant. By his meritorious obedience he is glorified.

When Jesus died on the cross, the books were opened and all the sins of the elect were paid for. Jesus' death was proleptic of the Final Judgment. When he died, the elect died. There the sinless one bore the sins of the many. On Golgotha, Jesus, as federal head under the Pactum Salutis, bore the eternal wrath of believers for their sins in Adam under the Covenant of Works. The crucifixion of Christ Jesus was Judgment Day for believers. As Paul writes,

> He made Him who knew no sin to *be* sin on our behalf, so that we might become the righteousness of God in Him. (2 Cor 5:21)

There is no coming Judgment Day for the believer. The cross was his Judgment Day. The believer's "old man" was crucified when Jesus was crucified (Rom 6:6, 8). All the sins of the believer faced the Final Judgment adjudication of the Covenant of Works in the crucifixion of Christ. Paul writes the Colossians,

> ... having canceled out the certificate of debt consisting of decrees against us and which was hostile to us; and He has taken it out of the way, having nailed it to the cross. (Col 2:14)

In the death of Christ, the believer was judged according to his works, and the sanction of damnation was rendered.

But the cross was also the fulfillment of the covenant stipulation under the Pactum Salutis by which Christ merited the eschatological blessing of the kingdom. So as the believer was judged by the Final Judgment on the cross, the believer is counted the heir of the kingdom through the meritorious covenant obedience of Christ that took him to the cross. The resurrection of Christ is the declaration that he is the righteous covenant heir; so Christ's resurrection is the believer's resurrection and declaration of covenant righteousness. Justification is not a general declaration of righteousness. Justification by faith is the participation of the believer in the declaration of covenant-keeping righteousness in his federal head, Christ Jesus.

The second book, the Book of Life, is the list of those whom Christ represents as federal head. For them he died; for them he obeyed. For them he is risen and exalted. Their names were written in the Lamb's Book of Life from the foundation of the world (Rev 13:8; 17:8). They will not be blotted out of the book of life. Jesus promises " I will not erase his name from the book of life" (Rev 3:5). Beale notes that none but the elect are ever written in the book of life.[29] The unbeliever's name was never written in the book of life (Rev 13:8; 17:8). In both verses, the perfect tense is used for "written."[30] Those who have their names in the book of life from the foundation of the world still have their name there. No one

---

29. Beale, *Revelation*, 280.
30. γέγραπται, *grapho*.

has their name erased. Their federal head took their place on the cross and merited the glory of heaven on their behalf. Everyone who believes in the Lord Jesus has already gone through the final Judgment Day.

Already/Not Yet

Jesus did tell parables that describe the difference between the believer transformed by grace and the unbeliever. He tells three parables recorded in Matthew 25 that speak of a general coming judgment. The virgins that were prepared and waiting for the bridegroom's coming entered the wedding feast, while those who were not watching for the groom's coming were shut out. Secondly, he tells the story of a master who gave talents to his servant and returned to judge and reward. Third, he tells the story of the sheep and the goats. He says,

> But when the Son of Man comes in His glory, and all the angels with Him, then He will sit on His glorious throne. ^{32} All the nations will be gathered before Him; and He will separate them from one another, as the shepherd separates the sheep from the goats; ^{33} and He will put the sheep on His right, and the goats on the left. (Matt 25:31–33)

The sheep he will welcome: "Come, you who are blessed of My Father, inherit the kingdom prepared for you from the foundation of the world" (Matt 25:34). But the goats he will send to "eternal punishment" (Matt 25:46). This generalized judgment is common in his teaching. Jesus warns against separating the wheat and tares before the harvest (Matt 13:30). And the coming judgment is like the separation of fish caught in a dragnet cast into the sea. He says,

> So it will be at the end of the age; the angels will come forth and take out the wicked from among the righteous, ^{50} and will throw them into the furnace of fire; in that place there will be weeping and gnashing of teeth. (Matt 13:49–50)

On the final day, the world will see clearly the separation of those in Christ and those not in Christ.

But there is something else that will be clear at that final day. Believers have already been judged in Christ and given eschatological life in Christ. The believer has already passed through the Final Judgment. Jesus says,

> Truly, truly, I say to you, he who hears My word, and believes Him who sent Me, has eternal life, and does not come into judgment, but has passed out of death into life. (John 5:24)

He uses the perfect tense for "has passed."[31] The believer has passed from death to life and the results remain. The believer is already a new creature (2 Cor 5:17). He already is a citizen of heaven (Phil 3:20; Heb 12:22–24). He is already a partaker of the eschatological glory as he is inhabited by the Holy Spirit. When the Lord Jesus appears, the believer will not undergo judicial review. Paul describes the believer's transformation as the "revealing of the sons of God" (Rom 8:19). He may look like a janitor in this world. She appears to this world as a commoner. But when the Lord Jesus comes, they will be transformed in glory as the children of God. Paul writes,

> Behold, I tell you a mystery; we will not all sleep, but we will all be changed, 52 in a moment, in the twinkling of an eye, at the last trumpet; for the trumpet will sound, and the dead will be raised imperishable, and we will be changed. 53 For this perishable must put on the imperishable, and this mortal must put on immortality. (1 Cor 15:51–53)

Faster than the eye blinks, in the twinkling of an eye, believers will be transformed to the imperishable, the immortal, the glorified image bearers of the Lord Jesus, who inherit the kingdom of God (1 Cor 15:50). There will not be a video review of their sins and obedient works. There will not be words of rebuke for their unbelief or ill intent. Likewise, there will not be any delay before believers are glorified possessors of the kingdom of God.

Though it remains to be seen. Not yet are believers glorified. Not yet are believers sinless. Not yet are believers recipients of their new bodies. Not yet are believers in the full eschatological glory of the royal temple of God. But already their sins were judged. Already they are new creatures. Already they are heirs of the kingdom. Already they are indwelt by the Holy Spirit. Already is God their Abba. Already is Christ their brother. Already are they living in the resurrection of Jesus. Already they have passed from death to life and will not come into judgment. They already enjoy the eschatological reward. Jesus told the disciples,

---

31. μεταβέβηκεν, *metabaino*.

> Truly I say to you, there is no one who has left house or brothers or sisters or mother or father or children or farms, for My sake and for the gospel's sake, **30** but that he will receive a hundred times as much now in the present age, houses and brothers and sisters and mothers and children and farms, along with persecutions; and in the age to come, eternal life. (Mark 10:29–30)

Already believers are blessed as the children of God in Christ. This is not a "name it and claim it" promise. This is the reality of the believer's life in the present age. God may provide a house or not; God may provide a life full of fellowship in the midst of persecution, but it is a life filled with the life of the resurrection in Christ in the present age. And certainly the covenant blessing is theirs in the age to come, eternal life. They already reign with Christ. John writes,

> Then I saw thrones, and they sat on them, and judgment was given to them. And I saw the souls of those who had been beheaded because of their testimony of Jesus and because of the word of God, and those who had not worshiped the beast or his image, and had not received the mark on their forehead and on their hand; and they came to life and reigned with Christ for a thousand years. (Rev 20:4)

Before the White Throne Judgment, they already reign with Christ.

To use a rough analogy, it would be like a coach telling the team that every player who is on next season's list will be given a new uniform and new equipment, but those who are being cut will have to clean out their lockers and leave the building. Coach will reveal who is who on July 1. Up until July 1, there are rumblings about who is going through and who is not, but on that day everyone will know. Some will stay and some will go. July 1 comes and all the players assemble. The team for the next season shows up dressed in their new uniform; the rest do not. Yes, Coach had told each person on next season's team ahead of time and had even given them their stuff as far back as the date that he announced what he was going to do. Johnny knew at the end of May, Stan at the beginning of June, etc. But on July 1, when they all show up, it is clear to all. Coach says, "This is the team!" The rest pack up and leave. They were already the team, but not yet.

But some will argue that a final justification remains before they enter the eternal kingdom of God. After all, was not Abraham "justified" by his works (Jas 2:24) after he was "justified" by faith (Jas 2:21–24; Gen 15:6)? Two points should be noted in answering this objection. First, Abraham's being "justified by works" (Jas 2:21) was not on the final Judgment Day. It was during the course of his life as a believer that he was "justified by works." Second, there is a theological equivocation between speaking of Abraham's justification and speaking of his being justified by works. This often happens when the meaning of a phrase is used with different meanings dependent on its biblical or theological context. An example would be the word "sanctify." Leviticus gives food laws and commands:

> They shall therefore keep My charge, so that they will not bear sin because of it and die thereby because they profane it; I am the LORD who sanctifies them. (Lev 22:9)

Israel's obedience to the dietary laws was part of their holiness to the Lord. Likewise, the believer grows in holiness out of a heart of faith and is sanctified. In this general sense, "sanctification" is about making holy. Unbelieving Israelites could be covenantally holy, "sanctified," if they obeyed the dietary laws of the Law. In the New Testament, there is also this broader covenantal use of "sanctified." Paul writes,

> For the unbelieving husband is sanctified through his wife, and the unbelieving wife is sanctified through her believing husband; for otherwise your children are unclean, but now they are holy. (1 Cor 7:14)

Or see the same usage in Hebrews regarding the apostate:

> How much severer punishment do you think he will deserve who has trampled under foot the Son of God, and has regarded as unclean the blood of the covenant by which he was sanctified, and has insulted the Spirit of grace? (Heb 10:29)

But when the discussion focuses on the *ordo salutis* in the believer's life, the meaning is narrowed. The unbelieving husband is not "sanctified" in this narrower sense. "Sanctification" in the *ordo salutis* refers to the definitive and progressive transformation of the believer into the image of the Lord Jesus. It is the spiritual transformation that only the true believer receives. Theological confusion ensues when the narrower use is imposed on the passages that have a broader meaning.

In the same way, "justify" has a broader usage. Jesus says,

> Yet wisdom is justified [ἐδικαιώθη, *dikaioo*] by all her children. (Luke 7:35 ESV)

The NASB proves the point by translating the word as "vindicated" in an effort that it not be confused with the evangelical understanding of "justified." Jesus is not suggesting that wisdom needs saving justification. But wisdom is proved to be right by her children. Just a few verses earlier, the people "justified" God. Luke writes,

> And all the people that heard him, and the publicans, justified [ἐδικαίωσαν, *dikaioo*] God, being baptized with the baptism of John. (Luke 7:29 KJV)

"Justify" means to declare righteous. Wisdom is proved by her children. God was acknowledged to be righteous. This is the broader use. Isn't it true that when believers are transformed into their glorified state, they will be manifest to be the righteous sons of God? But is it not true that when God created Adam, before he fell, God declared everything he made good. In this broader sense, Adam was declared to be the righteous image of God. In this broader sense, one could say Adam was "justified" before he sinned! It is in this broader sense that James can say that Abraham was "justified by works." His works demonstrated his faith. But Paul uses the word "justified" in the context of the relationship of the Covenant of Works, the Mosaic Law, the New Covenant with a narrow meaning. When Adam stood before the Spirit in the garden, he was not declared to be the covenant keeper in righteousness. He was a naked sinner in need of God's redemption. The Mosaic Law did not change the equation for anyone. All stood condemned in Adam. But now a righteousness from God is available through faith in Christ. This narrow use of justification refers to the covenant status under the Pactum Salutis that merits the sabbath reward. When the believer has reigned for ten million years, will not that glorious reign declare the righteousness the believer has in Christ? But it is not another "justification" in the narrow sense. In the *ordo salutis*, the believer is legally declared to be the covenant keeper because of a righteousness completely alien to his own works and found only in his federal head, the Lord Jesus Christ. There is one justification in Christ.

LAW OF THE HARVEST

Someone may object that Paul did teach a "law of the harvest." Paul writes,

> Do not be deceived, God is not mocked; for whatever a man sows, this he will also reap. (Gal 6:7)

This is not the only verse. Proverbs 22:8 teaches the same principle:

> He who sows iniquity will reap vanity,
> And the rod of his fury will perish.

Like others, Robert N. Wilkin tries to reconcile salvation by grace with reward for works when he writes,

> It is impossible to harmonize this text with Ephesians 2:8–9 if both are speaking of the same aspect of eternal life . . . Ephesians 2:8–9 refers to the *definite present possession* of it as a gift, whereas Galatians 6:7–9 speaks of the *possible future possession* of it as a reward for work done.[32]

But this approach sounds far too close to Charlie Anderson's Thanksgiving prayer in the movie *Shenandoah*. Jimmy Stewart plays Anderson, a Virginia farmer struggling to stay neutral during the Civil War. He prays,

> Lord, we cleared this land. We plowed it, sowed it, and harvested. We cook the harvest. It wouldn't be here and we wouldn't be eating it if we hadn't done it all ourselves. We worked dog-bone hard for every crumb and morsel, but we thank you Lord just the same for the food we're about to eat, amen.[33]

This is how Evangelicals sound when they talk about being saved by grace and rewarded for their works! But the believer has no boast in himself. His covenant blessing is the blessing merited by the seed. Paul's concern in Galatians is not merely whether Gentiles have to keep the ceremonial laws of the Old Covenant. Paul objects to bringing any of the Law into the equation of salvation. Christ is the seed promised Abraham, and the believer is heir in Christ. Any discussion of grace and Law being necessary to receive the promise is contrary to grace. The kingdom promised Abraham, and all its blessings, is received solely on the basis of Christ's meritorious obedience under the Pactum Salutis. He has done it; that is the good news.

Sow to works; reap destruction. Sow to the gospel; reap everlasting blessing. This contrast is seen in other passages. Jesus' words in Matthew 7:2 are a good starting point:

> For in the same way you judge others, you will be judged, and with the measure you use, it will be measured to you. (NIV)

---

32. Wilkin et al., *Judgment*, 40.
33. *Shenandoah*, directed by Andrew V. McLaglen (Universal Pictures, 1965).

Jesus is not suggesting that to the degree a believer is censorious, God will be censorious with him on Judgment Day. On the other hand, Jesus is not promising that God will be merciful to the believer to the degree that the believer has shown mercy. Who would be without judgment! All believers are in trouble if the mercy God will show them is dependent on the amount of mercy they have shown others! Rather, Jesus is contrasting the heart of the self-righteous Pharisee with the renewed heart of the believer. The Pharisee has only the Law; by it he justifies himself and condemns others. But the believer sees differently. As a recipient of God's grace, the believer counts himself righteous based on nothing he himself has done and sees his own need for Christ when he sees the sin of others. There are "measures." The self-righteous Pharisee measures himself and others by obedience to the righteous requirements of God. The believer sees sin, but knows he has been forgiven, and knows that God is saving others.

The same language is used in Luke. Jesus says,

> Judge not, and you will not be judged; condemn not, and you will not be condemned; forgive, and you will be forgiven; ^{38} give, and it will be given to you. Good measure, pressed down, shaken together, running over, will be put into your lap. For with the measure you use it will be measured back to you. (Luke 6:37–38 ESV)

Parallel to Matthew 7:2, Jesus says the censorious self-righteous will be judged accordingly. He says the same thing four times:

> Judge not, and you will not be judged
> Condemn not, and you will not be condemned
> Forgive, and you will be forgiven
> Give, and it will be given to you. (Luke 6:37–38)

In contrast to the condemning self-righteous, the believer forgives and gives! There is one topic here: the contrast between the self-righteous religious and the believer transformed by grace. The prior verses give the fuller context to understand Jesus' exhortation to "give." Jesus says,

> But I say to you who hear, love your enemies, do good to those who hate you, ^{28} bless those who curse you, pray for those who mistreat you. ^{29} Whoever hits you on the cheek, offer him the other also; and whoever takes away your coat, do not withhold your shirt from him either. ^{30} Give to everyone who asks of you, and whoever takes away what is yours, do not demand it back. ^{31} Treat others the same way you want them to treat you. ^{32} If

> you love those who love you, what credit is *that* to you? For even sinners love those who love them. ³³ If you do good to those who do good to you, what credit is *that* to you? For even sinners do the same. ³⁴ If you lend to those from whom you expect to receive, what credit is *that* to you? Even sinners lend to sinners in order to receive back the same *amount*. ³⁵ But love your enemies, and do good, and lend, expecting nothing in return; and your reward will be great, and you will be sons of the Most High; for He Himself is kind to ungrateful and evil *men*. ³⁶ Be merciful, just as your Father is merciful. (Luke 6:27–36)

Jesus is talking about a lot more than generosity in Christian service! He is calling the disciples to be like their Father in their attitude and actions toward their enemies! When the believer's rights are on the line, he responds with grace! This is not the way of the world. Even among the moral of the world, there is the understanding, "I did this for you; you owe me!" The world responds, "You never did anything for me! Why should I do anything for you?" But the kingdom of God and its children of the Most High are different! Jesus says, "Give to everyone who asks." Tit for tat is not the ethic of God's kingdom. Loving those from whom you receive is no different than the world. "Love your enemies." The believer gives because by God's grace he has! Great is the eschatological hope that is his in Christ—"your reward will be great." In this the believer evidences that he knows grace and is a child of the King—"because he is kind to the ungrateful and wicked." So, Jesus says, "Rather than judging like the world, extend grace as you have received grace! Don't judge or condemn! Forgive and give!" There is no discussion of Christian stewardship or degrees of reward for Christian service! Much more foundationally, Jesus teaches that the children of the kingdom live in mercy to others as their Father has shown them his mercy! In contrast to talking about some greater rewards for Christian works, Jesus promises the great reward that belongs to all believers! The believer's mercy to others is only returned to the believer overflowingly, "running over."

Paul too is not teaching some additional blessing when he writes,

> Do not be deceived, God is not mocked; for whatever a man sows, this he will also reap. ⁸ For the one who sows to his own flesh will from the flesh reap corruption, but the one who sows to the Spirit will from the Spirit reap eternal life. ⁹ Let us not lose heart in doing good, for in due time we will reap if we do not grow weary. ¹⁰ So then, while we have opportunity, let us

do good to all people, and especially to those who are of the household of the faith. (Gal 6:7–10)

Paul has spent the whole epistle refuting the Judaizers, who would mix works of the Law with the gospel. At length, he has contrasted the promise to Abraham and fulfillment in Christ to the Mosaic Law to show the difference between righteousness by grace in Christ and righteousness by obedience. The two are contrasted with "Spirit" and "flesh." The two terms are not contrasting between the immaterial and bodily parts of a man, but rather the legal standing all have in Adam—"flesh"—and the standing believers have in Christ—"Spirit." So now that he concludes the letter, it is ludicrous to think that Paul is saying,

> Don't be deceived, God is not mocked; to the degree that one lives for the flesh, their rewards will be diminished, but to the degree one obeys God, God will gain eternal rewards from God!

That is exactly what Paul has been vehemently fighting against for the previous five chapters! This erroneous view is exactly why he wrote the Galatians! Yes, theologically it is stated with different theological nuance, but it is still "in by grace, rewards according to works." Paul is actually saying exactly the opposite! "Flesh" is reward by merit; "Spirit" is reward by pure grace, not based on the believer's works! He warns those who live in the former that the result is only "corruption." But those who live in the gospel of grace will be given "eternal life." Degrees are not at issue; damnation and glorification with the Glory of the Lord Jesus are.

THE SAVIOR'S INVITATION

When the Lord Jesus comes to judge the nations, he also comes with his reward—his people. In Isaiah 40 they are pictured as sheep in his arms. Isaiah writes,

> Behold, the Lord GOD will come with might,
> With His arm ruling for Him.
> Behold, His reward is with Him
> And His recompense before Him.
> 11 Like a shepherd He will tend His flock,
> In His arm He will gather the lambs
> And carry *them* in His bosom;
> He will gently lead the nursing *ewes*. (Isa 40:10–11)

He purchased them from every nation. John writes,

> And they sang a new song, saying, "Worthy are You to take the book and to break its seals; for You were slain, and purchased for God with Your blood *men* from every tribe and tongue and people and nation. **10** You have made them *to be* a kingdom and priests to our God; and they will reign upon the earth." (Rev 5:9–10)

He paid the price for sinners. He did the meritorious work to obtain the kingdom. Theirs is the kingdom because of his work.

God, the Trinity, did what Adam did not do. In the Pactum Salutis, God became incarnate to be the Second Adam. Isaiah writes, "the Lord God will come." God the Son became a man and obeyed God the Father on behalf of the elect, thereby meriting the eschatological sabbath glory Adam failed to obtain. The Second Adam is the faithful priest-king who crushed the head of the serpent at the cross. His is the reward.

The Lord Jesus says,

> Behold, I am coming quickly, and My reward [*misthos*, wage] is with Me, to give to each as the work is His.[34] **13** I am the Alpha and the Omega, the first and the last, the beginning and the end. (Rev 22:12–13 AT)

The Lord Jesus fulfilled the Pactum Salutis and the reward/wage is his to give to all who believe. God has come and done what Adam did not do. The invitation is set forth:

> Blessed are those who wash their robes, so that they may have the authority to the tree of life,[35] and may enter by the gates into the city. **15** Outside are the dogs and the sorcerers and the immoral persons and the murderers and the idolaters, and everyone who loves and practices lying. (Rev 22:14–15 AT)

The reader is invited to enter the kingdom and partake of the tree of life. The finished work of Christ's blood can make one clean and give right to the tree. Again, here is succinctly stated the passive and active obedience of Christ. His obedience on the cross paid for the sins of the elect and merited the kingdom. So the believer is made clean and has "authority to the tree of life." Not only is the believer given entrance to the kingdom. By the meritorious work of the Lord Jesus, the believer is made clean and exalted to have "authority to the tree of life." Jesus is the faithful servant.

---

34. ὡς τὸ ἔργον ἐστὶν αὐτοῦ.
35. ἵνα ἔσται ἡ ἐξουσία αὐτῶν ἐπὶ τὸ ξύλον τῆς ζωῆς.

So outside the kingdom are all the unholy. Jesus is the faithful king. John writes,

> I, Jesus, have sent My angel to testify to you these things for the churches. I am the root and the descendant of David, the bright morning star. (Rev 22:16)

Again Isaiah is referenced. What was purchased by the Lord Jesus belongs to all who believe. John writes,

> The Spirit and the bride say, "Come." And let the one who hears say, "Come." And let the one who is thirsty come; let the one who wishes take the water of life without cost. (Rev 22:17)

Isaiah 55 says,

> Ho! Every one who thirsts, come to the waters;
> And you who have no money come, buy and eat.
> Come, buy wine and milk
> Without money and without cost.
> ^{2} Why do you spend money for what is not bread,
> And your wages for what does not satisfy?
> Listen carefully to Me, and eat what is good,
> And delight yourself in abundance.
> ^{3} Incline your ear and come to Me.
> Listen, that you may live;
> And I will make an everlasting covenant with you,
> According to the faithful mercies shown to David.
> ^{4} Behold, I have made him a witness to the peoples,
> A leader and commander for the peoples.
> ^{5} Behold, you will call a nation you do not know,
> And a nation which knows you not will run to you,
> Because of the Lord your God, even the Holy One of Israel;
> For He has glorified you. (Isa 55:1–5)

Isaiah writes to those who have felt the curse of the Old Covenant. He offers the blessing of the New Covenant purchased by Christ. It cost him all; it cost them nothing. He is the descendant promised David. He will bring into existence the kingdom from people who did not know him but will run to him in faith. As Jesus said, "And I, if I am lifted up from the earth, will draw all men to Myself" (John 12:32). So the Spirit and the bride say, "Come."

10

The Temple Builder
1 Corinthians 3

THE PROBLEM

THE LORD JESUS KEPT the Pactum Salutis as Second Adam and is enthroned in Glory at the right hand of the Father. He merited the eschatological blessing and secured the glorification of those He represented as federal head. Now he gathers the Gentiles from the ends of the earth to be the kingdom people of God. Clothed with the Glory-Spirit, he sends forth his Spirit to transform Jew and Gentile into the holy temple of the King.

The good news is that Jesus merited and secured the outcome! The toil is present every day in the labor of evangelism and ministry. Paul knew as well as anyone the certainty of the coming day of glory! But as well, he lived the difficulty of building the living temple the Lord Jesus purchased. Paul starts 1 Corinthians by calling the believers at Corinth "saints." From the two letters we have of the four he wrote them, it is immediately clear that calling them "holy" or "sanctified" was not descriptive of their behavior! Their doctrinal and ethical errors were numerous! They were divisive, eschewed suffering as beneath them, and allowed immorality among their members. They participated in idolatry, boasted in their spiritual gifts, and turned the Lord's Supper into a reason for their own chastisement. Paul notes, "when you come together as a church, I hear that divisions exist among you" (1 Cor 11:18). Paul starts his first epistle by addressing their divisiveness in chapters 1–4.

After his customary opening to the letter, Paul writes,

> Now I exhort you, brethren, by the name of our Lord Jesus Christ, that you all agree and that there be no divisions among you, but that you be made complete in the same mind and in the same judgment. ¹¹ For I have been informed concerning you, my brethren, by Chloe's *people*, that there are quarrels among you. ¹² Now I mean this, that each one of you is saying, "I am of Paul," and "I of Apollos," and "I of Cephas," and "I of Christ." (1 Cor 1:10-12)

Again, in the midst of his argument, Paul writes,

> For when one says, "I am of Paul," and another, "I am of Apollos," are you not *mere* men? (1 Cor 3:4)

Not only is it interesting that Paul starts his corrections by addressing their divisiveness, but his correction is based on a thorough and detailed theological argument from the Pactum Salutis.

THE LORD'S TEMPLE

Paul's Gospel

Because Paul's letters are occasional, one can lose sight of the cohesive gospel message in Paul's writings. Paul's gospel is more than that God sent his Son into the world to pay for sin, that Jesus rose on the third day and is exalted to the right hand of the Father, and that all who put their faith in Christ will be saved. Though this is wonderfully true, it leaves much to be said! One gets a glimpse of the bigger picture in Romans or Galatians, but all the elements are present in 1 Corinthians.

One the immediate clues to the bigger panorama is the introduction (1 Cor 1:1–9). Paul references his own role as "apostle of Jesus Christ through the will of God," the Corinthian believer's calling as the "sanctified in Christ Jesus," the "Lord Jesus Christ," "grace and peace," and that the Corinthians are "not lacking in any gift, awaiting eagerly the revelation of our Lord Jesus Christ." Failure to see the gospel as the Lord Jesus' fulfillment of the Pactum Salutis leaves the reader with a collection of diffuse, loosely related truths that roll around in the same box like marbles but fail to provide the powerful message of Paul's gospel.

Paul argues against believer dragging believer to pagan courts from the fact that believers will judge the angels (1 Cor 6:3). He addresses their immorality by reminding them that the unrighteous will not inherit the kingdom (1 Cor 6:9). Their bodies are the temple of the Holy Spirit (1 Cor 6:19). Their focus on spiritual gifts is redirected, for there are "varieties of gifts, but the same Spirit. [5] And there are varieties of ministries, and the same Lord" (1 Cor 12:4–5). Central to the gospel is Jesus' exaltation as Second Adam (1 Cor 15:45). But when the pieces are examined without theological context, one is left with confusion.

A notable example of a verse that has led to bewilderment when divorced from its theological context is 1 Corinthians 15:28:

> When all things are subjected to Him, then the Son Himself also will be subjected to the One who subjected all things to Him, so that God may be all in all.

Stripped from its theological context, this verse has led many to hold that the Son is eternally subordinate to the Father. So too, there is confusion regarding passages that refer to the Son and God the Father. In 3:5 the Lord Jesus is the one who distributes ministry to Paul and Apollos, but in 3:9 the ministers are God's fellow workers. Paul writes that "Christ belongs to God" (1 Cor 3:23). In 4:4–5, Paul says it is the Lord Jesus who "examines" and who "will bring to light the things hidden in darkness." Then God will give believers praise. So how do all the parts fit together?

The Pactum Salutis is the covenant of the Trinity to save sinners and glorify them as the people of God and bride of Christ. The triune God before creation covenanted within the Trinity to create heaven and earth, and to bring man into an everlasting relationship with God in glory. The Father would be King in heaven. The Son would be the image of the Father and fulfill the role of the Second Adam. The Spirit would manifest the Glory of God in heaven, and recreate that Glory in man on earth, which would culminate with the new heavens and new earth—one royal dwelling of God and his people. Forever the Father would be manifest in creation on the throne. Forever the Son would be the God-man, who is the exalted Second Adam with his bride, the church. Forever the Spirit would manifest the holy Glory of God, filling the new creation and its people. Forever the triune God who exists in himself, Creator of all things, would live with his creatures in the creation.

Specifically, the Son would be the vassal image of the Father, the King of Heaven. While there is no subordination of the Son ontologically in the Trinity, the Son would enter creation in a role of subordination. He would image the righteousness of the King and build the royal temple on earth to mirror the royal temple of the King in heaven. The Second Adam would obey the King and both propitiate God's wrath against sinners and merit their eschatological glory. As federal head, he would take their damnation sanctioned under the Covenant of Works, and merit their covenant inheritance under the Pactum Salutis. Having obeyed the stipulation to death on the cross, he was pronounced faithful vassal son by the resurrection and enthroned as Son of Man at the right hand of the King of Heaven. Clothed in the Glory of the King, the Lord Jesus sent the Spirit to bring the elect to glory. As previously noted, in the application of redemption by the Holy Spirit, the believer puts on the finished work of the Second Adam.

First Corinthians' introduction overflows with references to this work of God in Christ Jesus. Paul himself is the representative with all the authority of the one he represents, the Lord Jesus. He is an apostle. The believers at Corinth have been made to be the holy people, "sanctified" "saints" along with everyone who worships the Lord Jesus. By "grace" they receive that which he merited. To glory and sabbath "peace"[1] they will be brought. God has given to them in Christ all knowledge of God's work. Like a purchase attested by purchase contract, so God confirms that they have been purchased by Christ. The presence and gifts of the Spirit at work among them attest they are being built to be the living temple that will be revealed when the Lord Jesus comes again. When the Lord Jesus comes and has completely subjected all things, then he will, as Son of Man and Second Adam, be subject to the King of Heaven. So he will remain with his bride with the God the Father, King of Heaven, in the Glory of the Spirit forever.

Power and Wisdom of God

So how could the Corinthians live in division, and boast in men? They were baptized in the name of the Lord Jesus, not the teacher's name (1 Cor 1:13ff.). When they were baptized, they were baptized in the name of the Redeemer. That itself put them in immediate contrast to the way the world thinks. The world's wisdom is all about what one can achieve and what credits one has to one's name. Significance and blessing are based on who you are and what you have. The Jews looked for signs—attesting

---

1. OT: *shalom.*

power. The Greeks looked for wisdom. But redemption in Christ is not based on the power and wisdom of the world.

God intentionally chose what the world counted foolish to demonstrate his wisdom and power. He chose the weak, the base, the things that are not. Believers have no boast in what they have done. Their boast is in what God has done for them in Christ (1 Cor 1:26–31). The cross is the great leveler of grace. The Corinthians could not look to anything they or their teachers had done to bring redemption. In the cross, God came in power and wisdom to bring redemption and glory to sinners! Isaiah contrasts the worthless idols of the nations with the power of God. Christ brought righteousness to sinners through his covenant obedience. Christ was exalted to be Lord and sent his Spirit to transform the elect to be the living stones of the temple of God. In Christ, believers are redeemed from bondage (1 Cor 1:30–31).

Paul continues his argument by appealing to his own ministry to substantiate the contrast between the way the world thinks and the kingdom of God. The gospel message shapes the content and manner of Paul's preaching. He did not come offering the wisdom of the world (1 Cor 2:1). His message was contrary to what the world proclaims. He spoke things unknown to the world given to him by God (1 Cor 2:10–11). He preached the gospel "predestined before the ages to our glory" (1 Cor 2:7). He revealed in his preaching a glory promised the believer that exceeded anything anyone has ever seen or dreamed of (1 Cor 2:9). And it was not the achievement of man, but the glory "GOD HAS PREPARED FOR THOSE WHO LOVE HIM" (1 Cor 2:9).

This message was a scandal to the Jews and foolish to the Greeks (1 Cor 1:23). God purposed to bring sinners to everlasting glory through the death of the Lord Jesus Christ. This is not a message from this world. It is the wisdom of God revealed through his Spirit about the work of his Son. It is not of this world! It is not about what believers do, but about what is "freely given to us by God" (1 Cor 2:12). Only those who are citizens of the coming kingdom are able to understand; but indeed believers have the mind of Christ and understand!

So the big story is that the Lord Jesus fulfilled the Pactum Salutis and merited the eschatological blessing for believers. He has sent his Spirit to apply his redemption to the elect that they might be built into the dwelling of God's Glory, his temple. When the temple is finished, the Lord Jesus will present it to the King of Heaven. Then the Lord Jesus,

Second Adam, and his bride, the dwelling of God's Glory, will be subject in Glory to the Father forever in order that God be all in all!

Temple Builders

When Paul begins to directly discuss the divisions over the various teachers in 1 Corinthians 3, Paul is actually at the climax of the argument that started in chapter 1! Rather than the Corinthian believers' minds being renewed to think in accord with the wisdom of God in the cross, they still think like the world. Paul gave them milk because they were like babies, unable to understand (1 Cor 3:1–2). Their divisiveness evidences that they walk according to the wisdom of the world. When they chose different teachers to follow over others, they found their identity the way the world does. If only they could understand the big picture of what God was doing in Christ! Paul so patiently instructs. He first explains that he and Apollos are just teachers the Lord Jesus used to bring them to faith and teach them (1 Cor 3:6). Paul and Apollos are just servants. But it is God who was at work causing them to grow in the faith. It is God who planned their redemption. It is God who became incarnate to atone for their sin and merit their blessing. It is God the Holy Spirit who was at work in them and through them. Just like the Corinthian believers, Paul and Apollos are individually accountable to God and will receive their pay (*misthos*) from him! Like servants on a farm, they have labored in expectation of the blessing that is theirs in Christ! It is not their works that will be recompensed to them, but Christ's. So, as Jesus promised, "Great is your wage [*misthos*]" (Matt 5:12). But Paul and Apollos are not just servants of the Lord Jesus harvesting souls to redemption. The Lord Jesus, Lord of Glory, has purchased sinners to be living stones of the eschatological temple of God. The Lord Jesus is building that temple. Paul writes,

> For we are God's fellow workers; you are God's field, God's building. [10] According to the grace of God which was given to me, like a wise master builder I laid a foundation, and another is building on it. But each man must be careful how he builds on it. [11] For no man can lay a foundation other than the one which is laid, which is Jesus Christ. (1 Cor 3:9–11)

Paul, Apollos, and the other teachers are doing more than evangelizing and discipling a harvest of believers. They are engaged in the work of their master, the Lord Jesus. The spiritual gifts the Corinthians are in awe over are not powers to utilize for their own entertainment. The Lord is exalted to the throne, and has sent his Spirit and given gifts (see 1 Cor 3:5) for the building of the eschatological temple of God! The believers are that temple! Paul finally writes the obvious:

> Do you not know that you are a temple of God and *that* the Spirit of God dwells in you? (1 Cor 3:16)

God gifted Paul to be "like a wise master builder" to lay the foundation, Jesus Christ! Others are building on that foundation. Paul has already elaborated on that foundation of the cross in chapter 1. The temple the Lord Jesus is building is built on the gospel of the cross. The cross is the focal point of the work of Christ in the Pactum Salutis. But teachers have come into the Corinthian church and are preaching the wisdom of the world rather than the cross. In 2 Corinthians 11:5 Paul refers to them as "super-apostles."[2] Paul warns the Corinthians, as they think like the world and are being led astray, that those who build the temple will be held to account to build on the foundation of the cross, the finished work of Christ. There isn't any other foundation on which these teachers can build.

Paul continues the contrast between the wisdom of the world and the wisdom of God as he contrasts the building materials of the gospel teachers and the building materials of the false teachers:

> Now if any man builds on the foundation with gold, silver, precious stones, wood, hay, straw, [13] each man's work will become evident; for the day will show it because it is to be revealed with fire, and the fire itself will test the quality of each man's work. [14] If any man's work which he has built on it remains, he will receive a reward. [15] If any man's work is burned up, he will suffer loss . . . (1 Cor 3:12–15)

Paul says there is a "day" that will show the teachers' work for what it was. On that "day" it will be clear whether they were building the temple either with temple materials, gold, silver, and precious stones, or building with material inappropriate to the temple, wood, hay, straw. Building the temple of the Lord Jesus requires building consistent with the message of the grace of the Lord Jesus found in the cross. The false teachers are building with the wisdom of the world, not the gospel.

The "day" refers to the final Judgment Day. Paul uses the same language when he writes the Thessalonians, "But you, brethren, are not in

---

2. λογίζομαι γὰρ μηδὲν ὑστερηκέναι τῶν ὑπερλίαν ἀποστόλων.

darkness, that the day would overtake you like a thief..." (1 Thess 5:4).[3] And when he writes the Romans, "The night is almost gone, and the day is near" (Rom 13:12). This is the common reference among the New Testament writers. The author of Hebrews writes,

> ... not forsaking our own assembling together, as is the habit of some, but encouraging *one another*; and all the more as you see the day drawing near. (Heb 10:25)

The broader context makes Paul's reference clear. In 1 Corinthians 4, he writes,

> But to me it is a very small thing that I may be examined by you, or by *any* human court; in fact, I do not even examine myself ... ⁵ Therefore do not go on passing judgment before the time, *but wait* until the Lord comes who will both bring to light the things hidden in the darkness and disclose the motives of *men's* hearts; and then each man's praise will come to him from God. (1 Cor 4:3, 5)

Paul had started the letter with reference to the "day" when he wrote, "who will also confirm you to the end, blameless in the day of our Lord Jesus Christ" (1 Cor 1:8). Malachi pictures the day as God coming as a consuming fire (Mal 3:2; 4:1). In addition, Malachi says in that day, "And the Lord, whom you seek, will suddenly come to His temple..." (Mal 3:1). God, the consuming fire, will come to his eschatological temple. Malachi asks the obvious question: "who can endure the day of His coming?" (Mal 3:2).

When the Day of Judgment comes, Paul warns that the teacher's work will be evident. The gold, silver, and precious stones will endure the fire, while the wood, hay, and straw will be consumed. The faithful teacher building with the gospel on the foundation of the gospel will, as all believers, receive his wage (*misthos*) purchased by the blood of Christ. But the false teacher who has been propounding a temple not built on the gospel will suffer loss of any wage.

Paul does not here present a spectrum of outcomes, but rather the binary outcome[4] of the false teacher not receiving a wage for his work versus the gospel teacher receiving his wage (*misthos*). He uses an example from the life of a building owner. Paul is the architect. The subcontractors

---

3. See 1 Thess 5:2.

4. Fee, *First Corinthians*, 142–43 notes the "antithetical parallels" between the gospel teacher versus the teacher of the world's wisdom.

come and build. But on the day the owner comes, he evaluates the work. The work that was done to specifications is paid; the work that was substandard is not.

But the consequences Paul sets forth are considerably more serious than degrees of reward or even that the unfaithful workman will "suffer loss" of his reward. Paul doesn't use some word equivalent to the modern-day notion of "reward." As has already been argued, *misthos* is the common word for a wage earned, not a bonus for doing a good job. The later notion is absent from classical Greek literature's use of the word. The notion is absent from the use in the LXX. Paul is simply saying the faithful worker is paid his wage. Complimenting this language is the penalty for the unfaithful worker. His work is burned up, but that is not the "loss." That is the basis for the "loss."

The antithetical parallel is:

| faithful worker | work endures | paid a wage |
| unfaithful worker | work consumed | ζημιωθήσεται (zemioo) |

Almost universally, English translations translate ζημιωθήσεται (*zemioo*) as "suffer loss." But BDAG gives "be punished" for ζημιόω (*zemioo*) here. A. Stumpff, while arguing for "loss," nevertheless acknowledges,

> The natural opposite of "to receive a reward" would seem to be "to suffer punishment"... but it is doubtful from the context whether the word should be taken in its juridical sense.[5]

But that is exactly the context—the Final Judgment! Liddell and Scott gives the meaning "punish," but in a financial context, "to fine."[6] So Paul actually writes,

> εἴ τινος τὸ ἔργον μενεῖ ὃ ἐποικοδόμησεν, μισθὸν λήμψεται [15] εἴ τινος τὸ ἔργον κατακαήσεται, ζημιωθήσεται
> If one's work remains which he built, he will receive a wage; if one's work is consumed by the fire, he will be fined.

The parallelism then is:

---

5. Stumpff, "ζημιόω," 2:890.
6. Liddell and Scott, *Greek-English Lexicon*, s.v. "ζημιόω," 198.

faithful worker	work endures	paid a wage
unfaithful worker	work consumed	fined or punished

Paul does not say that the unfaithful worker will just suffer the loss of his work. Paul says that, in contrast to the faithful worker, who is paid a wage, the unfaithful worker is fined or punished for his work. The problem is not just that the unfaithful workman's work doesn't last, but that it actually damages the temple being built (1 Cor 3:16–17). So he is fined! This portrayal of hell as a fine to pay is common to Jesus' teaching. Jesus warned the unforgiving, "Truly I say to you, you will not come out of there until you have paid up the last cent" (Matt 5:26). Or as Jesus says,

> And his lord, moved with anger, handed him over to the torturers until he should repay all that was owed him. **35** My heavenly Father will also do the same to you, if each of you does not forgive his brother from your heart. (Matt 18:34–35)

This contrast between the wage and the fine is supported by the use of the two terms in classical Greek. Jay Shanor's examination of over fifty ancient sources supports this conclusion. Shanor translates one source from the fourth century BC that is particularly helpful. The requirements of the workmen working on the temple of Athena are given. One of the requirements Shanor translates:

> If anyone should oppose the allotment of the jobs [ἔργων], or should do harm, doing damage [φθήρων] in any way, let those who made the allotments fine [ζαμιόντω] him, whatever fines [ζαμ(αι)] seem right to them, and let them publicly announce it as their determination and summon him into the presiding court for the full sum of the fine [ζαμίαν].[7]

Shanor concludes that Paul uses the same wage-fine contrast in 1 Corinthians 3. Shanor writes,

> Since the Greek word, μισθός, is the term most commonly used for 'wages', it is important and appropriate to retain that sense here as well. It seldom, if ever, carries the connotation 'reward' in the customary sense of that word.[8]

Shanor continues,

---

7. Shanor, "Paul," 462.
8. Shanor, "Paul," 469.

Equally important to the present discussion is the opposite case, i.e., that in which the builder's work fails to stand the test of fire. In that case, we are told that 'he will suffer loss.' The term utilized here is that which is used in the inscription of a fine imposed by those who issue the contracts when, for any reason, an assigned piece of work has not been completed, or has extended beyond the time specified for any segment of the work. If this contextual meaning is applied to the Corinthian passage, it reads, '. . . he shall be fined', a rendering which is more suitable to the context than the more traditional, but less pointed, '. . . he shall suffer loss'.[9]

Shanor sees the active penal force of what has usually been softened as mere "loss" of rewards. The gospel teacher will be paid; the teacher of the world's wisdom will be fined in perdition.

David W. Kuck acknowledges,

> The word ζημιουν by itself can refer to punishment, even eternal damnation. It can equally well refer to a loss such as a payment of fine.[10]

Euripides writes, "For whoe'er, of mortal men, Dares impious deeds, him the gods punish" (ζημιοῦσιν *zemioo*).[11] Josephus uses the word to refer to capital punishment.[12] Jesus uses the word when he says,

> If anyone wishes to come after Me, he must deny himself, and take up his cross and follow Me. 25 For whoever wishes to save his life will lose [ἀπόλλυμι *apollymi*] it; but whoever loses his life for My sake will find it. 26 For what will it profit a man if he gains the whole world and forfeits [ζημιόω *zemioo*] his soul? Or what will a man give in exchange for his soul? 27 For the Son of Man is going to come in the glory of His Father with His angels, and will then repay every man according to his deeds. (Matt 16:24–27)[13]

---

9. Shanor, "Paul," 469.

10. Kuck, *Conflict*, 182–83.

11. Euripides, *Ion*, quoted from *Complete Greek Drama*, 1138 (Greek line 441, p. 22, ed. Jerram).

12. Josephus, *Antiquities*, quoted from *Works of Josephus*, 3:351 (Greek section 15.2); "κρινόμενον ὅτι καὶ μέλλοντα θανάτῳ ζημιοῦσθαι τοῦ κινδύνου" (15:2.16, p. 235, ed. Niese).

13. ὃς γὰρ ἐὰν θέλῃ τὴν ψυχὴν αὐτοῦ σῶσαι ἀπολέσει αὐτήν· ὃς δ᾽ ἂν ἀπολέσῃ τὴν ψυχὴν αὐτοῦ ἕνεκεν ἐμοῦ εὑρήσει αὐτήν. 26 τί γὰρ ὠφεληθήσεται ἄνθρωπος ἐὰν τὸν κόσμον ὅλον κερδήσῃ τὴν δὲ ψυχὴν αὐτοῦ ζημιωθῇ.

As verse 27 makes clear, Jesus is not just asking what profit there really is if one gains the world and loses oneself! The question is what profit there really is if one is punished with eternal damnation to gain the world! Jesus' use of ζημιόω (*zemioo*, "punishes") in verse 26 is clearly in distinction from "loses" (ἀπόλλυμι, *apollymi*) in verse 25. The Contemporary English Version comes close to conveying Jesus' words in verse 26: "What will you gain, if you own the whole world but destroy [ζημιόω, *zemioo*] yourself?" The Coverdale Bible of 1535 translates it "suffred harme." The Catholic Public Domain Version also brings out the active penal aspect when it translates as "suffers damage." Jesus is quite literally saying,

> If anyone wishes to come after Me, he must deny himself, and take up his cross and follow Me. **25** For whoever wishes to save his life will lose it; but whoever loses his life for My sake will find it. **26** For what will it profit a man if he gains the whole world and his soul be punished?[14] Or what will a man give in exchange for his soul? **27** For the Son of Man is going to come in the glory of His Father with His angels, and will then repay every man according to his deeds. (Matt 16:24–27 AT)

Jesus' words in verse 26, "be punished," are then reinforced by verse 27, "repay every man." The recompense is not just loss of the soul, but punishment.

So then, the contrast Paul presents is between the worker, who is paid his wage, and the unfaithful worker, who is punished. The following words bring home the dire consequence of building with the wisdom of the world.

Saved, as Through Fire

Paul's next words have been misunderstood by large segments of the church, both Roman Catholic and Protestant. Paul is not teaching purgatory. Paul is not saying the false teacher is "saved" in the soteriological sense. Paul is not saying that he is "barely saved" like someone escaping a burning building. As the context and the words themselves make clear, Paul says that the false teacher is "saved" from being totally annihilated like his work. He is kept or preserved to go through the unending fires of hell. Paul elaborates on the punishment of the false teacher:

> εἴ τινος τὸ ἔργον κατακαήσεται, ζημιωθήσεται, αὐτὸς δὲ σωθήσεται, οὕτως δὲ ὡς διὰ πυρός.

---

14. δὲ ψυχὴν αὐτοῦ ζημιωθῇ; passive subjunctive.

> If anyone's works are consumed by fire, he will be punished, and he himself will survive, and in this manner as through fire. (1 Cor 3:15 AT)

First, it should be observed that Paul says the false teacher will be punished, and (*de*, δὲ) the false teacher will be "saved." Paul does not use the stronger adversive, ἀλλά (*alla*, "but"),[15] but uses the enclitic δέ (*de*, "but" or "and"). If Paul were contrasting "suffer loss" with the teacher being soteriologically saved, Paul could have used the stronger conjunction to contrast the loss and the salvation. But he doesn't use a strong adversive conjunction. He uses δέ. Regarding δέ, A. T. Robertson notes, "there is in the word no essential notion of antithesis or contrast."[16] Paul says the false teacher will be punished and he himself will be "saved." Paul's use of δέ provides a continuity of thought from the failure of the false teacher's work to pass the judgment, the resulting fine he will pay, and the future state of the false teacher himself. The use of the intensive αὐτός ("he himself") shifts the focus from the failure of his work and the resulting fine to the state of the false teacher himself. He would not merely pay a fine and that would be the end of it. He would himself be "kept, and in this way as through fire!"

Second, Paul's context clarifies his use of "saved" (σώζω, *sozo*). The New Testament is full of examples where σώζω is not translated "saved" in the soteriological sense. Often σώζω describes physical healing. Matthew 9:21 says regarding the woman who had been bleeding twelve years, "for she was saying to herself, 'If I only touch His garment, I will get well [σώζω].'" Or when Jesus heals the man with the shriveled hand on the sabbath, and the Pharisees object, Mark says,

> And He said to them, "Is it lawful to do good or to do harm on the Sabbath, to save [σώζω] a life or to kill?" (Mark 3:4)

The disciples say to Jesus regarding Lazarus,

> Lord, if he sleeps, he will get better [σώζω]. (John 11:12 NIV)

When Jesus goes into the towns, the people cry out to him and try to touch his cloak for healing. Mark writes, "as many as touched it were being cured [σώζω]" (Mark 6:56). But the word is used just for deliverance. When the storm threatens to engulf the boat, the disciples wake Jesus and

---

15. Smythe, *Greek*, 644.
16. Robertson, *Grammar*, 1184.

say, "Save [σῴζω] us, Lord; we are perishing!" (Matt 8:25). When Peter is walking on the water to Jesus and begins to sink, he cries out, "Lord, save [σῴζω] me!" (Matt 14:30).

In classical Greek, the broader use as "preserve" (σῴζω) is well attested. Aristophanes writes, "Keep thou safely [σῴζω] the dog."[17] Homer uses σῴζω when Telemachus tells his father to "keep alive" the herald when they are killing others.[18] Jesus says the judgment on Jerusalem would be terrible. Matthew records Jesus' warning:

> If those days had not been cut short, no one would survive [σῴζω], but for the sake of the elect those days will be shortened. (Matt 24:22 NIV)

What is particularly interesting about the NIV's translation of σῴζω here as "survive"[19] is that it comes close to Paul's use in 1 Corinthians 3:15. Just as Jesus says no one would continue to live or exist in Jerusalem if the days of the Romans siege were not cut short, so Paul says the false teacher's work is consumed by the judgment fire, and the teacher will be punished, "and he himself will survive" (σῴζω), i.e., continue to exist. Then Paul immediately describes the eternal state of the false teacher:

> If anyone's works are consumed by fire, he will be punished, and he himself will continue to exist, and in this manner as through fire. (1 Cor 3:15 AT)

Paul is clear. He writes, οὕτως δὲ ὡς διὰ πυρός (1 Cor 3:15). Again, he continues the flow of thought with δὲ ("and" or mild adversive "but"). Then he uses the adverb of manner, οὕτως ("in this manner"). The following phrase then is descriptive of σῴζω ("survive"). The question is what Paul means by διὰ πυρός (*dia puros*, "through fire").

Decisive against the notion of purgatory are two points, even for a Catholic. This is the Final Judgment. There is no purgatory after the Final Judgment. Second, only the false teacher is affected διὰ πυρός. But what true teacher of the gospel passes into the eschatological state without error in doctrine or failure in ministry! Prominent today is the interpretation that it is either an idiom for "barely" or metaphorical for "saved by

---

17. Aristophanes, "Knights," 142–43 (Greek line 1017). σώζεσθαί σ᾽ ἐκέλευσ᾽ ἱερὸν Κύνα καρχαρόδοντα."

18. Homer, *Odyssey*, 166 (Greek section 22.357). καὶ κήρυκα Μέδοντα σαώσομεν, ὅς τέ μευ αἰεὶ.

19. "to continue to exist." *Merriam-Webster.com Dictionary*, s.v. "survive," https://www.merriam-webster.com/dictionary/survive.

the skin of one's teeth."[20] Arthur Stanley calls it a "proverbial expression in Hebraistic Greek."[21] Archibold Robertson and Alfred Plummer call it a "quasi-proverbial expression."[22]

The LXX uses διὰ πυρός in Psalm 66. The psalmist writes,

> You made men ride over our heads;
> We went through fire [διήλθομεν διὰ πυρὸς] and through water,
> Yet You brought us out into *a place of* abundance. (Ps 66:12)

God had delivered Israel from their Egyptian oppressors. They had passed through the judgment ordeal and been brought to the promised land. But this was true of all who came out in the exodus. Paul obviously is using διὰ πυρός in a more restricted sense than to say that the unfaithful teacher will be saved as one who passed through the judgment fire.

Often Amos 4:11 and Zechariah 3:2 are appealed to for supporting an idiomatic use. Thiselton quotes Cripps' comments on Amos: "being rescued at the last moment. The expression was a proverbial one."[23] Amos 4:11 says,

> I overthrew you, as God overthrew Sodom and Gomorrah,
> And you were like a firebrand snatched from a fire;[24]
> Yet you have not returned to Me," declares the Lord. (AT)

Note, Amos doesn't use διὰ πυρός (*dia puros*, "through fire"); he uses ἐκ πυρός (*ek puros*, "out of the fire"). God snatched them "out of the fire." Zechariah writes,

> Is this not a brand plucked from the fire? (Zech 3:2)[25]

Again, Zechariah doesn't use διὰ πυρός (through fire); he uses ἐκ πυρός (out of the fire). It's hard to make a case for διὰ πυρός being idiomatic of "barely" when the cited verses don't use the same words! Secondly, Zechariah says that God saved the remnant from the consuming exile judgment they all deserved! This is true of all believers, plucked from the fire by God's grace. Paul doesn't use this language of being plucked ἐκ πυρός ("out of the fire"), and certainly this would be true of the faithful

---

20. Fee, *Corinthians*, 144. Witherington, *Conflict*, 134.
21. Stanley, *Corinthians*, 68.
22. Roberrtson and Plummer, *Corinthians*, 65.
23. Thiselton, *First Corinthians*, 315; Cripps, *Critical Commentary on Amos*, 175.
24. ὡς δαλὸς ἐξεσπασμένος ἐκ πυρός.
25. οὐκ ἰδοὺ τοῦτο ὡς δαλὸς ἐξεσπασμένος ἐκ πυρός.

believer as much as the unfaithful believer. Paul must have something more restricted in view. Jude 23 fits with Amos and Zechariah, but not Paul. Jude 23 says,

> ... save others, snatching them out of the fire....

Here, too, ἐκ πυρός ("out of the fire") is used. Peter uses the phrase in 1 Peter 3:20 διεσώθησαν δι᾽ ὕδατος ("saved through water"). But whereas Peter says Noah's family was saved in the ark through the flood waters, there was no snatching! They were in the ark many days! Paul does not say that the teacher will be saved through the fire. So will the faithful teacher!

Josephus writes regarding a Romans deserter,

> ... though they made him pass through a fiery [διὰ πυρός] trial of his enemies in his examination, yet would he inform them nothing of the affairs within the city.[26]

As the deserter was put on trial, they made him "go through the fire." Though Whiston translates διὰ πυρὸς as "fiery," that is an adverbial description in English for the prepositional phrase in Greek. He went through the judgment fire in his trial. Plutarch writes,

> ... set fire by night to the house where he was living, and shot him down, as has been described, when he dashed out through the fire [διὰ τοῦ πυρὸς ἐξαλλόμενον].[27]

There is no idiom here. He actually ran out of the burning house, as is clear from the text.

In Aristophanes' *Lysistrata*, Calonice says, " I am willing to walk even through fire [διὰ τοῦ πυρός], if I must; but not what you ask," when asked to forsake sexual relations with her husband until the war is over.[28] She is saying she would rather walk in the fire than be without her husband.

Demosthenes writes,

> Conon, a man of this sort, is certainly not to be believed when he takes an oath, far from it. Rather, the man who of his own free will makes no oath, not even an honest oath, and would not even dream of swearing an oath on his children's heads, which

---

26. Josephus, *Wars*, 3.7.33 (in Josephus, *Works*, 1:254); μηδὲν διὰ πυρὸς ἐξερευνῶσι (3.321, ed. Niese).

27. Plutarch, *Plutarch's Lives*, 114 (Greek section 39.5).

28. Aristophanes, *Lysistrata*, 14 (Greek lines 134–35, ed. Leeuwen).

> is not sanctioned by your custom, but would suffer anything rather than do that—if an oath is in fact necessary—he is more to be believed than a man who swears by his children, even going through fire [διὰ τοῦ πυρός].[29]

Here, not only is διὰ τοῦ πυρός not an idiom for "barely," but it actually refers to the self-maledictory oath made by passing through the fire. In so doing, the oath swearer actually takes upon himself the fire curse if he should fail to keep the oath. Similarly, Sophocles writes, "We were ready even to lift red-hot iron in our hands, pass through fire [πῦρ διέρπειν] and swear oaths to the gods."[30]

Anthony Thiselton refers to J. Weiss's reference to Euripides to support an idiomatic usage.[31] Euripides uses διὰ πυρός in *Andromache* and *Electra*. *Andromache* is the tragedy about Andromache after the death of her husband, Hector, their son Astyanax, and the fall of Troy. She is a slave concubine to Neoptolemos. His wife, Hermione, despises her and the son, Molossus, she bore Neoptolemos. Andromache hides Molossus out of fear that Hermione's father, Sparta's King Menelaus, will kill him. The chorus says,

> The Laconian[32] of Menelaus the commander showed us: For through fire [διὰ γὰρ πυρός] she came against the other bed, and she is putting to death the poor Trojan girl and her son because of hateful strife.[33]

This is translated "burns to kill" by Slavitt and Bovie.[34] Hermione is not barely escaping. In fact, she is on fire in anger against Andromache. Andromache is the one who escapes!

Euripides' tragedy *Electra* is the story of matricide and revenge. Electra's mother, Clytemnestra, and her lover, Aegisthus, had murdered Electra's father, the Greek general Agamemnon, upon his return from the Trojan War. When suitors begin calling on Electra, Clytemnestra and

---

29. Demosthenes, "Conon," 78; Greek 54.40, *Demosthenes Private Orations*, vol 3, translated by A. T. Murray, Cambridge: Harvard, 1939, 156.

30. Rayor, *Sophocles'*, 14; Greek 264–65, *The Antigone of Sophocles*, translated by R. C. Jebb, Cambridge University, reprinted by Vassar College, 1893, 24.

31. Thiselton, *Corinthians*, 315 cites, Weiss, *Der erste Korintherbrief*, 83 n. 1.

32. Land of Sparta.

33. Line 486, *The Andromache of Euripides*, by A.R.F. Hyslop, London: Macmillan, 1900, 21.

34. Euripides, *Andromache*, 181.

Aegisthus marry her off to a peasant, afraid that Electra's offspring would seek revenge for Agamemnon's murder. They send her brother, Orestes, off to live with the king of Phocis.

Orestes, now grown, returns, and he and Electra plot to avenge their father's death and murder Clytemnestra and Aegisthus. Once they have killed them, they are filled with guilt and grief. Electra says to Orestes,

> Mournful matters indeed O brother, but I am the cause. Through fire [διὰ πυρὸς] I have wretched gone against this my mother, who gave me, her daughter, birth!³⁵

There is no image of being plucked from the fire; she was engulfed in red-hot anger against her mother!

What is clear from this survey is the absence of διὰ πυρὸς being used in Scripture or in classical Greek as an idiom for "barely" or "by the skin of the teeth." To be fair, Weiss may well have meant that it was idiomatic for being red hot like a firebrand, then linked that to Zechariah 3:2. But it is quite a jump to say that the Greeks were thinking of a firebrand whenever they used διὰ πυρὸς. Just because something is red hot or on fire doesn't mean it is a firebrand. And just because something is a firebrand doesn't mean it is snatched from the fire!

Demosthenes used the phrase to refer to the self-maledictory oath taken by passing through the fire. If the oath was broken, such was the end of the person—an existence going through the fire! Sophocles also used διὰ πυρὸς to refer to making an oath. The wives in Aristophanes' *Lysistrata* preferred to go through the actual fire than swear oaths denouncing intimate relations with their husbands. They preferred the actual judgment pictured by the oath making than to make that oath. Paul was not only educated in Jewish scholarship, but was well acquainted with the Greeks. Paul was a Roman citizen and his hometown, Tarsus, was the seat of a university known for its Greek philosophy. Paul evidenced his knowledge when he quoted the Stoic philosopher Aratus and Cretan philosopher Epimenides when he addressed the Athenians.³⁶

Rather than διὰ πυρὸς being used as an idiom for a narrow escape, the more obvious actual usage fits with the ancient Near Eastern use in the context of covenant oaths. Clearly Paul's Hebrew background supports this linguistic context, but so does his Greek background. Historian

---

35. Euripides, *Electra*, quoted from *Alcestis and Electra*, 79 (Greek line 1182, p. 111, ed. Keenes).

36. Acts 17:28.

Judith Fletcher notes the prevalence of the oath promise in all of Greek social and political life: law, commerce, civic, international treaties, private life. This is well attested by the thousands of extant texts.[37] Greek historian Peter Karavites references the centrality of covenant to Socrates famous response to Crito. Would Socrates break his promise,

> You are breaking your covenants and agreements with us, which you made under no compulsion and undeceived ... And now, then, will you not abide by your agreements? You will if you obey us, Socrates; do not make yourself ridiculous by leaving the city.[38]

The Greeks used the same elements in their oath covenants as their ancient Near Eastern civilizations.[39] Going through the fire, the water, or a sacrificial knife was part and parcel with covenant making in that world, including Greece. Where the evidence for understanding of διὰ πυρὸς as an idiom for "barely" is notably absent, the actual attestation supports a covenant understanding. This covenant usage is also evident in the Bible.

Psalm 66:12 and Isaiah 43:2 are not generic assurances that God is with his people Israel. Rather, they are the covenant affirmations by their suzerain that he is with Israel as they pass through the covenant judgment ordeals. As God saved Noah and his family as they went through the ordeal waters of the flood (1 Pet 3:20), so Peter assures believers that "baptism now saves you" (1 Peter 3:21). The flood ordeal is a type[40] of the baptism waters. Peter continues, "not the removal of dirt from the body but the pledge of a clear conscience toward God" (1 Pet 3:21 NIV). In baptism, the judicial covenant oath is made before God.[41] So the psalmist and Isaiah assure Israel that God is with them as they pass through the judgment ordeals of water and fire. God brought them on dry ground through the judgment waters in the exodus. God brought Shadrach, Meshach, and Abednego through fire in the furnace. Though διὰ πυρὸς may merely mean "on fire," the evidence suggests Paul is actually referencing the actual curse of going through the fire. For the false teacher, the judgment fire means the destruction of his work, his own punishment, and

---

37. Fletcher, *Performing*, 1, 3.
38. Karavites, *Promise-Giving*, 1.
39. Karavites, *Promise-Giving*, 11.
40. ὃ καὶ ὑμᾶς ἀντίτυπον νῦν σῴζει βάπτισμα, οὐ σαρκὸς ἀπόθεσις ῥύπου ἀλλὰ συνειδήσεως ἀγαθῆς ἐπερώτημα εἰς θεόν, δι' ἀναστάσεως Ἰησοῦ Χριστοῦ.
41. See Kline, *Oath*, 65–67.

his unending future existence in the fire! The following verses require an eternal penal interpretation.

Don't You Know?

Paul continues his argument as he writes,

> If anyone's works are consumed by fire, he will be punished, and he himself will continue to exist, and in this manner as through fire. 16 Do you not know that you are the temple of God and the Spirit of God dwells in you? 17 If anyone destroys the temple of God, God will destroy this one, for the temple of God is holy, which you are. (1 Cor 3:15–17 AT)

Commonly, interpreters disassociate the judgment on this temple destroyer and the fire revealing the work of the false teacher in verses 10–15. First, the reference to the temple in verse 9, "house," of which Jesus is the "foundation" (v. 10), and the clear identification of the Corinthian believers as the temple in verse 16ff. argues for the continuity of thought.

Second, and more significant for the argument, is Paul's use of "Do you not know" (Οὐκ οἴδατε, *ouk oida*). Paul uses this phrase as a question ten times in 1 Corinthians. In each case, the reason given after the question is in support of the argument that led up to the question. The question does not introduce a change in the argument.

In chapter 5, Paul is rebuking their tolerance of immorality in the church. So Paul writes,

> Do you not know that a little leaven leavens the whole lump *of dough*? (1 Cor 5:6)

He then directs them to clean out the old leaven and celebrate the crucifixion with sincerity and truth. In chapter 6, Paul admonishes the believers for taking each other to court before the world's judges. He writes,

> ... do you not know that the saints will judge the world? (1 Cor 6:2)

Paul then calls on them to settle the disputes among themselves. He immediately adds a reason for their competence:

> Do you not know that we will judge angels? How much more matters of this life? (1 Cor 6:3)

Continuing the same argument, he asks why they defraud each other, and then gives the supporting argument,

> Or do you not know that the unrighteous will not inherit the kingdom of God? (1 Cor 6:9)

He moves to another matter they presented to him. They said anything is lawful for their bodies. He responds that Jesus redeemed their bodies, and their bodies are members of Christ Jesus:

> Do you not know that your bodies are members of Christ? Shall I then take away the members of Christ and make them members of a prostitute? May it never be! (1 Cor 6:15)

Then he adds another argument:

> Or do you not know that the one who joins himself to a prostitute is one body *with her*? For He says, "THE TWO SHALL BECOME ONE FLESH." (1 Cor 6:16)

Then he gives a third argument:

> Or do you not know that your body is a temple of the Holy Spirit who is in you, whom you have from God, and that you are not your own? (1 Cor 6:19)

Though he piles up arguments, the point is the same. Then in chapter 9, Paul challenges the Corinthians to live out the gospel in giving up their rights for the sake of the gospel. Paul argues that he has rights as an apostle to monetary support. Then he appeals to the support of the temple priests and Levites:

> Do you not know that those who perform sacred services eat the *food* of the temple, *and* those who attend regularly to the altar have their share from the altar? (1 Cor 9:13)

But Paul has not used his rights; he has given them up for the sake the gospel. He continues to elaborate on how this motive has shaped his ministry. He finally says that he lives this faith that he may not just preach it to others but himself partake in its promises. Then he writes,

> Do you not know that those who run in a race all run, but only one receives the prize? Run in such a way that you may win. (1 Cor 9:24)

He then applies this truth to them, and calls them to give up their rights for the gospel.

Paul uses the same language in Romans 6:16 when he calls for them to live the resurrection life in Christ. He appeals to the knowledge of his Jewish audience and makes the case that the Mosaic Law only had jurisdiction on them prior to the cross (Rom 7:1ff.). In Romans 11:2 he appeals to their knowledge of Elijah and God's faithfulness to keep a remnant by faith.

In each case, Paul is not transitioning the argument or changing topics. The question "Do you not know?" in each case introduces an argument to support what Paul has just said. This continuity with the prior argument is also true with Paul's use in 1 Corinthians 3. Paul has argued that the teachers are just servants of the Lord Jesus to build his temple. The teachers are like workmen and the Judgment Day will make clear if they were building with the wisdom of God or the wisdom of the world. The true teachers will receive their eschatological inheritance. The false teachers will be evident in that day. Their work will be consumed in judgment; they will be punished as they themselves go through the judgment fires forever. Paul then confronts the Corinthians with the seriousness of their situation: "Do you not know you are the temple" Jesus is building? You are the dwelling place of the Spirit of God! These false teachers have been seeking to destroy the temple with their teaching, not building it! God will give them recompense for their "destructive" opposition to his temple building.

Paul uses "destroys" (φθείρω *phtheiro*) to describe the teaching of the false teacher. His "wood, hay, and straw" teaching has been destructive to the temple God is building. It is beyond convoluted to think that in verses 10–15 Paul is discussing believers being rewarded according to their works and then in verse 17 he is talking about the destruction that God will bring on the false teacher! The false teacher, who did not build rightly on the foundation of Jesus Christ crucified, is the topic throughout! So Paul brings the argument together when he writes,

> If anyone destroys [φθείρω] the temple of God, God will destroy [φθείρω] this one, for the temple of God is holy, which you are. (1 Cor 3:17 AT)

The false teacher will be repaid in kind for his works. God is building his temple, the redeemed, and no one will stop him.

Then Paul returns to the bigger argument he has been making since chapter 1 to contrast the wisdom of the world with the wisdom of God:

> Let no man deceive himself. If any man among you thinks that he is wise in this age, he must become foolish, so that he may become wise. **19** For the wisdom of this world is foolishness before God. For it is written, "*He is* THE ONE WHO CATCHES THE WISE IN THEIR CRAFTINESS"; **20** and again, "THE LORD KNOWS THE REASONINGS OF THE WISE, THAT THEY ARE USELESS." (1 Cor 3:18–20)

Their fleshly thinking has led them to think the way the world does—"My teacher is better than your teacher." They have found their righteousness in what they have done! But the wisdom of God is different! The wisdom of God strips man of his boast, and gives all glory to God. Paul admonishes the Corinthians to become fools to be wise. They do not want to be on the wrong side of the conflict between God and the wisdom of the world. The wisdom of the world, in the end, is "useless." But the wisdom of God in the cross of Christ has given them "all things." Paul writes,

> So then let no one boast in men. For all things belong to you, **22** whether Paul or Apollos or Cephas or the world or life or death or things present or things to come; all things belong to you, **23** and you belong to Christ; and Christ belongs to God. (1 Cor 3:21–23)

They have thought like babies. They have no idea! If only they knew what is theirs in Christ. The wisdom of the world has given them division and useless counsel. The wisdom of God in the cross has given them "all things." "All things belong to you"! The world offers rewards based on who one is and what one does. Death is the outcome. But the gospel is that the Lord Jesus has paid for the believer's sin and has merited the eschatological inheritance as federal head, federal representative, of the elect. All things are his, so all things are the believer's. As Paul writes, "all things belong to you, and you belong to Christ." And as Christ is the faithful servant in the Pactum Salutis, he "belongs to God." Where then is boasting among believers? The finished work of the Lord Jesus has secured the temple that is being built. Glorious will be the day when that temple is revealed in all his Glory!

11

The Hope of Glory

For the grace of God appeared, salvation to all men, ¹² teaching us that having denied ungodliness and worldly passions to live in this age sensibly and righteously and piously, ¹³ awaiting the blessed hope and appearance of the Glory of the Great God and our Savior Jesus Christ, ¹⁴ who gave himself for us in order that he might redeem us from all lawlessness and to purify for himself an especial people, zealous for good works. (Titus 2:11–14 AT)

IN THESE BRIEF VERSES, Paul outlines the believer's hope. God has fulfilled the Pactum Salutis through the redemptive work of Christ. In Christ the grace of God has come and is bringing salvation to the ends of the earth. Recipients of this gospel message put their hope in the Savior instead of this age's worldly passions. They live in expectation of the covenant blessing merited by Jesus on their behalf. They look for the day when their Savior Jesus Christ will come, and they will enter the Glory of their great God.

THE APPEARANCE OF THE GLORY

New Heavens and New Earth

The apostle Peter connects the believer's life in this current age to the eschatological hope:

> But the day of the Lord will come like a thief, in which the heavens will pass away with a roar and the elements will be destroyed with intense heat, and the earth and its works will be burned up. 11 Since all these things are to be destroyed in this way, what sort of people ought you to be in holy conduct and godliness, 12 looking for and hastening the coming of the day of God, because of which the heavens will be destroyed by burning, and the elements will melt with intense heat! 13 But according to His promise we are looking for new heavens and a new earth, in which righteousness dwells. (2 Pet 3:10–13)

When Jesus comes, this cosmos will be radically changed and transformed into a "new heavens and a new earth." This earth will burn up along with its works. "Earth will wear out like a garment" (Isa 51:6). Certainly this sinful world must be cleansed and replace by a cosmos in which righteousness dwells. But even at creation, before the fall of Adam, this cosmos was never intended to be man's home forever. This is evidenced by both the way God constructed the visible world and his explicit promise. First, note that apart from the fall and consequence of death, the propagation of the Adamic family would have filled the earth. Second, the visible world itself was created with movement toward entropy. Third, Adam was promised the sabbath eschatological glory enthronement. Fourth, the sabbath eschatological enthronement would be in the glorified heaven/earth royal temple of God. Heaven would no longer be invisible.

This cosmos was designed as the stage for the pre-glorification kingdom building. If Adam had fulfilled his kingdom-building mandate, he, his human family, and the visible world would have been transformed into sabbath glory. So the Second Adam, having fulfilled the kingdom-building mandate, brings the redeemed to eschatological glory, where heaven and earth are one. As Peter describes, the old heaven and earth are no more. There is a new heaven and earth. The transient temporary old creation is replaced with the creation designed to be the eternal dwelling of God's people. As the believer's resurrection to glory has elements of continuity to the prior body, so the glorious new creation has continuity with the first creation. But the discontinuity of the glorious new creation is much more radical than merely removing sin and evil. The new creation, the new cosmos, will be designed for physical existence for eternity in the Glory of God. It is not just a prettier earth. The new cosmos will be filled with the Glory of God, and the glorified, physically luminous redeemed enthroned with the Lord Jesus over the angels of God's court.

The Glory of the Great God

Revelation 21 describes the final glorified creation:

> Then I saw a new heaven and a new earth; for the first heaven and the first earth passed away, and there is no longer *any* sea. (Rev 21:1)

In this new creation, John sees the realization of the sabbath glorification:

> And I saw the holy city, new Jerusalem, coming down out of heaven from God, made ready as a bride adorned for her husband. ³ And I heard a loud voice from the throne, saying, "Behold, the tabernacle of God is among men, and He will dwell among them, and they shall be His people, and God Himself will be among them." (Rev 21:2-3)

No longer will heaven and earth be the invisible separated from the visible, the King of Glory separated from man on earth. Through Christ, the bride of Christ has become the citizens of heaven dwelling with God. She is clothed with the Glory of God (Rev 21:11). Filled with the Glory of God, she is portrayed as the mega-temple of God (Rev 21:3, 15ff.). There is no moon in this new creation, and no sun, for the Glory of God will be its light, and there will be no night. There believers will see God (Matt 5:8). This glorified Eden (Rev 22:1ff) is the realization of the sabbath glorification enthronement of believers. There is no earthly temple. John writes, "I saw no temple in it, for the Lord God the Almighty and the Lamb are its temple" (Rev 21:22). The Glory of the Father, the great King of Heaven, and the Glory of the Lamb, the image of the Father, is the Glory dwelling of the redeemed.

THE LORD OF GLORY

When Jesus returns, he comes as exalted Son of Man, the Lord of Glory. He is the image of the King of Heaven, clothed in the Glory. Isaiah 11 presents him as the king clothed with the Spirit of God. He will strike the earth with the "Spirit" of his lips (Isa 11:2, 4), or as Paul writes in 2 Thessalonians, "the Spirit of His mouth" (2 Thes 2:8). He brings the sabbath rest, Glory (Isa 11:10). So his Glory is the believer's. Peter encourages,

> If you are reviled for the name of Christ, you are blessed, because the Spirit of glory and of God rests on you. (1 Pet 4:14)

Jesus is the faithful vassal son who has now been exalted to receive the covenant blessing in Glory. When he comes again, he comes as the Lord of Glory with the angelic army of the King of Heaven. Matthew writes,

> For the Son of Man is going to come in the glory of His Father with His angels . . . (Matt 16:27)

He comes with the clouds, accompanied by the angels:

> . . . they will see the Son of Man coming on the clouds of the sky with power and great glory. (Matt 24:30)

As the Glory was manifest in the "cloud" in the Old Testament and at the transfiguration (Matt 17:5), so now the exalted Second Adam will come clothed in Glory. He will forever be enthroned as the image of the King of Heaven, the faithful Son of Man:

> And Jesus said to them, "Truly I say to you, that you who have followed Me, in the regeneration when the Son of Man will sit on the throne of His glory . . ." (Matt 19:28 AT)

And again:

> But when the Son of Man comes in His glory, and all the angels with Him, then He will sit on throne of His glory. (Matt 25:31 AT)

He is the image of the King of Glory. So Paul writes,

> . . . the light of the gospel of the glory of Christ, who is the image of God . . . [6] For God, who said, "Light shall shine out of darkness," is the One who has shone in our hearts to give the Light of the knowledge of the glory of God in the face of Christ. (2 Cor 4:4, 6)

The gospel is that the Son of Man, the image of God, has been enthroned in the Glory of God. The Glory of the King of Heaven clothes the Lord of Glory. That same Glory-Spirit that clothes Christ Jesus shines in the heart of the believer, transforming him from glory to glory.

THE ESPECIAL PEOPLE

The believer awaits the day when the Lord of Glory will bring him into the everlasting Glory. In that day, the believer himself will be forever glorified in the image of Christ, who is the image of God. He will finally and perfectly image the God of Glory. As God is love, he will forever live in love. As God is truth, he will forever live in truth. As God is King, he will forever be enthroned in union with the Lord of Glory. As God is life, forever he will breathe the Spirit of life.

Have you ever been in a conversation you didn't want to end, or seen a beautiful painting that you wanted see more? Have you ever heard a song that left you wanting more? Have you ever found the relationships of this world leaving you in pain? The coming life in the Glory of God is beyond comprehension. Paul, who had seen the "third heaven," references Isaiah 64:4 and 65:17 when he writes,

> THINGS WHICH EYE HAS NOT SEEN AND EAR HAS NOT HEARD,
> AND which HAVE NOT ENTERED THE HEART OF MAN,
> ALL THAT GOD HAS PREPARED FOR THOSE WHO LOVE HIM.
> (1 Cor 2:9)

Not only is that eternal home going to be wonderful, but the people of God will be perfectly at home.

When Moses returned from being in the presence of God on Mt. Sinai, so bright was the glory of his face that it had to be covered! When Stephen stood and bore witness to the Jews, his face shone with glory as the Lord of Glory received him into heaven (Acts 6:15). When the three disciples ascended the mountain, they beheld Jesus glorified:

> He was transfigured before them; and His face shone like the sun, and His garments became as white as light. (Matt 17:2)

Daniel describes the future glorification of believers when he writes in Hebraic parallelism,

> . . . will shine brightly like the brightness of the expanse of heaven,
> . . . like the stars forever and ever. (Dan 12:3)

John says that when the believer sees Jesus in his coming, the believer will then be like Jesus in Glory:

> We know that when He appears, we will be like Him, because we will see Him just as He is. (1 John 3:2)

Paul writes of this great transformation to Glory:

> ... who will transform the body of our humble state into conformity with the body of His glory, by the exertion of the power that He has even to subject all things to Himself. (Phil 3:21)

When he is revealed, so the believer will be revealed in Glory:

> When Christ, who is our life, is revealed, then you also will be revealed with Him in glory. (Col 3:4)

So great is this message of grace that the believer has yet to know the depth of God's love in Christ. Paul, describing how the union of husband and wife pictures the union of Christ and the church in Ephesians 5, can only say, "This mystery is great..." (Eph 5:32). But it is wonderfully through this redemptive union that the triune God lives in union with man.[1]

---

1. Kline, *Glory*, 220; see John 17:22f.

Bibliography

Alcorn, Randy. "The Believer's Judgment According to Works." https://www.epm.org/resources/1994/Jan/1/believers-judgment-works/.
Aristophanes. "The Knights." In *The Comedies of Aristophanes*, vol. 1, edited by Benjamin Hickley Rogers. London: George Bell, 1910.
———. *Lysistrata*. Edited by J. van Leeuwen. Lugduni Batavorum: Apud A. W. Sijthoff, 1903.
———. *Lysistrata by Aristophanes*. Adapted and arranged by Winifred Ayres Hope. New York: Samuel French, 1915.
Augustine. *City of God*. In vol. 2 of *Nicene and Post-Nicene Fathers*, 1st ser., edited by Philip Schaff. Grand Rapids: Eerdmans, 1978.
———. *Homilies on the Gospel of St. John*. In vol. 7 of *Nicene and Post-Nicene Fathers*, 1st ser., edited by Philip Schaff. Grand Rapids: Eerdmans, 1978.
Babylonian Talmud: Tractate Sanhedrin. Folio 38. http://www.halakhah.com/sanhedrin/sanhedrin_38.html.
Bavinck, Herman. *Reformed Dogmatics*. Vol 4. Grand Rapids: Baker, 2008.
Beale, G. K. *The Book of Revelation: A Commentary on the Greek Text*. Grand Rapids: Eerdmans, 1999.
———. *The Temple and the Church's Mission: A Biblical Theology of the Dwelling Place of God*. Downers Grove, IL: InterVarsity, 2004.
Beasley-Murray, George R. *John*. Word Biblical Commentary 36. Waco, TX: Word, 1987.
Block, Daniel I. "Eden: A Temple? A Reassessment of the Biblical Evidence." In *From Creation to New Creation: Biblical Theology and Exegesis: Essays in Honor of G. K. Beale*, edited by Daniel M. Gurtner and Benjamin L. Gladd, 3–30. Peabody, MA: Hendrickson, 2013.
Blomberg, Craig L. "Degrees of Reward in the Kingdom of Heaven?" *JETS* 35.2 (June 1992) 159–72.

———. *1 Corinthians*. Grand Rapids: Zondervan 1994.

———. *Matthew*. Nashville: Broadman, 1992.

Boyce, James P. *Abstract of Systematic Theology*. 1887. Reprint, Bibliotech, 2019.

Brown, Francis. *A Hebrew and English Lexicon of the Old Testament*. Oxford: Clarendon, 1975.

Bruce, F. F. *The Epistle to the Hebrews*. Grand Rapids: Eerdmans, 1964.

Calvin, John. *Commentary on the Gospel According to John*. Translated by William Pringle. Vol 1. Grand Rapids: Baker, reprinted 1979.

Carr, G. Lloyd. "שָׁלֵם (shalem)." In *Theological Wordbook of the Old Testament*, edited by R. Laird Harris, Gleason Archer, and Bruce Waltke, 2:930–31. Chicago: Moody, 1980.

Cripps, R. S. *A Critical and Exegetical Commentary on the Book of Amos*. London: SPCK, 1929.

Curtis, Byron G. "Hosea 6:7 and Covenant-Breaking like/at Adam." In *The Law Is Not of Faith*, edited by Bryan D. Estelle, J.V. Fesko, David Van Drunen, 170–209. Phillipsburg, NJ: Presbyterian and Reformed, 2009.

Cyril of Alexandria. *Commentary on the Twelve Prophets*. Edited by Thomas P. Halton et al. Fathers of the Church 115. Washington, DC: Catholic University of America Press, 2007.

Demosthenes. "Against Conon." 54.40. In *Demosthenes, Speeches 50–59*, translated by Victor Bers, 66–80. Austin: University of Texas Press, 2003.

Disley, Emma. "Degrees of Glory: Protestant Doctrine and the Concept of Rewards Hereafter." *JTS* 42.1 (April 1991) 77–105.

Euripides. *Alcestis and Electra*. Edited by Edward Brooks Jr. Philadelphia: David McKay, 1900.

———. *Andromache*. Edited by David R. Slavitt and Bovie. Philadelphia: University of Pennsylvania, 1998.

———. *The Electra of Euridipes*. Edited by Charles Haines Keene. London: George Bell, 1893.

———. *Ion*. Edited by C. S. Jerram. Oxford: Clarendon, 1896.

———. "Ion." In *The Complete Greek Drama—All Extant Tragedies of Aeschylus, Sophocles and Euripides, and the Comedies of Aristophanes and Meander*, vol. 1, edited by Whitney J. Oates and Eugene O'Neill Jr. New York: Random House, 1938.

Fee, Gordon D. *The First Epistle to the Corinthians*. Grand Rapids: Eerdmans, 1987.

Fesko, J. V. *Death in Adam, Life in Christ*. Geanies House, UK: Mentor, 2016.

Fletcher, Judith. *Performing Oaths in Classical Greek Drama*. Cambridge: Cambridge University, 2012.

Harper, William Rainey. *A Critical and Exegetical Commentary on Amos and Hosea*. ICC. Edinburgh: T. & T. Clark, 1905.

Herodotus. *Histories*. Vol. 4. Edited by A. D. Godley. London: Heinemann, 1930.

Holliday, William L. *A Concise Hebrew and Aramaic Lexicon of the Old Testament*. Grand Rapids: Eerdmans, 1972.

Homer. *The Illiad*. Vol. 2. Edited by A. T. Murray. London: Heinemann, 1925.

———. *Odyssey*. Vol. 2. Edited by W. W. Merry. Oxford: Clarendon, 1882.

Irenaeus. *Against Heresies*. Ante-Nicene Fathers 1. Grand Rapids: Eerdmans, 1977.

Irons, Charles Lee. *The Son of God: Three Views of the Identity of Jesus*. Eugene, OR: Wipf & Stock 2015.

Josephus, Flavius. *Flavii Iosephi Antiquitatum iudacarum epitoma*. Edited by Benedictus Niese. Berlin: Weidmann, 1896.

———. *The Works of Flavius Josephus: In Four Volumes*. Translated by William Whiston. Grand Rapids: Baker, 1974.
Karavites, Peter. *Promise-Giving and Treaty-Making: Homer and the Near East*. Leiden: E.J. Brill, 1992.
Kline, Meredith G. *By Oath Consigned*. Grand Rapids: Eerdmans, 1968.
———. "The Covenant of the Seventieth Week." In *The Law and the Prophets: Old Testament Studies in Honor of Oswald T. Allis*, edited by J. H. Skilton. Nutley, NJ: Presbyterian and Reformed, 1974.
———. "Double Trouble." *JETS* 32.2 (June 1989) 171–79.
———. "The Feast of Cover-Over." In *Essential Writings of Meredith G. Kline*, 151–67. Peabody, MA: Hendrickson, 2017.
———. *Genesis*. Peabody, MA: Hendrickson, 2016.
———. *Glory in Our Midst*. Overland Park, KS: Two Age, 2001.
———. *God, Heaven and Har Magedon*. Eugene, OR: Wipf & Stock, 2006.
———. "Gospel until the Law: Rom 5:13–14 and the Old Covenant." *JETS* 34 (1991) 433–46.
———. *Images of the Spirit*. Grand Rapids: Baker, 1980.
———. *Kingdom Prologue*. Eugene, OR: Wipf & Stock, 2006.
———. *The Structure of Biblical Authority*. 2nd ed. Grand Rapids: Eerdmans, 1972.
———. *Treaty of the Great King*. Eugene, OR: Wipf & Stock, 2012.
Kline, Meredith M. "The Holy Spirit as Covenant Witness." ThM thesis, Westminster Seminary, Philadelphia, 1972.
Kuck, David W. *Judgment & Community Conflict*. Leiden: Brill, 1992.
Lane, William L. *The Gospel of Mark*. NICNT. Grand Rapids, Eerdmans, 1974.
Liddell, H. G., and R. Scott. *Greek-English Lexicon*. Oxford: Oxford University, 1977.
Lincoln, Andrew T. *Ephesians*. Word Biblical Commentary 42. Waco, TX: Word, 1990.
Lutzer, Erwin W. *Your Eternal Reward*. Chicgo: Moody, 1998.
MacRae, Allan. "עוֹלָם (olam)." In *Theological Wordbook of the Old Testament*, vol. 2. edited by R. Laird Harris, Gleason Archer, and Bruce Waltke, 2:672–73. Chicago: Moody, 1980.
Marshall, Edward. *The Middle Wall*. Toronto: Langton & Hall, 1904.
McGrath, Alister E. *Iustitia Dei*. New York:Cambridge, 2005.
Merrill, Eugene. *Kingdom of Priests*. Grand Rapids: Baker, 1987.
Moo, Douglas. *Romans*. Grand Rapids, Baker, 1996.
Morris, Leon. *The Apostolic Preaching of the Cross*. Grand Rapids: Eerdmans, 1955.
———. *The Gospel According to John*. NICNT. Grand Rapids: Eerdmans, 1971.
Motyer. J. Alec. *The Prophecy of Isaiah*. Downers Grove, IL: InterVarsity, 1993.
Murray, John. "The Adamic Administration." In *Collected Works of John Murray*, 2:47–59. Carlisle, PA: Banner of Truth, 1977.
———. "Justification." In *Collected Works of John Murray*, 2:202–22. Carlisle, PA: Banner of Truth, 1977.
Ortland, Dane C. "Justified by Faith, Judgment According to Works: Another Look at a Pauline Paradox." *JETS* 52.2 (June 2009) 323–39.
Packer, J. I. *Knowing God*. Downers Grove, IL: InterVarsity, 1973.
Plutarch. *Plutarch's Lives*. English translation by Bernadotte Perrin. Cambridge, MA: Harvard University Press, 1916.
———. *Plutarch's Nicias and Alcibiades*. English translation by Bernadotte Perrin. Cambridge, MA: Harvard University Press, 1912.

Pratt, Richard L. *He Gave Us Stories*. Brentwood, TN: Wolgemuth & Hyatt, 1990.

Rayor, Diane J. *Sophocles' Antigone: A New Translation*. Cambridge: Cambridge University Press, 2011.

Ridderbos, Herman. *Paul: An Outline of His Theology*. Translated by John Richard DeWitt. Grand Rapids: Eerdmans, 1975.

Robertson, Archibold, and Alfred Plummer. *First Epistle of St. Paul to the Corinthians*. 2nd ed. Edinburgh: T. & T. Clark, 1914.

Robertson, A. T. *A Grammar of the Greek New Testament in the Light of Historical Research*. Nashville: Broadman, 1934.

Robertson, O. Palmer. *The Christ of the Covenants*. Phillipsburg, NJ: Presbyterian and Reformed, 1980.

Rogers, Cleon. "שָׂכָר (sakar)." In *Theological Wordbook of the Old Testament*, edited by R. Laird Harris, Gleason Archer, and Bruce Waltke, 2:878. Chicago: Moody, 1980.

Russell, Walter Bo, III. *The Flesh/Spirit Conflict in Galatians*. Lanham, MD: University Press of America, 1997.

Shanor, Jay. "Paul as Master Builder Construction Terms in First Corinthians." *NTS* 34 (1988) 461–71.

Smythe, Herbert Weir. *Greek Grammar*. Cambridge, MA: Harvard University Press, 1976.

Sophocles. *Sophocles*, vol. 1, *Oedipus the King, Oedipus at Colonus, Antigone*. English translation by F. Storr. Loeb Classical Library 20. London: Francis Storr, 1912.

Spurgeon, Charles H. "The Two Talents." Sermon delivered January 31, 1858. The Spurgeon Center, Midwestern Seminary. https://www.spurgeon.org/resource-library/sermons/the-two-talents/#flipbook/.

Stanley, Arthur Penrhyn. *The Epistles of St. Paul to the Corinthians*. Reprint of 1858 2nd ed. Minneapolis: Klock, 1981.

Stanley, Charles. *Eternal Security*. Nashville: Thomas Nelson, 1990.

Stott, John. *Life in Christ*. Chicago: Tyndale, 1991.

Strack, Herman L,. amd Paul Billerbeck. *Kommentar zum Neuem Testament* Vol. 1. Munich: Beck, 1926.

Stumpff, Albrecht, "ζημιόω." In *Theological Dictionary of the New Testament*, edited by Gerhard Kittel and Gerhard Friedrich, translated by Geoffrey W. Bromiley, 888–92. Grand Rapids: Eerdmans, 1964.

Thiselton, Anthony. *The First Epistle to the Corinthians*. NIGTC. Grand Rapids: Eerdmans, 2000.

Ton, Josep. *Suffering, Martyrdom, and Rewards in Heaven*. Reprint. Wheaton, IL: Romanian Missionary Society, 2000.

Thucydides. *Thucydides*. Vol 1. Edited by John William Donaldson. New York: Harper, 1861.

Vos, Geerhardus. *Biblical Theology*. Grand Rapids: Eerdmans, 1948.

Waltke, Bruce K. *The Book of Proverbs*. 2 vols. NICOT. Grand Rapids: Eerdmans, 2004.

Warfield, Benjamin. "Hosea VI.7: Adam or Man?" In *Selected Writings*, 1:116–29. Nutley, NJ: Presbyterian and Reformed, 1970.

Weiss, Johannes. *Der erste Korintherbrief*. Göttingen: Vandenhoeck & Ruprecht, 1925.

Wesley, John. "The Righteousness of Faith." https://www.hopefaithprayer.com/faith/the-righteousness-of-faith-john-wesley/.

Wilkin, Robert N., Thomas R. Schreiner, James D. G. Dunn, and Michael P. Barber. *Four Views on the Role of Works at the Final Judgment*. Grand Rapids: Zondervan, 2003.

Witherington, Ben, III. *Conflict and Community in Corinth: A Socio-Rhetorical Commentary on 1 and 2 Corinthians*. Grand Rapids: Eerdmans, 1995.

Woolsey, Andrew. *Unity and Continuity in Covenantal Thought*. Grand Rapids: Reformed Heritage, 2012.

Young, Edward J. *The Book of Isaiah*. Vol 3. Grand Rapids: Eerdmans, 1972.

Scripture Index

OLD TESTAMENT

Genesis

1–3	ix, 18, 19
1–2	21, 36
1	7, 39, 214
1:1—2:4	100
1:1—2:3	3, 44–48
1:1ff	20
1:1	3, 6, 12, 13, 20, 45
1:2	3, 6, 7, 8, 10, 11, 12, 20, 40, 44, 49, 63
1:26ff	3, 44, 49
1:26	14, 16–17
1:27	40
1:28	52, 163
2	49, 214
2:1–3	20, 32, 33, 42
2:1	20
2:2	42
2:3	21
2:4—3:24	48–54
2:4–14	48
2:4ff	44, 105
2:7	15, 16, 49
2:9	44, 48
2:12	48
2:15–17	48
2:15	17
2:16–17	49, 50
2:17	44
2:18–25	48
2:19	48
2:23	52
2:24	52
3	49, 97
3:1–6	48
3:1	54
3:4–5	54
3:7–8	53
3:7	48
3:8–21	48
3:8	49, 51
3:9–19	49
3:14	97
3:15	75, 98, 163
3:16	97
3:17–19	98
3:18	45
3:20	99

Genesis (cont.)

3:22–24	3, 48
3:22	14, 49
3:24	17, 49, 50, 52
4–7	ix
5	53, 163
5:1–5	53
5:1ff	105
5:1	14
5:3	14
5:8	53
5:11	53
5:14	53
5:17	53
5:20	53
5:27	53
5:31	53
6:2	15
6:4	15
6:9ff	105
6:9	112
7:1	112
8–11	ix
8:21–22	47
9	47
9:9	46
10	42
10:1ff	105
11	163
11:7	3, 14
11:10ff	105
11:27–32	106
11:27ff	105
12–22	112
12:1—15:20	106, 107
12:1–5	106
12:1–3	106
12:3	42, 119
12:6—13:17	106
12:7	107, 111, 112
12:16	107
12:20	107
13:2	107
13:14	112–13
13:18—14:24	106
15	108, 136
15:1–20	106
15:1	184
15:5	108
15:6	121, 235
15:7	108, 113
15:8	108
15:13–21	108
15:18	113
16:1–16	106
16:7ff	107
17:1—22:19	106, 107
17:1–27	106
17:1	107
17:6	119
17:7–8	120
17:8	113
17:13	120
17:19	120
18:1—19:38	106
18:1–2	138
18:1	107
18:12	107
18:18	119
18:23	107
20:1—21:34	106
20	110
22:1–19	106
22:6	184
22:12	109
22:14	109, 121
22:16–18	109, 111–12
22:17	29, 30
22:18	120, 182
22:20—25:11	106
25:12ff	105
25:19ff	105
26:3	112, 113
26:5	112, 182, 184
26:22	113
28:13	113
28:15	113
29:15	184
30:16–18	183
30:18	183, 184
30:28	183, 184
30:32f	184
31:7–8	184
32:1–2	4
36:1ff	105
37:2ff	105
46:3	114

49:8–12	31	23:20–23	138
49:10	101	24:7–8	136
49:11f	101	24:15–18	9–10
49:15	42	25–31	42
		31:16–17	32, 32–33
		31:18	40

Exodus

		33	40, 138
1:5–8	114–15	33:10–11	41
1:12	115	33:19–23	40
1:20–21	115	35–40	42
1:22	182	40:33	42
2:9	184	40:34–38	10, 144
2:24–25	137		
3:1–6	137		

Leviticus

3:2	137	4:6	66
3:4	137	8:11	66
3:6	137, 138	10:1–3	128
4:20	130	14:7	66
4:22–23	15	16:2	41
4:22	151	18:5	136
8:19	40	19:13	67
10:21–23	42	22:9	236
12:2	41	25:13	147
12:12–13	141	25:28	147
12:12	142	26	65, 220
12:13	142	26:3–13	133
12:23	141, 142	26:14–33	134–35
12:29	142	26:41	220
14:19–24	9	26:42	147
14:19–20	142	26:43	147
14:19ff	41		

Numbers

14:19	138		
14:21–22	42	1:53	17
14:28	182	3:8	17
15:6	41	3:10	17
15:8	41	3:32	17
17	129	4:23	220
17:6	129	6:26	171
17:9	130	7:8–9	41
19:4–6	42	8:26	17
19:4	11	9:17	41
19:6	42	10:33–36	42
19:16–18	51	12:5	41
19:16	52	14:24	181
19:19	51	18:3ff	17
20	132	20	127, 129, 130
20:8–11	21, 32	20:8	127
20:13	155	20:9–12	127
21:36	209		

Numbers (cont.)

20:11	129
20:23–29	128
22:28	139
22:29	139
22:30	139
22:31	140
23:10	116
24	101
24:17–24	101
31:30	17
31:47	17
36:4	147

Deuteronomy

1:10	115
1:37	128
4:12	51
4:21	128
4:33	51
5:22–26	51
6:10	116
6:13	86
6:14–15	116
6:16	85
6:17–18	116
7:2	36
7:12–13	182
8:3	85
9:4	115
9:5	115
10:22	115
12:9	42
21:23	88
22:30	38
26:15	6
28	65
28:1–14	133–34
28:15–68	135
28:15–19	135
29:23	28
30:17–18	116
31:15	41
32	7, 10, 44
32:8	42
32:10–11	7, 8, 40, 142
32:11	11
32:51–52	127
34:4	113

Joshua

1:6	113
1:13	42
3	28
3:16	28
5:6	113
5:13–15	4, 139
10:1	210
21:43–45	113–14
23:12–16	116

Judges

2:1	140
6:12	140
6:22–23	140
13:6	140
13:18	140
13:20	140
21:25	101

Ruth

3	37–38
3:9	38

1 Samuel

7:1	17
8:4–5	42
8:5	101
8:7–8	42
9:2	101
13:14	101
16:13	102
17:39–40	102
26:23–24	186
27:8	32

2 Samuel

5:24	51–52
7:11–16	32
7:12–13	69, 102
7:13	120
12:6	182
14:17	51
19:36–37	184
23:5	32

Scripture Index

1 Kings

3:9	50–51
3:12–14	185
3:28	51
4:20	116
4:21	114
4:25	103
6:2	14
6:38	103
7:1	103
8:10–11	144
8:27	14
12:25–33	28

2 Kings

4:7	209
12:9	17
15:25	28
19:35	140
23:3	43–44

1 Chronicles

23:32	17
28:2	20, 41

2 Chronicles

2:6	14
6:18	14
6:41	20
15:7	67
34:9	17

Nehemiah

9:6	4
9:7–8	114
9:18–20	8

Job

7:1	220
10:17	220
14:14	220
19:25	100
25:6	82
31:33	28
34:11–12	211

Psalms

2:7–8	71
2:7	161
8	63
8:4	81
8:5	47
11:4	6
14:5	28
18:20–24	183
18:20	186
19:1–6	45–46
19:4	6
19:7	186
19:11	181, 184, 186
28:4	211
40:15	181, 182
45:6–7	103
50:14	209
51:5	35
62:9–10	209
62:12	209, 221, 258, 262
65:12–13	45
66:12	258
78:69	143
80:17	81
83:5	70
89:3	32
93	19
106:32	128
110	91
110:1	153
103:19–21	4
104:1–2	11
105:39	38
105:42–44	115–16
106:32	128
110:4	70
132:7–8	20
132:7	41
132:13–14	20
137:8	211
148:1–4	4

Proverbs

3:2	186
3:16	186
8	12, 14
8:22–30	13

Proverbs (cont.)

11:18	67, 182, 184
15:33	186
18:12	186
22:4	182, 185
22:8	238
24:11–12	210
24:12	221

Ecclesiastes

2:9	103
2:11	103
4:9	184

Isaiah

1–39	65
1–12	64
2:2–4	65
4:2–4	65
4:2	65, 69
5:23	181
6:1–4	5
6:5	14
6:8	65
6:10	88
7:14	65
8:13–15	128
8:14	68
9:1–2	87–88
9:6	65
11	270
11:1–16	65
11:1	69
11:2	270
11:4	270
11:10	270
13–35	65
19:10	182
19:25	65
22:22	154
24–27	31
24:1	31
24:2	32
24:3	31
24:4–6	32
24:4	45
24:5	27, 31, 31–32, 32, 33, 65
25:6–8	65
28:5	195
29:17–19	117
29:22	117
31:5	142
35:1–6	66
36–39	65
40–66	65
40	81
40:1–2	220
40:1	65, 79
40:2	220
40:3	65, 79, 81
40:9	65
40:10–11	220, 241
40:10	66, 67, 79, 222, 223
40:21–23	5–6, 19
41:8–9	81
41:8	65
41:17–18	65
41:21–22	14
42:1–9	66, 67
42:1–4	66
42:1	81
42:5–12	65
42:6	66, 81, 88
42:18–25	65
43:2	262
44:1–2	81
44:1	66
44:21	66, 81
45:4	66, 81
48:20	81
49:1–18	66
49:1–7	66, 67
49:3	81
49:6	66, 81, 88
50:4–11	66
50:4–9	66, 67
50:4–7	66
50:7	86
51:2	65
51:3	17, 49, 66
51:6	268
51:12	82
51:17	89

52:13—53:12	66, 67, 220	**Ezekiel**	
52:13	66	1:24–25	52
52:15	66	1:28	52
53:1	88	2:1	81
53:10–11	83	3:22–24	9
53:12	66, 83	8:1	9
55:1–5	243	9:3	41
58:8	88	10	144
59:16	174	10:4	41
59:18	174	10:18	41
59:20–21	174	11:5	9
60:1	88	11:23	144
62:11	66, 67, 68, 222, 223	16	36–39, 38, 39
63:9	138	16:8	37, 38
63:10–14	8–9	18:30	211
63:12	40	24:14	211
64:4	22, 271	28:13–16	48–49
65:13–15	158	28:13	17, 49
65:17	66, 271	28:14	17
66:1	4, 19, 20, 21, 159	29:18f	67
		31:8–9	17, 49
Jeremiah		33:20	211
2:2	37	36	16
3:16–17	159	36:27	16
7:24–26	116	36:35	16
17:10	221	37:1–10	16
23:5–6	69–70	37:9–10	16
25:15	89	37:14	16
25:30	6	40–47	18
29:11	171	40	159
31:16	67	40:2	159
31:32	37	40:3	159
31:33	36, 154	40:35	159
33:14–17	70	44:15f	17
33:20–26	120	47:7	49
33:20–22	46–47, 117	47:10	159
33:22	117	47:12	49
33:24	117	48:11	17
33:26	117		
50:15	212	**Daniel**	
50:29	212	1	144
51:24	212	1:20	145
		2	144
Lamentations		2:47	145
4:20	16	3	144
		3:28	145
		4	144
		4:37	145

Daniel (*cont.*)

5	144, 145
6	144
6:25–27	146
7	230
7:3–8	4
7:9–10	4–5
7:9ff	92
7:10	230
7:13–14	90, 230
7:14	152
7:26–27	230
7:27	152
8:15–17	40
9:1	147
9:2	146
9:5	170
9:17	146, 147
9:20	147
9:24	146, 147
9:25	147
9:26–27	148
9:26	147, 148, 149
9:27	147, 148
10:4–9	40
12	43, 230
12:1	230
12:3	271
12:5–7	40

Hosea

1–3	29
1:1–2	29
1:3–5	29
1:4	29
1:7	29, 30
1:8–9	29
1:10	28, 29, 30
1:11	30
2:1	30
2:2–5	30
2:6–13	30
2:6–8	30
2:9–13	30
2:14–23	30
2:23	30
2:20	28
2:25	28

3:1–3	30
4:3	29
4:15	28
5:1–2	28
5:8	28
5:14	29
6:4	31
6:5	31
6:6	31
6:7	23, 24, 27–31, 27, 29, 31
6:8	28
8:9	29
9:6	29
11:1	15, 151
11:8–11	31
11:8	29
12:2	210–11
12:3–6	29
12:9	31
13:14	31
14:2–8	31

Amos

4:4	28
4:11	258

Micah

1:2–3	6
3:1–2	51
6:6	156
6:8	156

Nahum

1:8–9	129

Haggai

2:5	9, 41, 43

Zechariah

1:12	140
2:1	159
3:2	258, 261
6:9–15	68–69
6:9–11	69
6:12–13	69, 70

Scripture Index

6:12	69
6:13	69, 70
6:14–15	69, 70
6:15	71

Malachi

3:1	81, 251
3:2	140, 251
4:1	142, 251

NEW TESTAMENT

Matthew

1:1	120
1:19	170
2:2	104
3:9	118
3:15	85
4:3	85
4:4	82, 85
4:5	84
4:6	85
4:7	85
4:8–9	85
4:10	86
4:15–16	88
5:3–10	157, 158
5:3	187
5:8	100, 187, 269
5:9	187
5:10	187
5:12	187, 228, 249
5:17–18	154
5:20	155, 187
5:21	155
5:22	155
5:23–25	155
5:26	253
5:27	155
5:29	155, 156
5:31	155
5:32	156
5:33	155
5:34–35	19
5:37	156
5:38	155
5:39	156
5:43	155
5:44–45	155–56
5:48	157
6:2–4	187
6:5–6	187
6:9	15
6:16–18	187
6:19–24	188
7:2	238, 239
7:15–20	187
7:21	190
8:10–12	118
8:12	198
8:25	257
9:21	256
10:19	56
10:40–42	188
11:1–5	66
12:6	84
12:28	40
12:36	207
13:30	233
13:41–42	198
13:49–50	198, 233
14:27	60
14:30	257
16:22–23	86
16:24–27	254, 255
16:25	255
16:26	255
16:27	218, 221, 225, 255, 270
17:2	271
17:5	83, 270
18:6–9	218
18:34–35	253
19:16—20:28	205
19:16	200
19:21	201
19:27	201
19:28–29	201
19:28	270
19:30	202
20:1–16	202–3
20:18–19	205
20:20–28	203–4
21:2	86
21:31–32	118
21:43	119

Matthew (cont.)

22:11–14	198–99
24:22	257
24:30–31	92
24:30	270
24:36	60
24:50–51	199
25	195, 233
25:14–30	197
25:31–33	233
25:31	270
25:34	58, 233
25:46	233
26:63–65	92
28:18–20	159
28:18	90

Mark

1:1	79
1:3	79
1:7	80
1:8	80
1:11	80
1:13	80, 85
1:16–20	80
1:24	80
1:27	80
1:35	82
2:10	83, 84
3:4	256
3:17	81
3:33–35	163
4:14–20	190
4:20	199
4:39	83
4:41	80
5:15	80
5:33	80
6:56	256
9:6	80
10:29–30	235
10:45	83
14:49	84
15:34	80
15:39	81
16:8	80

Luke

1:17	81
1:32–33	104
1:35	15, 83
1:54–55	81
1:69	104
2:11	104
2:13	4
2:25	104
2:30–32	104
2:32	81
2:36–38	104
2:46	84
2:49	82
3:4–6	81
3:8	118
3:16	81
3:22	81
3:38	14–15, 81
4:18–19	148
5:16	82
6:20–26	158
6:22–26	83
6:27–36	239–40
6:37–38	239
7:29	237
7:35	236
9:13–27	196
9:23–24	194
9:51	86
9:54	81
10:7	185
11:20	40
12:14	35
12:45–46	217
14:25–35	202
16:24	118
19	195
19:13–27	196
22:8–12	86
22:18–20	150
22:20	58
22:29–30	58, 150, 174
22:29	36, 58
22:37	83
22:42	88
24:27	127

John

1:1	60
1:1–3	13, 81
1:3	14, 60, 152
1:12	152, 163
1:14	14, 15, 81, 84, 152
1:23	152
1:29	152
1:49–51	152
2:16	83
2:19–21	84
3:2	75
3:4–8	74–75
3:13	82
3:17	82
4:34	82
5	61
5:17	83
5:18	60
5:19	83
5:24	234
5:25–39	92–93
5:27	219
5:30	60
6:29	82
6:31–35	192
6:38	82
6:42	82
6:57	83
6:67	190
6:68	190–91
8:33	118
8:42	59
8:56	121, 126
10:7	153
10:9	153
10:18	86
11:1–5	66
11:12	256
11:25	153
12:23	87
12:27–28	87
12:28	87
12:32	87, 243
12:35–36	87
12:38–41	88
13:3	82, 83
14:1–3	89
14:1–2	193
14:6	153
17:4–5	89–90, 162
17:22f	272
18:4–6	87
20:22	16

Acts

1:18	185
2:1–4	15
2:2	52
2:30–31	102
2:33–63	91
2:46	84
3:10	84
6:15	149, 271
7:48–50	149
7:56	149
13:33	161
17:28	261
17:31	218

Romans

1–3	167
1	33
1:3–4	167–68, 214
1:4	91, 161
1:5	168
1:8	168
1:16–17	168
1:16	173, 213
1:18	168, 213
1:19–21	216
1:19ff	214
1:20	33, 45, 213
1:21	213
1:23	168
1:25	168
2	33
2:1–5	33
2:1	169, 213
2:5–13	213–14
2:5	169, 214
2:6–10	32–33, 33
2:6	33, 161, 170, 215, 221
2:7–8	216

Romans (cont.)

2:7	33, 169, 170, 171
2:8-9	33
2:8	33, 169, 170
2:9-10	169
2:9	33, 170
2:10	33, 161, 169, 170, 171
2:11	33
2:12-24	33
2:13	161
2:23	215
3:9-10	33
3:9ff	169
3:10-11	216
3:10	122, 208, 214
3:19	216
3:21	169
3:23	171
3:24	169
3:25	169, 174
4	167
4:1-5	121-22
4:1ff	174
4:4	67, 180, 229
4:13	122, 170, 174
4:25	162, 170, 174
5	74, 167
5:1-11	34, 36
5:1-2	170-71
5:2	34, 171
5:12-21	34-36, 34, 36, 171
5:12ff	24, 174, 214
5:12	34-35, 35
5:15	35
5:16	35
5:17	35
5:18-19	72
5:18	35, 36
5:19	35, 36
5:13-14	34
5:15	172
5:18	172
5:21	172
6-8	74, 167
6	171, 174
6:6	214, 232
6:8	232
6:16	265
7	171
7:1ff	265
7:5-6	74
8	171, 172, 214
8:1-2	171
8:1	172, 174
8:2	165
8:9	172
8:10	172
8:11	39
8:14	172
8:15-23	175
8:15	15, 165, 172
8:17	172
8:18ff	173
8:19-22	32, 45
8:19	163, 234
8:28-30	39
8:29	164, 174
8:30	175
8:37-39	173
9-11	167, 173
9:5-9	174
9:24-26	119
9:27-29	173
9:33	173
10:5-6	136
10:11	173
10:15-16	173
10:20-21	173
11:1	174
11:2	265
11:8	173
11:15ff	174
11:26-27	173, 174
11:28	174
11:34	173
12-16	167
12:11	173
13:12	251
14:8	217
14:10-12	206, 217
14:10	218
14:13	217
14:15	217
15:12	173
15:14-21	173
15:21	173

16:20	175	6:19	16, 246, 264
		7:14	236
1 Corinthians		9:13	264
		9:22–27	193–94
1–4	244	9:22–23	194
1	249, 250	9:24	264
1:1–9	245	9:27	194
1:8	251	10:1–12	194
1:10–12	245	10:4	130
1:13ff	247	11:5	250
1:23	68, 248	11:18	244
1:26–31	248	12:4–5	246
1:30–31	248	15	36
2:1	248	15:20–28	73
2:6–7	22	15:22	36, 160
2:7	248	15:28	246
2:8	230	15:45–49	73, 74
2:9	22, 248, 271	15:45	246
2:10–11	248	15:49ff	47
2:12	248	15:50	234
3	228, 249, 253, 265	15:51–53	234
2:1–2	249	16:19–20	164
3:4	245		
3:5	246, 250	**2 Corinthians**	
3:6	249	3:3	40
3:9–11	249	3:9	165
3:9	246, 263	3:14–18	131
3:10–15	263, 265	3:14	154
3:10	263	3:17–18	154, 165
3:12–15	250	4:4	63, 270
3:15–17	263	4:6	270
3:15	227, 256, 257	5:1–4	15
3:16–17	253	5:10	206, 216, 218
3:16ff	263	5:11	217
3:16	16, 250	5:17	234
3:17	265	5:20	217
3:18–20	266	5:21	232
3:21–23	266	11:5	250
3:23	246		
4:3	251	**Galatians**	
4:4–5	246	3:6–9	122
4:5	207, 251	3:10–12	123
5:6	263	3:10	47
6:2	263	3:16–18	123
6:3	245, 263	3:16	163
6:9	246, 264	3:17	37
6:15	264	3:29	123
6:16	264	4:1–3	126
6:19–20	164		

Galatians (*cont.*)

4:6	15
4:26	164
6:7–10	240–41
6:7–9	238
6:7	237

Ephesians

1:3–4	57
1:3	58, 59
1:4	59
1:13–14	59, 166
1:21	90
2:6	160, 163
2:8–9	238
2:12–13	70–71
2:14	164
2:19–22	71, 84, 164
2:19	166
3:14–15	15
4:24	16, 47, 164
5:32	272

Philippians

2:6–11	89
2:8–9	161
2:9–11	59
3:20–21	166
3:20	234
3:21	272

Colossians

1:15	39, 63, 83
1:16	3, 4, 90
2:14	232
3:4	272
3:10	16
3:23–24	189

1 Thessalonians

2:19–20	194
5:2	251
5:4	251

2 Thessalonians

1:6–10	219
1:10	223
2:8	270

2 Timothy

1:8–10	58
1:12	193
4:8	195
4:14	221

Titus

2:11–14	267

Hebrews

1:1–4	62
1:1	62
1:2	62
1:3	63, 83
1:4	63
1:5–14	63
1:5	161
1:8	64
1:13	64
2	63
2:4	64
2:5–8	63
2:7–8	63
2:8	63
2:9–10	64
2:10	72, 166
2:11	163
2:14	64
2:17	64
2:18	64
3:1	152
3:5–6	151
3:6	64
4	21, 99
4:1	64
4:4	21
4:8–9	42
4:9	21
4:14–16	21
4:14ff	90
4:14	64, 91

6:13	153
6:17	152
8:13	149
9:7	70
9:11	143
9:15	132, 152
9:23–24	143
10:5–7	84
10:12–13	153
10:19–22	153
10:25	251
10:29	236
11:4	99
11:6	165
11:7	112
11:9–10	120
11:13–16	120
11:16	22
11:17–19	121
11:19	111
11:26	166, 188
12:19	52
12:22–24	166, 234
12:22–23	174

James

1:12	195
2:10	208
2:18	225
2:20	225
2:21–24	235
2:21	111, 236
2:24	235
5:1–6	158
5:4	185

1 Peter

2:4–8	84
2:5–8	68, 70
2:9	153
3:20	259, 262
3:21	262
3:18–22	112
4:14	270
5:4	195

2 Peter

3:10–13	268

1 John

2:2	72
3:2	272
4:10	72

2 John

1:7–9	189
1:8	189

Jude

23	259

Revelation

1–3	191
1:6	153
1:12–16	153–54
1:13ff	39
1:13–16	41
1:13–15	91
1:18	154, 219
2:1	219
2:5	191
2:7	49
2:8	219
2:12	219
2:16	191
2:17	192
2:18	219
2:22–23	191
2:26–27	192
3:1	191, 219
3:5	232
3:7	219
3:12	84, 159
3:14	219
3:17–18	191
3:17	191
3:21	192
4	5, 14
4:2	5
4:8	5
4:11	5

Revelation (cont.)

5:9–10	242
5:11–12	91
6:15–17	207
7:4	123
7:9	124
10	43
10:1–3	41
11:1	159
13:8	232
14:2	52
14:10–12	206
14:10	89
17:8	232
18:2	212
18:5	212
18:6–7	212
18:6	212
18:7	212
18:11ff	213
18:24	213
19:7–9	154
19:17–18	142
19:20	231
20:1–2	219
20:4	235
20:10	219, 231
20:11–12	207
20:11	5
20:12	221, 229
20:13	229
20:15	229, 231
21–22	18, 22
21	49, 143, 159
21:1	269
21:2–3	269
21:2	18
21:3	18, 269
21:10	18
21:11	269
21:15ff	269
21:19–21	154
21:22	84, 269
22	49, 221
22:1ff	18, 269
22:1–2	49
22:12–13	222, 242
22:12	221, 223
22:13	222
22:14–15	242
22:16	243
22:17	243

www.ingramcontent.com/pod-product-compliance
Lightning Source LLC
Chambersburg PA
CBHW071235230426
43668CB00011B/1442